# Social Contract Theory

READINGS IN SOCIAL AND POLITICAL THEORY

Edited by William Connolly and Steven Lukes

# Social Contract Theory

*Edited by* MICHAEL LESSNOFF

NEW YORK UNIVERSITY PRESS
Washington Square, New York

All rights reserved
First published in the U.S.A. in 1990 by
NEW YORK UNIVERSITY PRESS
Washington Square
New York, NY 10003

*Library of Congress Cataloging-in-Publication Data*

Social contract theory/edited by Michael Lessnoff.
    p. cm. — (Readings in social and political theory)
  Includes bibliographical references.
  ISBN 0−8147−5054−0 — ISBN 0−8147−5055−9 (pbk.)
  1. Social contract.   I. Lessnoff. Michael H. (Michael Harry)
II. Series.
JC336.S53   1990
320.1′ 1—dc20                                    90−33402
                                                    CIP

Typeset in Sabon on 10/11 pt
by Setrite Typesetters Ltd, Hong Kong
Printed in Great Britain by Billing & Sons Ltd, Worcester

# Contents

# Introduction: Social Contract

MICHAEL LESSNOFF

The concept of the social contract is a familiar and well-established element of our thinking about politics. The modern student of political ideas is almost certain to be introduced to a number of major 'social contract theorists', notably Hobbes, Locke and Rousseau; and several scholars have devoted themselves to tracing the history of the idea – in one well-known study (J. W. Gough's *Social Contract*, first published in 1937) over a period of more than 2,000 years.[1] More recently, social contract theory has been explicitly and self-consciously revived by the leading political philosopher of our day, John Rawls. Largely thanks to Rawls, social contract theory is now again a major focus of systematic and original political thought.

The concept of the social contract is current, not only in the rarefied world of academic scholarship, but also in the 'real world' of politics. It is invoked, not infrequently, to refer to live issues, problems and proposed solutions. The British Labour Party, for example, in an Election Manifesto published in the crisis-ridden year of 1974, proposed to 'save the nation' by means of a 'Social Contract', between itself as the government, and the British trade union movement.[2] In April 1987, according to a London newspaper (*The Financial Times*), officials of the Economy Ministry in Argentina were 'meeting union and business leaders to continue efforts aimed to create a social contract', that is, an agreement on economic policy aimed at ending a crippling wave of strikes.[3] And in June of 1987, a distinguished contributor to the *New York Review of Books*, discussing the economic problems confronting General Secretary Gorbachev in the Soviet Union, and particularly the need to reduce the huge, wasteful subsidies that have for decades been built into the system, noted that, nevertheless, 'these subsidies ... embody the social contract between citizen and state to ensure employment and very cheap necessities'. That Gorbachev's reform programme might have to 'come in conflict with the social contract' created, in this commentator's view, a danger of adding 'potentially explosive elements to the Soviet political equation'.[4] Other similar examples of analyses of contemporary politics in terms of the idea of the social contract could easily be given.

Yet well-established though the idea now is, at many levels of political thinking, nevertheless the use of the term 'social contract' seems in some respects misleading and inappropriate – and even slightly mysterious. Among the writers and works that make up the theory's historical lineage, hardly any use the phrase. The outstanding exception is Rousseau, author of the famous *Du contrat social*, published in 1762. His predecessors spoke of pacts and compacts, of covenants and, indeed, of contracts – but seldom if ever of a social contract. This does not mean that the 'history of social contract theory' is a sham – far from it. Rousseau was quite clearly developing – and combating – the ideas of the earlier writers. It may be that because of his great celebrity, and that of his book, it is Rousseau's terminology that has become standard.

Unfortunately, however, this terminology may give the impression that the theory (or theories) in question maintain that 'society' is the result of a contract made by (non-social or pre-social) individuals. Such a conception can easily be ridiculed, not just as historically inaccurate, but on the more fundamental ground that it is incoherent. Not only has man been always by nature a social animal, the concept of contract is itself a social concept, which presupposes social life among men. Pre-social men, if they could exist, could not even have the concept of a contract (or pact or covenant), and hence could not make one (they could not even have a language). True. But this (not infrequent) criticism of social contract theory is largely aimed at a straw man. Very few, if any, of the major contract theorists have actually argued in this way. Rather, they have been concerned with the origin and justification of specific sorts of social institutions, and indeed, above all, institutions of political authority, centralized government and positive law. Thus, for example, the state of 'war' posited by Hobbes as natural to men is clearly one of recognizable social interaction, though marked by intermittent fighting and constant fear of fighting. (Admittedly, Hobbes did, in one very famous sentence, describe men's natural condition as solitary; but it is obvious from his overall account that he meant this only in a relative sense.) Locke's 'state of nature' is even more obviously a social state, 'with a law of nature to govern it'. Rousseau himself did indeed (in the *Discourse on the Origin of Inequality*) depict man's original state as solitary and genuinely non-social – but society is there described as resulting from a spontaneous process, not from a contract. In his *Social Contract*, despite the name, he is concerned, like Hobbes and Locke before him, with the establishment of *political* (or civil) society.

*Social* contract theory, then, is a branch of *political* philosophy. A social contract theory can be defined as, most typically, one which grounds the legitimacy of political authority, and the obligations of rulers and subjects (and the limits thereof), on a premised contract or contracts relating to these matters. More accurately, this would be an acceptable definition of social contract theory in the pre-Rawls era. Rawls, however, has revived the theory with a distinctly non-traditional end in view – to furnish (from contractarian premises) principles of social justice. This is still, of course, a branch of political philosophy (Rawls's theory is intended as a standard for state action), but is actually more appropriately described as a *social* contract theory than in the case of the older writers. Not, however, in the sense that Rawls's contract has to do with the origin of society – but rather because its scope embraces the legitimacy not just of political institutions but of social institutions more generally.

Let us return to contract theory as a theory about political authority. Why is such a theory needed? Why does political authority require justification? Why posit limits to the obligations of subjects and the rights of rulers? One possible answer is that *all men are by nature free and equal*. In medieval Europe this principle was in fact widely accepted by theorists, largely through the influence of Roman law and the writings of the Christian fathers.[5] But it appears – at least at first sight – to be flouted by the existence of political authority, which means that some rule and others are ruled (hence all are not equal, and the ruled apparently are not free). Of course, many ways of justifying such a state of affairs are possible: what is peculiar to contract theory is to rest the justification on the agreement, in some sense, of the ruled. As Locke was to put it in the seventeenth century, 'no one can be ... subjected to the political power of another, without his own consent.' Subjection to political authority, in other words, is legitimate if and only if it actually results from the exercise of a man's equal natural freedom.

But there is more to contract theory than mere consent. Consent can be a unilateral act: contract is bilateral or multilateral. One may consent to an existing state of affairs: one contracts with another contracting party or parties, in order to bring about a new state of affairs. To rest political authority and political obligation on *contract*, therefore, is to rest it on *an* agreement — an agreement which actually creates that authority and that obligation. Typically, too, a contract establishes new rights and obligations, reciprocally, of all the contracting parties. It is an exchange of undertakings, or promises, by which each contractor acquires an obligation to act in a particular way, and a right that his fellow contractors also act in some particular way. And these rights and obligations are conditional — the right of each contractor is conditional on fulfilling his obligation, and his obligation on the others fulfilling *their* obligations. Such a relationship between parties is posited by social contract theory as the ground of political authority. The parties in question (as will be shown in more detail below) can be rulers, peoples, individuals or intermediate social units.

The idea of grounding political authority on a contract may or may not be valid, but there is one criticism — a further charge of incoherence — which can be immediately dismissed. Contract, it is sometimes said, is a *legal* concept. Hence political society cannot possibly be based on contract, for law is itself part and parcel of political society. Perhaps it is (though this might be disputed). But this criticism construes the term 'contract' in 'social contract theory' much too literally. As we have seen, many 'contract theorists' never used the term. What matters is the *concept*, which is that of a binding agreement or exchange of promises. *That* concept in no way presupposes either law or political authority.

But we must now mention another recurrent criticism of contract theory which cannot be so easily dismissed. A contract, as we saw, is a specific act which changes the rights and obligations of the contractors. To base political authority and obligation on contract, therefore, is to trace it to such an act or acts. In other words, social contract theory is a theory in which justification and history are necessarily and inextricably intertwined. The legitimacy of political authority is made to depend on its history — on how it was actually established. If this history is faulty, or irrelevant (both assertions have frequently been made), the theory appears to fall.

Before we can begin to assess these common criticisms, it is necessary to be aware of the range and variety of social contract theories. The first such theorist represented in this compilation — and according to some commentators, the first genuine or at least the first systematic contract theorist — is the German Calvinist Johannes Althusius, who wrote early in the seventeenth century.

But if Althusius was in some sense the first social contract theorist, he was certainly not the first to offer a contractarian analysis of political authority and obligation. Properly to appreciate Althusius and his successors, we need to know something of the most important of his forerunners.

## THE DEVELOPMENT OF CONTRACTARIAN THOUGHT

The earliest contractarian analyses of political authority are concerned with the relation between 'ruler' and 'people', who are the two contracting parties; and the writer who, according to our present knowledge, can claim to be the founder of this style of analysis is an Alsatian monk, Manegold of Lautenbach, who in the late eleventh century took up scholarly cudgels on behalf of his Pope, Gregory VII, against his perennial enemy, the Emperor. The oft-quoted words of this monk deserve to be quoted again:

> King is not a name of nature but a title of office: nor does the people exalt him so high above it in order to give him the free power of playing the tyrant in its midst, but to defend it from tyranny. So soon as he begins to act the tyrant, is it not plain that he falls from the dignity granted to him? Since it is evident that he has broken the contract by virtue of which he was appointed. If one should engage a man for a fair wage to tend swine, and he find means not to tend but to steal them, would one not remove him from his charge? ... Since no one can create himself emperor or king, the people elevates a certain one person over itself to this end, that he govern and rule it according to right reason, give to each one his own, protect the good, destroy the wicked, and administer justice to every man. But if he violates the contract under which he was elected, disturbing and confounding that which he was established to set in order, then the people is justly and reasonably released from its obligation to obey him.[6]

It is important to stress that, although Manegold in this passage had in mind one particular ruler — the Emperor Henry IV — nevertheless he has adumbrated a general theory about the relation between rulers and peoples, a contractual relation, whence derive limits to the former's authority and the latter's obligation to obey. A number of elements in the contemporary political situation enabled him to do so. Manegold's polemical intent was to justify rebellion by the German princes who were at odds with Henry. These princes were feudal vassals of the Emperor, and it is of prime importance that feudal vassalage was a contractual relationship which imposed obligations on both sides. If, Manegold says, a ruler acts tyrannically, any man who has sworn an oath of allegiance to him (as in a feudal contract) is thereby absolved from his oath, and the people is free to depose him. It is also clear that, in accord with contemporary conceptions, Manegold takes the rebel princes to be acting as the natural leaders of the 'people', and thus as its representatives. They were deemed to act as such when, as electors, they chose the Emperor, a point clearly in Manegold's mind, as our quotation shows. Indeed, election of a ruler by the 'people' in this sense was not, in early medieval Europe, confined to the Empire, but was a widely accepted element of the theory (if not always the reality) of kingship. The 'people', represented by its leading men, conferred kingship or at least ratified the succession of a new king, and swore allegiance on condition that the king ruled in accordance with the established laws and customs of the kingdom. The king, for his part, normally swore to do so in his coronation oath. These forms — or formalities — were doubtless in Manegold's mind when he wrote of the 'contract' by which a king or emperor is appointed.

To call this contract a contract between ruler and people may seem a pure fiction. But fictions can be powerful, and the idea was to be repeated again and again in the course of European history, at least up to the seventeenth century. Clearly a pivotal position in the concept is occupied by the magnates of the kingdom. On the one hand, they represent the people; on the other they are on a footing of equality with the king, who is but 'first among equals', and are able to contract with him, on the people's behalf, on equal terms. This view of politics is nicely expressed by the famous (even if probably spurious) 'oath of the Aragonese', supposed to have been uttered by the people of the old kingdom of Aragon when they accepted a new king: 'We, who are as good as you, make you our king and lord, on condition that you preserve our laws and liberties; and if not, not [*si no, no*].[7]

The contractarian argument of Manegold which we have quoted expresses a very clear view of political authority: that it exists to meet certain needs of the people, and the authority of *specific rulers* over their people stems from the latter's recognizing this fact, and therefore conferring on them a conditional authority, for the people's benefit. This idea was taken an important stage further by a later medieval contract theorist, Engelbert of Volkersdorf, abbot of a monastery in Austria, in the early fourteenth century. Engelbert went beyond Manegold by considering the *origin* of political authority. Clearly, reasons of the kind that, according to Manegold, motivate a people to choose a man as their ruler could also be a motive to establish rulership as such in the first place. Just this is what Engelbert asserted: all kingdoms and principates, he says, originated when men, following nature and reason, chose a ruler and bound themselves to (conditional) obedience in a 'contract of subjection' (*pactum subiectionis*), made 'in order to be ruled, protected and preserved'.[8] Engelbert can claim to be the first to enunciate an idea destined for a long career — what would later be called the 'original contract'. It was for breach of the 'original contract' between king and people, his enemies claimed, that King James II of England was stripped of his throne in the 'Glorious' Revolution of 1688–9.

Engelbert's *pactum subiectionis* (or original contract) implies the existence of a pre-political phase in human history — what later writers were to call the 'state of nature'. The same complex of ideas — if not the terminology — is involved in the work of another important political contract theorist, Mario Salamonio, a Roman jurist who wrote two centuries after Engelbert. In apparent contrast to Manegold of Lautenbach, Salamonio wrote his *De Principatu* (1511–13) *against* the power of the Pope: but the contrast is only apparent, for in Rome the Pope was also secular ruler. Salamonio, like Manegold (and most other writers in this tradition) used contractarian arguments to put limits on the power of princes. Princes, he stresses, did not always exist: at first, he notes, all men were created equal by God and nature; but later they found it necessary to institute kingdoms and princedoms 'by agreements of men'. But what makes Salamonio important in the history of contract theory is not these already familiar ideas. Rather, it is his conception of the political community or state (*civitas*), which he defines, in Roman law terms, as a *civilis societas*. *Societas* was the Roman law term for a partnership, made by free contract among the individual partners. Thus for Salamonio political or civil society is a partnership among individual citizens, created by contract among them — a *pactio inter cives*. The terms of the contract are the laws of the state, without which no state can exist, and which are binding on all its members — including the prince or ruler.[9]

Salamonio achieves a result somewhat similar to his predecessors, but by a different method — by making the formation of the political society and its laws *prior* to the creation of the prince.

This 'original contract' is not between ruler and people, but — for the first time — between individual citizens.

Shortly after the publication of Salamonio's *De Principatu*, the Pope had to face a much more serious challenge — that of Martin Luther and the Protestant Reformation. This epochal event deeply affected every facet of European history, including political theory. Naturally, it had its effect on contract theory and — most importantly — enormously increased its salience. This was largely the work not of the Lutherans, but of the Calvinists, who in most of Europe found themselves in opposition to established rulers, and whose theology disposed them to think in terms of 'covenants'. It is hardly surprising, therefore, that they resorted to contractarian arguments about politics. One of these is particularly famous — the *Vindiciae Contra Tyrannos* of 'Junius Brutus', a pseudonymous French Huguenot, written during the religious wars of the 1570s against the Catholic King of France, and translated and reprinted many times into the next century.

The *Vindiciae* is interesting both for what is old in it, and for what is new. 'Junius Brutus' reiterated the existence, in all realms, of 'a contract mutually obligatory between the king and [his] subjects, which requires the people to obey faithfully, and the king to govern lawfully', such that breach of faith by the prince releases the people from their obligation of obedience.[10] But prior to this, in Junius Brutus' view, is another contract (or contracts) — not between Salamonio's state-forming citizens, but rather reflecting the role of man and government in the divine plan of the universe, as seen through Calvinist eyes. This is a covenant between God on the one hand, and ruler and people on the other, in which the latter undertake 'to honour and serve God according to His will revealed in His word'.[11] 'Junius Brutus' invokes as evidence Old Testament descriptions of such covenants at the inauguration of Hebrew kings, but applies their implications to all rulers, though especially Christian ones. If a ruler destroys true religion, he may and must be resisted; not only is he in breach of the fundamental authorizing covenant, but also that covenant *requires* the people to resist such a ruler. Or rather, not the people, exactly, but their natural leaders and representatives, the great magnates of the kingdom — for they, unlike purely private persons, have a public 'calling' (in the Calvinist phrase).[12] These, of course, are the 'lesser magistrates' of Calvinist resistance theory (in the French religious wars, the Huguenot leaders were great feudal magnates); but they are also irresistibly reminiscent of the German princes considered by Manegold of Lautenbach to represent the people of the eleventh-century Empire.

Manegold, Engelbert, Salamonio, and 'Junius Brutus' each made a distinctive contribution to contractarian thinking about politics; but in the writings of the first three the contractarian element plays a relatively limited part, while the *Vindiciae Contra Tyrannos* is more polemical tract than philosophical treatise. With the last-named, however, we have arrived at the threshold of the first great flowering of social contract theory as political philosophy, which begins a generation later with the *Politics* of Althusius. As a Calvinist scholar deeply involved in the still-continuing religious strife of early seventeenth-century Europe, Althusius could not help but be aware of the arguments of the *Vindiciae*. Indeed, he incorporated into his own highly articulated and logically worked-out theory the main concepts of all four of the predecessors we have discussed above, besides adding much that was new. Thus, he bases the authority of all princes and kings on an original contract between each people and its first ruler, reaffirmed when later rulers succeed by election. Prior to these covenants is the covenant with God, which obliges the ruler to establish true religion, and the people to resist him if he does not. But prior to them also is the contract by which the political community itself — the people, commonwealth or realm — was first constituted, and its fundamental laws established. As with Salamonio, the ruler (or 'supreme magistrate') is bound by these laws — for Althusius this is part of the 'original contract' between ruler and people and its later reaffirmations. Otto Gierke, the scholar who did most to highlight the importance of Althusius, pointed out the logical necessity of some such explanation of how the people can become a unity capable of contracting with its ruler. Althusius, he claimed, was the first to provide a clear account combining in a coherent way these two successive contracts.[13]

In Althusius' theory, however, the parties to the prior, commonwealth-forming contract are not (as in Salamonio's) individuals. They are provinces and cities, lesser political units with their own government and laws, which Althusius sees as prior to the commonwealth, and formed in their turn out of prior private associations and, ultimately, contracting individuals. By this

pyramiding of contracts Althusius makes the authority of the
commonwealth, and particularly its ruler, the 'supreme magistrate',
a conditional delegation from its constituent units and their representatives. From this follows naturally the characteristic Calvinist
doctrine about the duty of 'lesser magistrates' (called 'ephors' by
the learned Althusius) to resist a tyrannical or ungodly king: these
ephors include the provincial estates and the great territorial magnates, who have powers in their provinces similar to those of the
king in his realm. In this way Althusius was able to justify the
rebellion of the Protestant Netherlands against their Catholic king,
Philip of Spain. What is not so clear, however, is exactly what the
political role of a province is or, to put it another way, why the
process of state-formation must go through the two stages, first
province, then commonwealth. Was the province at first intended
to be independent? If so, it was in effect a commonwealth. If not,
what was its function? Althusius' theory seems to be modelled too
closely on the particular political entities of the Europe of his day,
with their peculiar structure and historical development.

It is obvious that, up to the time of Althusius, contract theory in
politics was mainly invoked in order to justify resistance to rulers.
But soon after came the great exception – Thomas Hobbes.
Hobbes (however unwelcome his political views may be) was unquestionably the greatest of all the contract theorists (and possibly
the greatest of all political philosophers). He was also the sworn
enemy of all Calvinist and other rebels, whom he blamed for the
misery of England's seventeenth-century Civil War. Several features
of his theory are notable. First, he gives unprecedentedly close
attention to the nature of man, and to deducing from this the
'natural condition of mankind', or state of nature – the non-
political (or pre-political) state of man. The natural freedom and
equality of men in this condition make life intolerably insecure –
*therefore they must be abandoned.* Establishment of an unchalleng-
able sovereign is the imperative function of the original contract
(or covenant). For Hobbes only this can create a stable or tolerable
social structure; hence in the state of nature there can be only *one*
authorizing contract, the covenant among individuals that establishes the sovereign. There is no question of a people first constituting
itself, then contracting with its ruler, and thus imposing limits on
his power. Far from being constrained by any contract, says Hobbes,
the power of the sovereign is the only means to enforce contracts
and hence make them binding. With ruthless logic, Hobbes stripped
away all superfluous elements standing between his premises and
his desired conclusion. The result is impressive – just how impress-

ive can be judged by reading the second extract in the anthology. But there was also a theoretical price to pay, as will be discussed below.

Another seventeenth-century writer who sought to defend royal power on the basis of a contract theory was the great German jurist Samuel Pufendorf. But Pufendorf was in many ways critical of Hobbes. Men would not, he argued, institute a sovereign without receiving in return a promise of protection: hence (returning to older conceptions) there must first have been a contract to establish a political community, then a second contract between that community and its ruler. But − somewhat surprisingly − Pufendorf nevertheless concluded that resistance to the sovereign is practically never justified, relying here on two essentially Hobbesian arguments: the pre-political state of nature is intolerable; and the supreme political authority is by definition not accountable to, or punishable by, any human being. Pufendorf's elaborate re-multiplication of contracts turns out to be without significant consequences, and superfluous.

The logic of Pufendorf's objection to Hobbes was more cogently developed by another English theorist, John Locke, who returned contract theory to its traditional role as a justification of resistance to government. But he did not follow Pufendorf's reversion to multiple contracts. Rather he envisaged, like Hobbes, a unique original contract, but modified its terms in order to give a quite different conclusion. In the Hobbesian state of nature, men have complete natural liberty, which makes their life intolerable; hence they must entirely surrender it; but for Locke, 'the state of nature has a law of nature to govern it', which constrains (or defines) their equal liberty. What makes this state intolerable is the absence of any effective, centralized apparatus to enforce the law of nature. And that is Locke's definition of the state and its function − effectively to enforce the law of nature and thus protect the rights of individuals. What men must give up to enter a political community, therefore, is not their natural liberty, but only, as Locke puts it, their right to enforce the law of nature − that is, to judge and punish offenders. Locke has given a very clear statement of the function of the state, and the limits of its legitimate authority. These limits derive, not from any contractual obligation of the ruler, but from the (quasi-Hobbesian) premise that the authority of rulers derives wholly from rights voluntarily alienated by individuals, and also from the obligatory force of the law of nature, which for Locke is independent of any contract. The function of the legitimate state is called by Locke its 'trust': if the ruler breaches his trust, Locke says, government is dissolved and resistance justified. Clearly the ruler in Locke's mind was King James II of England, who lost his throne in the 'Glorious' Revolution of 1688—9.

## THE RELATION OF SOCIAL CONTRACT THEORY TO HISTORICAL FACT

Locke's contract theory, though stated less economically and consistently than that of Hobbes, may seem in its essentials the more convincing of the two. But now it is time to confront a problem which both share in an equal degree — the historicity of the contract. It is useful here to remind ourselves of the earlier contractarian ideas. The contract between ruler and people first mentioned by Manegold of Lautenbach, repeated so often thereafter, and incorporated into the theory of Althusius, was thought of (rightly or wrongly) as a specific historical event, re-enacted at the succession of every ruler. Obligations derive from such actual contracts as a matter of course, in accordance with the principle that persons are bound by their promises. Engelbert's addition of an original contract, which Althusius retains in his theory also, in a sense makes no difference, and creates no great problems, so long as it is only a model for the later contracts. But the great innovation of Hobbes (followed here by Locke) was to suppress the latter, and thus rest his argument mainly on the original contract alone. This raises in an acute form the problem of historicity. The problem is two-fold. Did this original contract actually take place? If it did, since we are talking only of an *original* contract, are persons now alive, not parties to it, bound by it? If the answer to either question is no (as seems not unlikely), how can political authority or political obligation be based on the contract?

Both Hobbes and Locke show evident signs of uneasiness about these problems. Locke, however, explicitly fends off doubts about the contract's historicity, and tries to relate it to present-day obligation by his (notoriously unsatisfactory) doctrine of 'tacit consent'. As for Hobbes, many commentators have seen clear signs that he did not really believe in the literal historicity of the contract. The issue, however, is not what Hobbes (in his heart of hearts) believed; it is the meaning of his words, and the logical structure of his argument. Hobbes devotes great care to defining what a contract is, and how rights and obligations derive from it (and from covenant); integral to his argument is the moral principle (or Law of Nature) 'that men perform their covenants made'; he clearly states that political obligations and liberties depend 'on what rights we pass away, when we make a commonwealth'; and that 'every subject in a commonwealth, hath covenanted to obey the civil law'. The conclusion seems inescapable that, according to Hobbes's argument, the original contract must be an actual historical event, whose terms are binding on 'every subject in a commonwealth'.

Such an argument — it was suggested above — is problematic, and was bound to provoke objections: objections which received a classical formulation from the eighteenth-century Scottish philosopher David Hume. Hume's famous essay 'Of the Original Contract' addresses both of the two problems noted above. Was government at first founded on a contract? To this Hume's answer is yes, at least in the sense that the first institution of government must have had the agreement of the governed, given men's natural equality and the evident advantages of government. Does men's political obligation *now* stem from this original contract? Hume's answer is no — it stems from the evident advantages of government. These advantages, which motivated the original contract, are the grounds of our present 'duty of allegiance' — directly. To refer to the original contract is an unnecessary and irrelevant detour.

The relation between Hume and social contract theory is roughly as follows. Contract theory sought to answer the questions why, and to what extent, we are obliged to obey government by looking to the reasons why government was established and accepted in the first place, that is, to the advantages of government compared to the pre-political condition of men. It then argued that men established government in order to secure these advantages, and agreed to obey governments so long as they did so. In earlier versions of the theory, it was supposed that this contract was periodically reaffirmed at the accession of each new ruler. Hobbes and Locke dropped this further element, but not the inference it seemed to license, that men are still bound by the original contract. Hume's proposal is that we should drop this too.

The logic of Hume's critique seems to be impeccable; nevertheless it does not follow that social contract theory must be totally abandoned. Rather, it may suggest that it be *reformulated*, in terms of a *hypothetical*, rather than an actual contract. For if Hume is right that the evident advantages of government are both the ground of political obligation and the motive of the original contract, may we not say that *if* human beings found themselves without government (in a 'state of nature'), they *would* contract to establish and accept a government that yields these advantages? Many commentators, indeed, have claimed that just this is the form of Hobbes's real argument, and even of Locke's too. For reasons already discussed, I do not believe this is so. Nevertheless, there is no reason why their theories, and other social contract theories, should not be thus reformulated, and considered in this hypothetical form.

At any rate, Hume's critique by no means put an end to social contract theory − on the contrary, its most famous manifestation was yet to come, in the form of Rousseau's *Du contrat social*. Whether Rousseau's contract theory is vulnerable to the Humean critique is not entirely easy to say. It may well not be. In Rousseau's first discussion of the subject, in the *Discourse on the Origin of Inequality*, he portrayed the original contract as a trick by which the rich were able to fasten their rule on the poor.[14] No more than Hume, therefore, does it seem that he saw the original contract as the basis for legitimate political authority. The social contract described in the later, more famous work is quite different, and is probably best thought of as an ideal rather than an actual historical event. This ideal contract is notable as an equality-preserving one: that is, the equality of the state of nature is preserved in Rousseau's ideal form of government as the equal legislative authority of all citizens, who make up the sovereign people. (According to Rousseau, such government also preserves the liberty of all citizens, replacing their natural liberty by civil liberty. That, however, is a highly debatable claim.) Rousseau's theory, like that of Hobbes and Locke, allows for only one contract among individual citizens, but with very different implications. Since it creates a *sovereign people*, there is no question of any subsequent contract between people and ruler, or people and government − the government can only be the agent of the sovereign people's will.

With Rousseau's successor Immanuel Kant, we at last reach a contract theory which is explicit in denying the historicity of the contract. It is, Kant says, an 'idea of reason'; but one which has 'undoubted practical reality', in the sense that 'it can oblige every legislator to frame his laws in such a way that they could have been produced by the united will of a whole nation.' This means that it is a test for good laws, but not that it can ever provide any justification for resistance − on this Kant was as conservative as Pufendorf. The practical utility of Kant's 'idea of reason' is in fact dubious. Kant uses it to deduce various 'ideal' constitutional and other laws, but the deductions are not particularly compelling. The exception, perhaps, is in the area of international law, in which Kant makes his most original use of contract theory, to argue for the establishment of supra-state organs to preserve international peace.

Is Kant's 'contract as an idea of reason' the same thing as the *hypothetical* contract, which, it was suggested above, is a possible reformulation of the theories of Hobbes and Locke? Not quite. According to Kant, 'pure reason ... legislates *a priori*, regardless of all empirical ends'. Since men have different conceptions of happiness, their empirical ends cannot be subsumed under any common principle, nor (therefore) be the ground of the social contract. Thus, in Kant's eyes, the justification of the state is that to leave the 'state of nature' is a moral obligation pure and simple. For Hobbes, too, it is a moral obligation: but it is so precisely *because* it is the common interest of all, and *necessary* to their happiness and achievement of their ends. Therefore, we may say, it is what rational, self-interested persons *would* agree to (even if actual persons have not, not having been given the opportunity). It is, in fact, debatable whether the Kantian version is a genuine contract theory at all. If the contract is determined by what is morally obligatory, independently of the contract, then the contract itself seems dispensable. The traditional point of contract theory was to *derive* (an aspect of) moral obligation *from* the contract. This feature, at least, is preserved by the hypothetical form of the contract. A social contract theory, in the traditional or 'hypothetical' sense, is one which deduces moral principles for society from what individuals motivated by self-interest agree to or would agree to.

### HEGELIAN AND MARXIAN CRITICISMS OF SOCIAL CONTRACT THEORY

The definition just given enables us, now, to confront a new range of objections to the whole idea of contract theory, objections of a Hegelian and Marxist cast. Neither Hegel nor Marx wrote about social contract theory at any length, but what they did write on the subject was highly critical. In essence, Hegel's objection is that the state, and the citizen's obligation to it, cannot be reduced to the self-interest of individuals. Contract is a concept suited to the economic, not the political sphere. It fails to do justice to the grandeur and majesty of the state, and the obligations it is thereby entitled to impose on the individual.[15] Hegel's argument, in fact, is put in a form that is so extreme as to be almost self-refuting. But a more moderate, quasi-Hegelian argument might carry more conviction: namely, that the relation between fellow citizens is or ought to be something more than the cold and calculating relation of self-interested contractors. A state, it may be said, should be a kind of *community*, with all that implies. But is social contract theory an implicit denial of this? Not necessarily. It would perhaps be so, if it purported to give a total account of the nature of the state. But if it is used simply as a device for working out certain specific political rights and obligations, that is not to deny that there is more to the state than that.

The Marxist critique of contract theory, unlike the Hegelian, has no desire to exalt the state — quite the contrary. Yet there are similarities. Marxists too find contract theory, especially in its classic seventeenth- and eighteenth-century form, a transposition from the economic into the political realm of a self-seeking individualism — or rather, of the self-seeking individualism of one particular economic system, capitalism. For Marxism (in contrast to Hegel) social contract theory is in a certain sense an appropriate political theory, given a contract-based capitalist market economy: but contract is not in an ultimate sense appropriate to any sphere of human life, because of its individualistic implications.

Marx's own comments relative to contract theory are few and brief. In the *Grundrisse*, he compared 'Rousseau's *contrat social*, which brings naturally independent, autonomous subjects into relation and connection by contract', to the emergent economy of free competition, and the individualistic economic theory of Adam Smith and Ricardo; and one letter to Engels contains an implicit analogy between nineteenth-century English capitalism and the Hobbesian state of nature.[16] Later Marxists, notably C. B. Macpherson, have developed such ideas much further;[17] and in the work of the Soviet legal philosopher Evgeny Pashukanis, social contract theory appears as a full-blown capitalist ideology. Pashukanis (quite reasonably, in historical terms) saw social contract theory as part and parcel of the theory of natural law, and was thus able to treat it in terms of his theory of law in general. In brief summary, he saw law as an outgrowth of bourgeois, 'commodity-producing' (that is, capitalist) society. It presupposes 'the conflict of private interests', and the individual rights of private law are the rights of 'isolated bearers of private egoistic interests' — that is, of owners of private property.[18] The legal contract is a device by which the desire of bourgeois property-owners for profit is facilitated.[19] Natural law theory, in Pashukanis's view, extends such concepts into the political sphere: for it 'deduces the state from [a] contract between isolated individuals'.[20] For Pashukanis, this is in part an ideological fiction (since the reality of the bourgeois state is the coercive rule of one class over another); but it is ideological also in the sense of reflecting one part, at least, of the economic reality of capitalism — the contractual relation between isolated, self-seeking individuals.[21] Social contract theory, in the view of Pashukanis, seeks to legitimate the bourgeois state — which safeguards the self-seeking of property-owners — in the name of the self-interest of all. It thus rests on, and endorses, a conception of man as selfishly acquisitive.

Both Hegelians and Marxists, then, object to a legitimation of the state in terms of individual self-interest (the former, because this demeans the state; the latter, because it precludes the state-less communist society). But here, so far as social contract theory is concerned, two issues have to be distinguished: individualism, and egoism. The theory is indeed (in its classical form) an individualistic theory, but it is not an endorsement of egoism. On the contrary, it calls for restraint on egoism, in the name of moral obligation. A contract, freely entered into, is presumably to the advantage of *all* parties to the contract: the obligation to abide by contractual undertakings is an obligation not to injure the interests *of others* — in the case of social contract theory, of one's fellow citizens. At least, this is so if the contract is understood historically: if it is understood hypothetically, the obligation is to accept political institutions that (since all affected would agree to their establishment) are presumed to be in the *interests of all*. This is not egoism, but a universalistic individualism, concerned with the interests of all individuals equally.

### SOCIAL CONTRACT, SOCIAL JUSTICE AND SOCIAL MORALITY

The Humean, Hegelian and Marxist critiques of contract theory help to explain why the theory almost disappeared from view in the nineteenth century; yet, paradoxically, they also suggest the reason for its renaissance in the twentieth. For the Humean critique (as was indicated above) suggests a way to reformulate the theory so as to avoid some obvious objections, and a consideration of the Hegelian and Marxist critiques throws light on some of its virtues. To adopt as a standard of legitimacy in social institutions what all those affected could rationally agree to is a procedure well adapted to ensure that the interests of all are properly protected. John Rawls, the principal begetter of the recent revival, has seized on just this feature of contractarianism in order to emphasize its superiority over utilitarianism, with its exclusive attention to aggregate, as distinct from individual, benefit.[22] Nevertheless, Rawlsian contract theory involves a marked change of direction. In its older versions, the theory was in essence concerned with the *common* interests of all men — the state (or a certain kind of state) is in the interests of all, by comparison with a state-less society (the 'state of nature'). It did not address the problem of *conflicting* interests. Or rather, it saw the contract as an outcome of a common interest in escaping from the intolerably conflicting interests of the state of nature; but not as a method of settling any such disputes. Rawls's innovation has been to adapt contract theory to precisely this purpose. His suggestion is that (appropriately modified) it can do so in a 'manner which, again, ensures that the interests of all will be properly protected. To resolve conflicting interests in a way that adequately protects the interests of all is to ensure *justice*. Hence, Rawls's contract theory is a theory of justice.

The Rawlsian contract is a hypothetical contract, but with a difference. The reason is that Rawls is not satisfied with the moral principles underlying traditional contract theory — that one is bound either by one's (actual) contract, or by the contract that all would make in a hypothetical situation (such as the 'state of nature'). For a contract can be invalidated — morally and even legally — if the relation of the contracting parties is *already* so unequal as to give one or some an undue advantage. It is Rawls's view, indeed, that no actual or even hypothetically possible situation, such as a state of nature, can place contractors in a position of initial equality sufficiently thoroughgoing for his purposes. Hence his introduction of the famous 'veil of ignorance', which goes so far as to hide from his hypothetical contractors all knowledge that could give them a bargaining advantage. Clearly the Rawlsian 'original position', in which his contract is to be made, is neither actual nor 'natural' nor even possible — it is a carefully designed fiction intended to ensure that the contract is fair. In the fair original position, his contractors are to choose principles for the distribution of 'primary social goods' (such as liberties, power, and wealth). In brief, his argument is that inequalities in social distribution are just if and only if they would be acceptable to all in an original position of equality as defined by the veil of ignorance.

Viewed from this perspective, James Buchanan's version of social contract theory, in his *Limits of Liberty*, seems notably unconcerned with the fairness of the initial contracting situation. Although similar to Rawls in that his contract is explicitly hypothetical and is concerned with the distribution of rights and of wealth, Buchanan unlike Rawls reverts to a hypothetical state of nature as his starting-point — one which is Hobbesian in its a-morality and is explicit in eschewing any presumption of equality among the contracting parties. Buchanan is even willing (with scant consistency) to consider the actually existing status quo as the starting-point for a valid social contract.

Given that he is concerned with problems of the distribution of goods of a kind where conflicting interests are involved, Buchanan's cavalier attitude to the problem of fairness is a crippling defect; but on the other hand Rawls's attempt to cope with it by means of the 'veil of ignorance' has been intensely controversial. For Robert Nozick (himself the author of a famous theory of justice), the Rawlsian contract is just as much of a trick as the historical 'original contract' seemed to be to Rousseau — not, however, a trick played by the rich on the poor, but almost the other way round. More precisely, Nozick charges that it enables the 'poorly endowed' to exploit the 'well endowed'.[23] For the Rawlsian veil of ignorance conceals all knowledge of unequal endowment (including natural endowment) and so prevents the well endowed from reaping the full reward from their talents and legitimately acquired resources, a reward which, in Nozick's view, they are morally entitled to. Rawlsian justice, in practice, requires governmental intervention to ensure that *all* benefit from the wealth-creating activities of *all* members of society. In other words, government must *re*distribute wealth from the 'well endowed' to the 'poorly endowed', or from rich to poor. To Nozick, this amounts to robbery. In this controversy, James Coleman's article suggests a plausible compromise position: even without the Rawlsian veil of ignorance, and in full knowledge of relative endowment, contractors could still unanimously agree on *some* measure of redistribution from the rich to the poor. After all, knowledge of one's endowment and that of others does not remove all uncertainty about how one will fare in society in economic terms, especially in the free market system favoured by Nozick. It would be rational even for the well endowed to accept some redistribution as an insurance policy — for even they might need it.

By common consent, the most noteworthy contribution to social contract theory since the publication of Rawls's *Theory of Justice* has been David Gauthier's *Morals by Agreement*. This difficult work does not easily yield an extract suitable for inclusion here, and so its argument is represented instead by Gauthier's article 'Justice as Social Choice'. Like Coleman's, it can be seen as a response to the disagreement between Rawls and Nozick, and in a sense a compromise between them. Gauthier's principle of 'maximin relative benefit' has a Rawlsian ring (Rawls argues for a maximin principle of economic distribution, meaning that that system is just which maximizes a society's lowest or minimum level of wealth), even if he arrives at it by a quite different argument. Indeed, if Gauthier's argument were sound, it could be used to buttress Rawls, because in Rawls's argument the maximin principle depends crucially on his controversial 'veil of ignorance'. Gauthier, on the other hand, claims to derive his principle of 'maximin relative benefit' from a hypothetical ideal bargain among rational self-interested individuals, in which the veil of ignorance is not required. Unfortunately, it does not seem to me that the argument succeeds, for it requires the highly dubious premise that a rational, self-interested person cannot demand of another person known to be rational and self-interested anything that is not acceptable to himself.

Gauthier's contract theory of justice differs from that of Rawls in another, much more important way. While Rawls's maximin principle is supposed to apply to the whole economic product of a society, that of Gauthier is to apply only to what he calls the 'cooperative surplus',[24] that is, to the *increase* in economic product brought about by social cooperation. In the phrase 'maximin relative benefit' the last word means benefit to the individual, compared to what he or she could achieve or acquire, in the absence of social cooperation — the latter is the 'starting-point' for each individual entering Gauthier's bargaining process. This 'absence of social cooperation' is a kind of state of nature, and one might think that, if Hobbes is right, the individual in the state of nature could achieve almost nothing by his own efforts. Gauthier, however, stipulates that the appropriate state of nature (or starting-point for his contract) is not Hobbesian but Lockean. But this is misleading — what he means is not really the Lockean state of nature with its inconveniences, infringement of property rights, and risk of war, but rather a state in which Lockean property rights are respected (and Lockean property rights are also Nozickian property rights). The upshot is that, according to Gauthier, each person is entitled to whatever he or she could get in an ideal free market, plus a share of the cooperative surplus determined by the principle of maximin relative benefit. Otherwise put, the latter principle applies only to the distribution of benefit from public goods.

Gauthier's argument has at least this advantage over Nozick's, that (unlike Nozick) he is aware that public goods exist. Nevertheless, it is deeply puzzling. Public goods are, by definition, non-exclusive: that is, it is impossible or impracticable to limit their consumption to those who (voluntarily) pay for them (national defence and lighthouses are the standard examples). This makes it necessary (it is usually argued) to organize their provision by means of a coercive central agency, normally the state. But — by definition — no question can arise about the distribution of public goods: they are such because, if provided at all, they are provided for everyone. What *could* be in question is the distribution of the *costs* of public goods. Perhaps Gauthier's argument could be adapted to this question, but he has not shown how. If so, it would become purely and simply a theory of just taxation.

It seems, therefore, that the scope of Gauthier's theory is a good deal narrower than is suggested by the title of his book, *Morals by Agreement* (and even that of his article, 'Justice as Social Choice'). Nevertheless, and largely under the influence of Rawls, there have been not a few recent attempts to extend social contract theory from the sphere of political or public morality to moral theory more generally. A distinguished example is the article by B. J. Diggs included here. Diggs upholds a contractarian social morality as the one best accommodated to our ideal of individual moral autonomy, or 'respect for persons'. The contractarian moralist, according to his definition, is one who seeks 'to find or to invent a set of restrictions that it would be reasonable to include in the morality by which he governs himself if almost all were willing to accept these restrictions — or ... to determine articles of morality that it would be reasonable for all persons together freely to subscribe to'. The contractarian moral agent is enjoined to respect the viewpoint of all other persons equally with his own, and to resolve moral issues as if he were an impartial 'moral judge'. Diggs claims that this version of contractarianism, which does not use the idea of a 'veil of ignorance', nor of an agreement between self-interested bargainers, gives a foundation as strong as or stronger than Rawls's for some Rawlsian conclusions, such as toleration or equal liberty: but unlike Rawls and Gauthier he does not claim that such conclusions can be *deduced* from his premises — rather, the latter function as a *guide*. This, he suggests, is the best that the nature of the problem allows. And in another way also, Diggs's contractarianism is more modest than Rawls's and, indeed, most of the contractarian tradition — it yields, he says, results which are 'pragmatic' and 'contextual' (not universal). The moral restrictions people can reasonably accept depends on what goals and ideals they happen to have. Hence, Diggs recognizes, they are likely to be different in different times and societies. Contractarian moral reasoning, therefore, has to be done piecemeal and repeatedly, rather than all at once and for all time. The more modest results that follow from this are, in Diggs's view, the best that can be achieved.

CONCLUDING REMARKS

The differences between Diggs's version of contractarianism and that of Rawls are instructive, and a consideration of them will take us to the heart of some central problems of social contract theory. One problem may be expressed thus: in what way should the theory relate moral obligation and self-interest? It was argued above that traditional social contract theory solved that problem by restricting its attention to matters of *common* interest, and by postulating (or deducing) a duty to share in promoting this common interest, on the presumption that one either has agreed, or would agree, to do so, out of self-interest. (In effect, this is an obligation not to be a 'free rider'.) Rawls retained the presumption of self-interested motivation, but, in order to cope with the issue of *conflicting* interests, took pains to place his contractors in a fair original position, incorporating the 'veil of ignorance'. Diggs, by contrast, takes individuals just as they are, with their (partly) conflicting interests *and* moral beliefs.

Diggs's contractarianism seems to have this advantage over Rawls's, that while his contract (or rather contracts) are just as imaginary, his contractors are real people. The question, however, is whether his method can produce definite results. Diggs is at pains to argue that it can: a case in point being, he claims, the principle of toleration. For his contractarianism requires us to seek principles all can reasonably agree on, hence to respect the views equally of all. Intolerance, Diggs suggests, contradicts such an attitude. But does it? Or rather, does equal respect for all persons imply equal respect for all views? Diggs seems to under-rate what might be called the problem of the 'moral paternalist', the person concerned that *others* should live rightly, as *he* or *she* understands living rightly. Why should such a person find it reasonable to agree to a principle of tolerance? Diggs's answer, it appears, would be that 'moral paternalism' is incompatible with truly respecting others as persons. This might be disputed: but if granted, it means that the apparent advantage of Diggs's contractarianism — that his contractors are real people — involves a heavy theoretical price: some (perhaps many) people have to be excluded from the contract. It is necessary, apparently, to exclude those with inappropriate moral attitudes, such as moral paternalists. From this point of view, Rawls's approach has the distinct advantage that *all* his contractors are envisaged as concerned purely with their own plan of life — they are quite uninterested, therefore, in the (self-regarding) behaviour of fellow contractors. At the same time the veil of ignorance forces them to treat all possible plans of life impartially. The conclusion of tolerance seems to be more firmly based on these Rawlsian premises (admittedly, it still does not follow ineluctably).

In another respect, however, Diggs's version of contractarianism seems to me to be preferable to that of Rawls. Diggs seems right to say that what can reasonably be agreed by persons must depend on their goals and values. (By 'values' here I mean, not moral principles, but conceptions in terms of which persons define their *own* interests.) A long-standing, and well founded, complaint against the social contract tradition is that it seems to assume that all men are alike in this regard — or at least, sufficiently alike that all can agree on one particular contract.[25] Hobbes, for example, assumed that the most powerful 'passion' of all men is the fear of premature death, and the assumption is crucial to his whole argument, and to the universal validity he claimed for it. We know, however, that many people are willing to risk death for the sake of goals both noble and ignoble. A similar problem besets Rawls's contract theory: why shouldn't his contractors be willing to risk their 'guaranteed minimum' of liberty and material wealth for the sake of other goods? Such adventurous spirits would not be willing parties to the Rawlsian contract any more than to the Hobbesian.

Since social contract theory, by definition, derives norms from agreeement actual or hypothetical, the derived norms have to be in some way limited by the values of the contractors, which are non-universal and have to be taken as given. Insofar as social contract theory is a part of *political* philosophy, the most promising strategy may therefore be to limit its application to particular political communities or states, taken one at a time (which is not, of course, to deny that the same contractarian argument could be applicable in several different states). One may hope that, within a given political community at a given time, there is sufficient uniformity of fundamental values to give a basis for general agreement — that is, for a social contract. At any rate there is a better chance of this in a single political community than there is in relation to all humanity.

It should not be thought that such a contractarianism, relatively modest though it would be, is intended to abstract from conflicts of interest, or to return to the concern of the older contract theory with common interests only. We may imagine, for example, a society all of whose members desire economic wealth and material security *for themselves*. Despite similarity of values, such a society manifests conflicting interests. Indeed, it is arguable that the problem of coflicting interest cannot be avoided by social contract theory – even the traditional form of the theory which focused on the common interest of all in leaving the 'state of nature' to enter civil society. Even if we grant that (almost) everyone has such an interest, serious conflicts of interest may still exist. These would be likely to manifest themselves in support for different *terms* of entry into civil society, or in other words, different constitutions thereof. Questions of distribution of wealth, for example, could hardly be avoided. Should a Lockean solution be adopted, endorsing and protecting private property rights no matter how unequal, so long as the property was acquired in appropriate ways? Or should the Rawlsian solution be preferred, with its requirement of government action to secure a 'social minimum'? Or should everything be left to the decision of the sovereign (Hobbes), or the sovereign people (Rousseau)? It can hardly be contended that different individuals, differently circumstanced, will be indifferent as between these alternatives. In this sense, it seems that every social contract theory (or at least, every theory in whch the contracting parties are individuals) *must* be a theory of justice. It is a weakness of the older theories that they appear not to recognize this – and a corresponding strength of Rawls that he does.

If this is correct – if every social contract theory must reckon with conflicting interests and the terms of their resolution – then it seems to follow that the theory must incorporate some such device as the Rawlsian veil of ignorance. The veil of ignorance is designed, in part, to make the problem of conflicting interests *manageable*, without abolishing it.[26] It has to be admitted, however, that it greatly changes the form and nature of the conflict, and does so in a way that is intensely controversial. According to Rawls, the contracting situation which it creates is fair to all parties, while to Nozick it is a monstrous injustice to the 'well endowed' (see above). Whether Rawls or Nozick is right is, ultimately, a matter of individual judgement. But without the veil, or something like it, it appears that social contract theory can cope with common interests only, and hence can arrive only at conclusions of a very general kind – for example, that government (in some form) is desirable) and perhaps (if Coleman's argument is right) that some sort of social security system is (in certain societies) desirable. Such results, no doubt, are not negligible; but they would fall well short of the ambitions typical of social contract theory, old and new.

### NOTES

1   J. W. Gough, *The Social Contract* (Oxford: Clarendon Press, 1937).
2   Cf. *The Times Guide to the House of Commons, October 1974*, pp. 300—1.
3   *Financial Times*, 24 April 1987.
4   Peter G. Peterson, 'Gorbachev's Bottom Line', *New York Review of Books*, 34: 11 (25 June 1987), p. 3.
5   See M. H. Lessnoff, *Social Contract* (London: Macmillan, 1986), pp. 23—4.
6   Quoted in D. G. Ritchie, *Darwin and Hegel* (London: Sonnenschein, 1893), p. 203; and A. J. Carlyle, *Medieval Political Theory in the West*, 3 (London: Blackwood, 1915), pp. 163—6.
7   R. A. Giesey, *If Not, Not* (Princeton UP, 1968), p. 247.
8   G. B. Fowler, *Intellectual Interests of Engelbert of Admont*, 2nd edn (New York: Columbia UP, 1967), pp. 167—70.
9   M. Salamonio, *De Principatu* (Milan: Giuffre Editore, 1955), esp. pp. 27—9. See also J. W. Gough, *Social Contract*, p. 47.
10  Junius Brutus, *A Defence of Liberty Against Tyrants*, ed. H. Laski (London: Bell, 1924), p. 179. This is a reprint of the 1689 English translation of the *Vindiciae Contra Tyrannos*.
11  Ibid., p. 72.
12  Ibid., pp. 109, 111, 199, 212.
13  O. Gierke, *The Development of Political Theory* (London: Allen & Unwin, 1939), pp. 98—102.
14  J.-J. Rousseau, *The Social Contract and Discourses* (London: Dent, 1973), pp. 88—9.
15  G. W. F. Hegel, *Philosophy of Right* (Oxford, Clarendon Press, 1952), pp. 57—9, 122—3, 126.
16  K. Marx, *Grundrisse* (Harmondsworth: Penguin Books, 1973), p. 83; L. R. Page, *Karl Marx and the Critical Examination of his Works* (London: The Freedom Association, 1987) p. 124.
17  C. B. Macpherson, *The Political Theory of Possessive Individualism* (Oxford: Clarendon Press, 1962), chs. 2 and 5.
18  E. B. Pashukanis, *Law and Marxism* (London: Ink Links, 1978), pp. 82, 81, 103. First published in Russian, 1924; the English edn is a translation from the German version of 1929.
19  Ibid., p. 121.
20  Ibid., p. 144.
21  Ibid., pp. 137—47.
22  J. Rawls, 'Justice as Fairness', in P. Laslett and W. G. Runciman,

*Philosophy, Politics and Society* (second series) (Oxford: Blackwell, 1962), pp. 149–56.

23  R. Nozick, *Anarchy, State and Utopia* (Oxford: Blackwell, 1974), pp. 192–8.

24  D. Gauthier, *Morals by Agreement* (Oxford: Clarendon Press, 1986), pp. 130, 133–4, *passim*.

25  This point is discussed at greater length in M. H. Lessnoff, *Social Contract* (London: Macmillan, 1986), pp. 103–4, 143, 145–7, 151–4.

26  Ibid., pp. 135–6, 140–2, 154.

# 1

# Human Association and Politics

JOHANNES ALTHUSIUS

## Politics

THE GENERAL ELEMENTS OF POLITICS
*(Chapter 1)*

Politics is the art of associating men for the purpose of establishing, cultivating, and conserving social life among them. Whence it is called 'symbiotics'. The subject matter of politics is therefore association (*consociatio*), in which the symbiotes[1] pledge themselves each to the other, by explicit or tacit agreement, to mutual sharing of whatever is useful and necessary for the harmonious exercise of social life.

The end of political 'symbiotic' man is holy, just, comfortable, and happy symbiosis,[2] a life lacking nothing either necessary or useful. Truly, in living this life no man is self-sufficient, or adequately endowed by nature. For when he is born, destitute of all help, naked and defenceless, as if having lost all his goods in a shipwreck, he is cast forth into the hardships of this life, not able by his own efforts to reach a maternal breast, nor to endure the harshness of his condition, nor to move himself from the place where he was cast forth. By his weeping and tears, he can initiate nothing except the most miserable life, a very certain sign of pressing and immediate misfortune. Bereft of all counsel and aid, for which nevertheless he is then in greatest need, he is unable to help himself without the intervention and assistance of another. Even if he is well-nourished in body, he cannot show forth the light of reason. Nor in his

The volume from which these selections are taken (*The Politics of Johannes Althusius*, translated with an Introduction by Frederick S. Carney, and originally published by Eyre and Spottiswoode in 1965) will be republished in the near future by the University Presses of America in association with The Center for the Study of Federalism at Temple University in Philadelphia. Extracts reprinted by permission of Frederick S. Carney.

adulthood is he able to obtain in and by himself those outward goods he needs for a comfortable and holy life, or to provide by his own energies all the requirements of life. The energies and industry of many men are expended to procure and supply these things. Therefore, as long as he remains isolated and does not mingle in the society of men, he cannot live at all comfortably and well while lacking so many necessary and useful things. As an aid and remedy for this state of affairs is offered him in symbiotic life, he is led, and almost impelled, to embrace it if he wants to live comfortably and well, even if he merely wants to live. Therein he is called upon to exercise and perform those virtues that are necessarily inactive except in this symbiosis. And so he begins to think by what means such symbiosis, from which he expects so many useful and enjoyable things, can be instituted, cultivated, and conserved. Concerning these matters we shall, by God's grace, speak in the following pages ...

The symbiotes are co-workers who, by the bond of an associating and uniting agreement, share among themselves whatever is appropriate for a comfortable life of soul and body. In other words, they are participants or partners in common life.

This mutual sharing, or common enterprise, involves (1) things, (2) services, and (3) common rights by which the numerous and various needs of each and every symbiote are supplied, the self-sufficiency and mutuality of life and human society are achieved, and social life is established and conserved ... The communion of right (3) is the process by which the symbiotes live and are ruled by just laws in a common life among themselves.

The communion of right is called the law of association and symbiosis ...

The law of association in its first aspect is, in turn, either common or proper. Common law (*lex communis*), which is unchanging, indicates that in every association and type of symbiosis some persons are rulers (heads, overseers, prefects) or superiors, others are subjects or inferiors. For all government is held together by imperium and subjection; in fact, the human race started straightway from the beginning with imperium and subjection. God made Adam master and monarch of his wife, and of all creatures born or descendant from her. Therefore all power and government is said to be from God ...

The ruler, prefect, or chief directs and governs the functions of the social life for the utility of the subjects individually and collectively ... Therefore, as Augustine says, to rule, to govern, to preside is nothing other than to serve and care for the utility of others, as parents rule their children, and a man his wife. ...

Government by superiors considers both the soul and the body of inferiors: the soul that it may be formed and imbued with doctrine and knowledge of things useful and necessary in human life, the body that it may be provided with nourishment and whatever else it needs. The first responsibility pertains to education, the second to sustentation and protection. Education centres on the instruction of inferiors in the true knowledge and worship of God, and in prescribed duties that ought to be performed towards one's neighbour; education also pertains to the correction of evil customs and errors ... Protection is the legitimate defence against injuries and violence, the process by which the security of inferiors is maintained by superiors against any misfortune, violence, or injury ...

Proper laws are those enactments by which particular associations are ruled. They differ in each species of association according as the nature of each requires.

Thus the needs of body and soul, and the seeds of virtue implanted in our souls, drew dispersed men together into one place. These causes have built villages, established cities, founded academic institutions, and united by civil unity and society a diversity of farmers, craftsmen, labourers, builders, soldiers, merchants, learned and unlearned men as so many members of the same body. Consequently, while some persons provided for others, and some received from others what they themselves lacked, all came together into a certain public body that we call the commonwealth, and by mutual aid devoted themselves to the general good and welfare of this body. And that this was the true origin first of villages, and then of larger commonwealths embracing wide areas, is taught by the most ancient records of history and confirmed by daily experience. (Opposed to this judgement is the life and teaching of recluses, monks, and hermits, who defend their error and heresy by an erroneous appeal to Luke 1: 80; 10: 41; Hebrews 11: 38; I Kings 19: 8. But scripture places this kind of life among its maledictions. Deuteronomy 28: 64, 65; Psalms 107 and 144; Code X, 32, 26. Note also that a wandering and vagabond life was imposed upon Cain in punishment for his fratricide. Genesis 4: 14.)

From what has been said, we further conclude that the efficient cause of political association is consent and agreement among the communicating citizens. The formal cause is indeed the association brought about by contributing and sharing one with the other, in which political men institute, cultivate, maintain, and conserve the fellowship of human life through decisions about those things useful and necessary to this social life. The final cause of politics is the enjoyment of a comfortable, useful, and happy life, and of the common welfare — that we may live with piety and honour a peaceful and quiet life, that while true piety toward God and justice among the citizens may prevail at home, defense against the enemy from abroad may be maintained, and that concord and peace may always and everywhere thrive. The final cause is also the conservation of a human society that aims at a life in which you can worship God quietly and without error. The material cause of politics is the aggregate of precepts for sharing those things, services, and right that we bring together, each fairly and properly according to his ability, for symbiosis and the common advantage of the social life.

Moreover, Aristotle teaches that man by his nature is brought to this social life and mutual sharing. For man is a more political animal than the bee or any other gregarious creature, and therefore by nature far more of a social animal than bees, ants, cranes, and such kind as feed and defend themselves in flocks. ... No man is able to live well and happily to himself. Necessity therefore induces association; and the want of things necessary for life, which are acquired and communicated by the help and aid of one's associates, conserves it. For this reason it is evident that the commonwealth, or civil society, exists by nature, and that man is by nature a civil animal who strives eagerly for association ...

### THE FAMILY
#### (Chapters 2–3)

Thus far we have discussed the general elements of politics. We turn now to types of association or of symbiotic life. Every association is either simple and private,[3] or mixed and public.[4]

The simple and private association is a society and symbiosis initiated by a special covenant (*pactum*) among the members for the purpose of bringing together and holding in common a particular interest. This is done according to their agreement and way of life, that is, according to what is necessary and useful for organized private symbiotic life. Such an association can rightly be called primary, and all others derivative from it. For without this primary association others are able neither to arise not to endure.

The efficient causes of this simple and private association and symbiosis are individual men covenanting among themselves to share whatever is necessary and useful for organizing and living in private life ...

There are two types of simple and private association. The first is natural, and the second is civil.[5] The private and natural symbiotic association is one in which married persons, blood relatives, and in-laws, in response to a natural affection and necessity, agree to a definite community among themselves. Whence this individual, natural, necessary, economic, and domestic society is said to be contracted permanently among these symbiotic allies of life, with the same boundaries as life itself. Therefore it is rightly called the most intense society, friendship, relationship, and union, the seedbed of every other symbiotic association ...

There are two kinds of private and natural domestic association. The first is conjugal, and the second is kinship (*propinqua*). The conjugal association and symbiosis is one in which the husband and wife, who are bound each to the other, share the advantages and responsibilities of married life ... The kinship association is one in which relatives and in-laws are united for the purpose of sharing advantages and responsibilities ... He is called the leader (*princeps*) of the family, or of any tribe of people, who is placed over such a family or tribe, and who has the right to coerce the persons of his family individually and collectively ...

Certain political writers eliminate, wrongly in my judgment, the doctrine of the conjugal and kinship private association from the field of politics and assign it to economics. Now these associations are the seedbed of all private and public associational life. The knowledge of other associations is therefore incomplete and defective without this doctrine of conjugal and kinship associations, and cannot be rightly understood without it. I concede that the skill of attending to household goods, of supplying, increasing, and conserving the goods of the family, is entirely economic, and as such is correctly eliminated from politics. But altogether different from this is association among spouses and kinsmen, which is entirely political and general, and which shares things, services, rights, and aid for living the domestic and economic life piously, justly, and beneficially. Economic management, however, concerns merely household goods — how much and by what means they may be furnished, augmented, and conserved. By such management the skill is made available for cultivating fields, tending herds, ploughing, sowing, reaping, planting, pruning, and doing all kinds of agricultural work. But by politics alone arises the wisdom for governing and administering the family. It is politics that teaches what the spouses, paterfamilias, materfamilias, servants, and attendants may contribute and share among themselves — and what the kinsmen among themselves — in order that private and domestic social life may be piously and justly fulfilled.

So therefore economics and politics differ greatly as to subject and end. The subject of the former is the goods of the family; its end is the acquisition of whatever is necessary for food and clothing. The subject of the latter, namely politics, is pious and just symbiosis; its end is the governing and preserving of association and symbiotic life.

Furthermore, certain persons wrongly assert that every symbiotic association is public, and none private. Now this axiom stands firm and fixed: all symbiotic association and life is essentially, authentically, and generically political. But not every symbiotic association is public. There are certain associations that are private, such as conjugal and kinship families, and collegia. And these are the seedbeds of the public association. Whence it follows that the private association is rightly attributed to politics.

### THE COLLEGIUM
*(Chapter 4)*

This completes the discussion of the natural association. We turn now to the civil association, which is a body organized by assembled persons according to their own pleasure and will to serve a common utility and necessity in human life. That is to say, they agree among themselves by common consent on a manner of ruling and obeying for the utility both of the whole body and of its individuals.

This society by its nature is transitory and can be discontinued ... In it ... men of the same trade, training, or profession are united for the purpose of holding in common ... things they jointly profess as duty, way of life, or craft. Such an association is called a collegium.[6] ... It is said to be a private association by contrast with the public association ...

At the present time in many places the people of a provincial city, realm, or polity, by reason of their occupation or kind and diversity of organized life, are customarily distributed in three orders, estates, or larger general collegia. The first is of clergymen, the second of nobility, and the third of the people or plebs, including scholastic men, farmers, merchants, and craftsmen. Such general collegia and bodies contain within them smaller special collegia. Such are the particularly important collegia of judges and magistrates, the collegia of ministers of the church, and the collegia of various workers and merchants necessary and useful in social life, which we will discuss later ...

## THE CITY
### (Chapters 5–6)

With this discussion of the civil and private association, we turn now to the public association. For human society develops from private to public association by the definite steps and progressions of small societies. The public association exists when many private associations are linked together for the purpose of establishing an inclusive political order (*politeuma*) . . .

This public symbiotic association is either particular or universal. The particular association is encompassed by fixed and definite localities within which its rights are communicated. In turn, it is either a community (*universitas*) or a province.

The community is an association formed by fixed laws and composed of many families and collegia living in the same place. It is elsewhere called a city (*civitas*) in the broadest sense, or a body of many and diverse associations . . .

The members of a community are private and diverse associations of families and collegia, not the individual members of private associations. These persons, by their coming together, now become not spouses, kinsmen, and colleagues, but citizens of the same community.

Furthermore, this community is either rural or urban. A rural community . . . is either a hamlet, a village, or a town. An urban community . . . is called a city . . .

## THE PROVINCE
### (Chapters 7–8)

We have completed the discussion of the community. We turn now to the province, which contains within its territory many villages, towns, outposts and cities united under the communion and administration of one law . . .

The members of the province are its orders and estates, as they are called, or larger collegia. The provincials have been distributed in these orders and estates according to the class and diversity of life they have organized in keeping with their profession, vocation, and activity . . .

The provincial order or estate may be either sacred and ecclesiastical, or secular and civil. In Germany they are known as *der Geistlich und Weltlich stand*. These orders, together with the provincial head, represent the entire province. All weightier matters are guided by their counsel, and the welfare of the commonwealth is entrusted to them. They admonish the head of the province when he errs, correct the abuse of his power, and punish his seducers and base flatterers ...

The prefect of these sacred and secular provincial orders is the superior to whom is entrusted the administration of the province and of provincial matters. He receives his trust from the realm under which the province exists, and of which it is a member. He may be called a dynast, eparch, satrap, governor, president, rector, or moderator of the province ... Today in many places in Europe such prefects are called counts, and are designated by the name of the province entrusted to them, or of the principal fortress or metropolis of the province. Such are the counts of Nassau, Friesland, Schwartzenberg, Hanover, Mansfield, Oldenburg, and many others. In difficult matters involving the entire province, namely, of war, peace, imposition of taxes, publication of general law and decrees, and other such things, the prefect can do nothing without the consent and agreement of the provincial orders ...

Whenever two or more provinces are entrusted to the administration of one person, he is usually called a duke, prince, marquis, or landgrave ...

Even though these heads, prefects, and rectors of provinces recognize the supreme magistrate of the realm as their superior, from whom their administration and power are conceded, nevertheless they have rights of sovereignty in their territory, and stand in the place of the supreme prince. They prevail as much in their territory as does the emperor or supreme magistrate in the realm, except for superiority, pre-eminence, and certain other things specifically reserved to the supreme magistrate who does the constituting. Such is the common judgement of jurists. The head of a province therefore has the right of superiority and regal privileges in his territory, but without prejudice to the universal jurisdiction that the supreme prince has ...

The duty of the provincial head is, first, to exercise diligent watch and care over sacred and secular provincial affairs, and to provide that they be lifted up and directed to the glory of God and to the welfare of the entire province and the members thereof ... His duty, secondly, is rightly to administer justice to individual persons, with the power and the right of inflicting penalties of life, body, goods, and reputation, and of rewarding those who do good ...

POLITICAL SOVEREIGNTY, AND ECCLESIASTICAL COMMUNITY
*(Chapter 9)*

Now that we have discussed particular and minor public associations, we turn to the universal and major public association. In
this association many cities and provinces obligate themselves to
hold, organize, use, and defend, through their common energies
and expenditures, the law of the realm (*jus regni*) in the mutual
sharing of things and services. For without these supports, ... a
pious and just life cannot be established, fostered, and preserved
in universal social life.

Whence this mixed society, constituted partly from private,
natural, necessary, and voluntary societies, partly from public
societies, is called a universal association. It is a polity in the
fullest sense, an imperium, realm, commonwealth, and people
united in one body by the agreement of many symbiotic associations
and particular bodies, and brought together under one law. For
families, cities, and provinces existed by nature prior to realms,
and gave birth to them.

Many writers distinguish between a realm (*regnum*) and a
commonwealth (*respublica*), relating the former to a monarchical
king and the latter to polyarchical optimates.[7] But in my judgment
this distinction is not a good one. For ownership of a realm
belongs to the people, and administration of it to the king ...

We will discuss, first, the members of a realm and, then, its law.
The members of a realm, or of this universal symbiotic association,
are not, I say, individual men, families or collegia, as in a private
or a particular public association. Instead, members are many
cities, provinces, and regions agreeing among themselves on a
single body constituted by mutual union and association ...

The bond of this body and association is consensus, together
with trust extended and accepted among the members of the
commonwealth. The bond is, in other words, a tacit or expressed
promise to share things, mutual services, aid, counsel, and the
same common laws to the extent that the utility and necessity of
universal social life in a realm shall require ...

Such are the members of the realm. Its law is the means by
which the members, in order to establish good order and the
supplying of provisions throughout the territory of the realm, are
associated and bound to each other as one people in one body and
under one head. This law of the realm (*jus regni*) is also called the

right of sovereignty (*jus majestatis*). It is, in other words, the law of a major state or power as contrasted with the law that is attributed to a city or a province ...

The people, or the associated members of the realm, have the power of establishing this law of the realm and of binding themselves to it ... Without this power no realm or universal symbiotic life can exist. Therefore, as long as this right thrives in the realm and rules the political body, so long does the realm live and prosper. But if this right is taken away, the entire symbiotic life perishes, or becomes a band of robbers and a gang of evil men, or disintegrates into many different realms or provinces.

The law of the realm, or right of sovereignty, does not belong to individual members, but to all members joined together and to the entire associated body of the realm. For as universal association can be constituted not by one member, but by all the members together, so the right is said to be the property not of individual members, but of the members jointly ...

Bodin disagrees with our judgment by which supreme power is attributed to the realm or universal association. He says that the right of sovereignty, which we have called the right of the realm, is a supreme and perpetual power limited neither by law (*lex*) nor by time ...

This question concerns civil law and right. Should he who is said to have supreme power subordinate his imperium and high office to civil law? Bodin says no, and many others agree with him. In the judgment of these men there is supreme power above civil law and not limited by it ... I disagree. By no means can ... supreme power be attributed to a king or optimates, as Bodin most ardently endeavours to defend. Rather it is to be attributed rightfully only to the body of a universal association, namely, to a commonwealth or realm, and as belonging to it. From this body, after God, every legitimate power flows to those we call kings or optimates. Therefore, the king, prince, and optimates recognize this associated body as their superior, by which they are constituted, removed, exiled, and deprived of authority ... For however great is the power that is conceded to another, it is always less than the power of the one who makes the concession, and in it the pre-eminence and superiority of the conceder is understood to be reserved. Whence it is shown that the king does not have a supreme and perpetual power above the law, and consequently neither are the rights of sovereignty his own property, although he may have the administration and exercise of them by concession from the associated body. And only so far are the rights of sovereignty ceded and handed over to another that they never become his own property ... All have only the use and exercise of power for the benefit of others, not the ownership of it ...

Universal symbiotic communion is both ecclesiastical and secular. Corresponding to the former are religion and piety, which pertain to the welfare and eternal life of the soul, the entire first table of the Decalogue. Corresponding to the latter is justice, which concerns the use of the body and of this life, and the rendering to each his due, the second table of the Decalogue. In the former, everything is to be referred immediately to the glory of God; in the latter, to the utility and welfare of the people associated in one body. These are the two foundations of every good association ...

### THE EPHORS AND THEIR DUTIES
*(Chapter 18)*

We have thus far discussed communal law in the universal association. We now turn our attention to the administration of this law. This is the activity by which the rights of universal symbiotic association are ordered, properly administered, and dispensed by designated public ministers of the realm for the welfare of its members, both individually and collectively ... These public ministers of the realm are elected by the united and associated bodies or members of the realm ...

The people first associated themselves in a certain body with definite laws, and established for itself the necessary and useful rights of this association. Then, because the people itself cannot manage the administration of these rights, it entrusted their administration to ministers and rectors elected by it. In so doing, the people transferred to them the authority and power necessary for the performance of this assignment, equipped them with the sword for this purpose, and put itself under their care and rule ...

The rector and administrator of this civil society and commonwealth cannot justly and without tyranny be constituted by any other than the commonwealth itself. For 'by natural law all men are equal' and subject to the jurisdiction of no one, unless they subject themselves to another's imperium by their own consent and voluntary act, and transfer to another their rights, which no other person can claim for himself without a just title received from their owner. In the beginning of the human race there were neither imperia nor realms, nor were there rectors of them. Later, however, when necessity demanded, they were established by the people itself. We see examples of this in India and among the Ethiopians, as historians report ...

Indeed, it is evident that the supremely good and great God has assigned to the political community this necessity and power of electing and constituting. 'You shall establish judges and moderators in all your gates that the Lord your God gave you through your tribes, who shall judge the people with a righteous judgment.' 'I will establish a king over me.' 'So you shall establish a king over you.' ...

An administration is said to be just, legitimate, and salutary that seeks and obtains the prosperity and advantages of the members of the realm, both individually and collectively, and that, on the other hand, averts all evils and disadvantages to them, defends them against violence and injuries, and undertakes all actions of its administration according to laws ... This power of administering that these ministers and rectors established by the universal association have is bound to the utility and welfare of the subjects, and is circumscribed both by fixed limits, namely, by the laws of the Decalogue and by the just opinion of the universal association. Therefore, it is neither infinite nor absolute ...

Administrators are not permitted to overstep these limits. Those who exceed the boundaries of administration entrusted to them cease being ministers of God and of the universal association, and become private persons to whom obedience is not owed in those things in which they exceed the limits of their power ... These administrators exceed the limits and boundaries of the power conceded to them, first, when they command something to be done that is prohibited by God in the first table of the Decalogue, or to be omitted that is therein commanded by God. They do so, secondly, when they prohibit something that cannot be omitted, or command something that cannot be committed, without violating holy charity. The former commands and prohibitions are called impious, the latter wicked. The limits of their power are transgressed, thirdly, when in the administration entrusted to them they seek their personal and private benefit rather than the common utility and welfare of the universal association ...

The reason for refusing obedience to these administrators, as well as for denying absolute power to them, is their general and special vocation in which as Christian men they promised otherwise to God in baptism, which they are bound to fulfil. Moreover, administrators do not themselves have such great power, for no one gave them the power and jurisdiction to commit sin. Nor did the commonwealth, in constituting administrators for itself, deprive itself of the means of self-protection, and thus expose itself to the plundering of administrators. Besides, whatever power the people did not have it could not transfer to its administrators. Therefore, whatever power and right the administrators did not receive from the people, they do not have, they cannot exercise over the people, nor ought they to be able to do so. Finally, the wickedness of administrators cannot abolish or diminish the imperium and might of God, nor release the administrators from the same. For the power and jurisdiction of God are infinite. He created heaven and earth, and is rightly lord and proprietor of them. All who inhabit the earth are truly tenants, vassals, lessees, clients, and beneficiaries of his. 'The earth is the Lord's and the fulness thereof,' and is so by the right of creation and conservation. God is therefore called 'King of kings and Lord of lords.' . . .

Administrators of this universal association are of two kinds: the ephors and the supreme magistrate. Ephors are the representatives of the commonwealth or universal association to whom, by the consent of the people associated in a political body, the supreme responsibility has been entrusted for employing its power and right in constituting the supreme magistrate and in assisting him with aid and counsel in the activities of the associated body. They also employ its power and right in restraining and impeding his freedom in undertakings that are wicked and ruinous to the commonwealth, in containing him within the limits of his office, and finally in fully providing and caring for the commonwealth that it not suffer anything detrimental by the supreme magistrate's private attachments, hatreds, deeds, negligence, or inactivity.

These ephors, by reason of their excellence and the office entrusted to them, are called by others patricians, elders, princes, estates, first citizens of the realm, officials of the realm, protectors of the covenant entered into between the supreme magistrate and the people, custodians and defenders of justice and law to which they subject the supreme magistrate and compel him to obey, censors of the supreme magistrate, inspectors, counsellors of the realm, censors of royal honour, and brothers of the supreme magistrate.

From these things it is apparent that ephors, as the feet and foundations of the universal society or realm, are the means by which it is sustained and conserved during times of interregnum and peril, or when the magistrate is incapable of exercising imperium, or when he abuses his power, as Botero says. They do this in order that the commonwealth may not become exposed to dangers, revolutions, tumults, seditions, and treacheries, or occupied by enemies. For the ephors establish the head of the political body, and subject the king or supreme magistrate to law (*lex*) and justice. They establish the law, or God, as lord and emperor when the king rejects and throws off the yoke and imperium of law and of God, and ceasing as a minister of God, makes himself an instrument of the devil ... For the people has committed itself to these ephors for safety, and transferred all its actions to them, so that what the ephors do is understood to be the action of the entire people. The people does this because of utility and necessity. For it would be most difficult, as Diego Covarruvias says, to require individual votes of all citizens and parts of a commonwealth ...

Those persons should be elected ephors who have great might and wealth, because it is in their interest that the commonwealth be healthy, and they will act as custodians of the public welfare with greater love, concern, and care ...

The duties of these ephors are principally contained under five headings. The first duty is that they elect the general and supreme magistrate. The second is that they contain him within the limits and bounds of his office, and serve as custodians, defenders, and vindicators of liberty and other rights that the people has not transferred to the supreme magistrate, but reserved to itself. The third is that in time of interregnum, or of an incapacitated administration of the commonwealth, the ephors become a trustee for the supreme magistrate and undertake the administration of the commonwealth until another supreme magistrate is elected. The fourth is that they remove a tyrannical supreme magistrate. The fifth is that they defend the supreme magistrate and his rights ...

We see in the power and authority conceded to these few ephors for defending the rights of the people or universal association that the people has not transferred these rights to the supreme magistrate, but has reserved them to itself. For the universal association entrusted to its ephors the care and defence of these rights against all violators, disturbers, and plunderers, even against the supreme magistrate himself. The Dutch Wars of Independence offer examples of this care and defence by ephors during forty years of exploits against the King of Spain. Whence the office of these ephors is not only to judge whether the supreme magistrate has performed his responsibility or not, but also to resist and impede the tyranny of a supreme magistrate who abuses the rights of sovereignty, and violates or wishes to take away the authority of the body of the commonwealth ...

All these ephors and orders of the realm are distributed among two species. Some are general, and others special. General ephors are those to whom is entrusted the guardianship, care and inspection of the whole realm and of all its provinces. Such are imperial senators, counsellors, syndics, chancellors of the realm, and so forth . . .

Special ephors are those that undertake the guardianship and care of a province, region, or certain part of the realm. They recognize the supreme magistrate or commonwealth as their immediate superior. Such are dukes, princes, margraves, counts, barons, castellans, nobles of the realm, imperial cities (as they are called in Germany), and others that are named according to the province entrusted to them . . .

A special ephor has the same right and power in the province entrusted to his care and protection that the supreme magistrate has in the whole realm. He exercises in his territory those things that have been reserved to the emperor under the sign of the imperial crown . . .

### THE CONSTITUTING OF THE SUPREME MAGISTRATE
#### (Chapters 19–20)

So much for the ephors of the universal association. We turn now to its supreme magistrate. The supreme magistrate is he who, having been constituted according to the laws (*leges*) of the universal association for its welfare and utility, administers its rights (*jura*) and commands compliance with them. Although the rights of the universal association belong to the body of the universal association, or to the members of the realm, by reason of ownership and proprietorship, they also relate to its supreme magistrate to whom they have been entrusted by the body of the commonwealth by reason of administration and exercise . . .

The magistrate is called supreme because he exercises not his own power, but that of another, namely, the supreme power of the realm of which he is the minister. Or he is so called in relation to inferior and intermediate magistrates who are appointed by and depend upon this supreme power, and for whom he prescribes general laws. Whence he is said to have supereminence over all other superiors. Moreover, he is called supreme in relation to individuals. But he is not supreme in relation to his subjects collectively, nor to law, to which he is himself subject . . .

Three matters are henceforth to be considered; the constituting, the administration, and the types of the supreme magistrate. The constituting of the supreme magistrate is the process by which he assumes the imperium and administration of the realm conferred by the body of the universal association, and by which the members of the realm obligate themselves to obey him. Or it is the process by which the people and the supreme magistrate enter into a covenant concerning certain laws and conditions that set forth the form and manner of imperium and subjection, and faithfully extend and accept oaths from each other to this effect.

There is no doubt that this covenant, or contractual mandate (*contractum mandati*) entered into with the supreme magistrate, obligates both of the contracting parties, so much so that it is permitted to neither magistrate not subjects to revoke or dishonour it. However, in this reciprocal contract between the supreme magistrate as the mandatory, or promisor, and the universal association as the mandator, the obligation of the magistrate comes first, as is customary in a contractual mandate. By it he binds himself to the body of the universal association to administer the realm or commonwealth according to laws prescribed by God, right reason, and the body of the commonwealth. According to the nature of a mandate, the obligation of the people, or members of the realm, follows. By it the people in turn binds itself in obedience and compliance to the supreme magistrate who administers the commonwealth according to the prescribed laws.

The supreme magistrate exercises as much authority (*jus*) as has been explicitly conceded to him by the associated members or bodies of the realm. And what has not been given to him must be considered to have been left under the control of the people or universal association. Such is the nature of the contractual mandate. The less the power of those who rule, the more secure and stable the imperium remains. For power is secure that places a control upon force, that rules willing subjects, and that is circumscribed by laws, so that it does not become haughty and engage in excesses to the ruin of the subjects, nor degenerate into tyranny. . . . Absolute power, or what is called the plentitude of power, cannot be given to the supreme magistrate. For first, he who employs a plentitude of power breaks through the restraints by which human society has been contained. Secondly, by absolute power justice is destroyed, and when justice is taken away realms become bands of robbers, as Augustine says. Thirdly, such absolute power regards not the utility and welfare of subjects, but private pleasure. Power, however, is established for the utility of those who are ruled, not of those who rule, and the utility of the people or subjects does not in the least require unlimited power. Adequate provision has been made for them by laws . . .

The forms and limits of this mandate are the Decalogue, the

fundamental laws of the realm, and those conditions prescribed for the supreme magistrate in his election and to which he swears allegiance when elected.

Wherefore Fernando Vasquez and Lambert Daneau rightly say, and refute those who disagree, that the people is prior in time and more worthy by nature than its magistrate, and has constituted him. And so no realm or commonwealth has ever been founded or instituted except by contract entered into one with the other, by covenants agreed upon between subjects and their future prince, and by an established mutual obligation that both should religiously observe. When this obligation is dishonoured, the power of the prince loses its strength and is ended. Whence it follows that the people can exist without a magistrate, but a magistrate cannot exist without a people, and that the people creates the magistrate rather than the contrary. Therefore, kings are constituted by the people for the sake of the people, and are its ministers to whom the safety of the commonwealth has been entrusted. The magistrate or prince is mortal and an individual person; the realm or community is immortal. Upon the death of the king, the right of the realm returns to the estates and orders of the realm.

There are many precepts, examples, and rational evidences of this constituting a supreme magistrate by such a covenant or contract between the supreme magistrate and the ephors who represent the entire people of the associated bodies ...

This covenant or constitution by which the supreme magistrate is constituted by the ephors with the consent of the associated bodies has two parts. The first is the committing of the realm and its administration to a governor; the second is the promising of obedience and compliance by the people. The committing of the realm is the process by which the ephors, in the name of the people or associated body, confer and entrust the administration of the realm to the supreme magistrate. This is accomplished by two actions, namely the election of the supreme magistrate, and his inauguration or initiation.

The election, which is called αρχαιρεσια by the Greeks, is the process by which the ephors or magnates of the realm choose and designate, according to the laws and customs of the commonwealth, the supreme magistrate of the associated bodies or realm, and — invoking the name of God — offer and entrust to him, under fixed conditions and laws, the care and administration of the realm in accord with the established order of piety and justice. ... In this election conducted in the name of the associated people as the mandator, certain laws and conditions concerning subjection, and the form and manner of the future imperium, are proposed to the prospective magistrate as the mandatory. If he accepts these laws, and swears to the people to observe them, the election is considered firm and settled. This agreement entered into between magistrate and people is known as a mutually binding obligation ...

The conditions and laws of subjection, or the form, manner, and limits of the entrusted imperium, are customarily defined in certain articles that are publicly read and proposed by one of the ephors to the magistrate to be elected. Then this ephor asks whether the magistrate is willing to abide by these articles in the administration of the realm, and solemnly binds his assurances by a written oath ...

But if no laws or conditions have been expressed in the election, and the people has subjected itself to such a magistrate without them, then whatever things are holy, fair, and just, and are contained in the Decalogue, are considered to have been expressed, and the people is considered in the election to have subjected itself to the imperium of the magistrate according to them. Indeed, there is no instance in which a people has conferred upon a prince the unrestrained licence to bring about its own ruin. For a people when questioned could have doubtlessly responded that it had granted no power to accomplish its own ruin ...

I add that no one can renounce the right of defence against violence and injury. And the power of correcting an errant king, which the ephors have, has not been transferred to the king and cannot be so transferred. Nor can the supreme right in a commonwealth be transferred, because it is by nature incommunicable, and remains with the body of the universal association. Moreover, there is no power for evil or for inflicting injury. There is only power for good and for giving support, and thus for the utility and welfare of subjects. Therefore, the power that the people has, not a power that the people does not have, is considered to be given by this general wording ...

In the election of the supreme magistrate, the highest concern must be had for the fundamental law of the realm. For under this law the universal association has been constituted in the realm. This law serves as the foundation, so to speak, of the realm and is sustained by the common consent and approval of the members of the realm. By this law all the members of the realm have been brought together under one head and united in one body. It is indeed called the pillar of the realm.

This fundamental law is nothing other than certain covenants (*pacta*) by which many cities and provinces come together and agree to establish and defend one and the same commonwealth by common work, counsel, and aid. When common consent is withdrawn from these covenants and stipulations, the commonwealth ceases to exist, unless these laws are rejected and terminated by common consent, and new ones established, without harm to the commonwealth or impairment to its rights of sovereignty ...

The election of the supreme magistrate is in accord with either of two types. One is entirely free, and the other is restricted to persons of a certain origin from whom the choice is to be made. For rulers are to be elected either from all persons or from men of a certain kind, namely, from the nobility or from a certain family ...

The restricted election is one that has been limited by the agreement of the people and realm, or universal association, to persons of a certain origin. By established law, the right to be elected has been obtained for these persons, and it cannot later be withdrawn or transferred to another against their will, without injury and violation of trust ... The restricted election, by which ... a realm is called hereditary or successive, is either of two kinds. It may be limited to a certain nation and the nobles thereof, or to the heirs of the deceased supreme magistrate ...

If the people does not manifest obedience, and fails to fulfil the service and obligations promised in the election and inauguration — in the constituting — of the supreme magistrate, then he is the punisher, even by arms and war, of this perfidy and violation of trust, indeed, of this contumacy, rebellion, and sedition. But if the supreme magistrate does not keep his pledged word, and fails to administer the realm according to his promise, then the realm, or the ephors and the leading men in its name, is the punisher of this violation and broken trust. It is then conceded to the people to change and annul the earlier form of its polity and commonwealth, and to constitute a new one. In both cases, because a proper condition of the agreement and compact is not fulfilled, the contract is dissolved by right itself. In the first case, the prince will no longer treat such rebels and perfidious persons as his subjects, and is no longer required to perform toward them what he has promised. In the other case, likewise, the people, or members of the realm, will not recognize such a perfidious, perjurous, and compact-breaking person as their magistrate, but treat him as a private person and a tyrant to whom it is no longer required to extend obedience and other duties it promised. The magistrate loses the right to exact them justly. And it can and ought to remove him from office. Thus Bartolus says that a legitimate magistrate is a living law, and if he is condemned by law he is condemned by his own voice. But a tyrant is anything but a living law ...

### ECCLESIASTICAL ADMINISTRATION
#### (Chapter 28)

The administration of the public functions of the realm is either ecclesiastical or secular. ... This administration is imposed upon the magistrate by the mandate of God, as we have said. Consequently, the magistrate before anything else, and immediately from the beginning of his administration, should plant and nourish the Christian religion as the foundation of his imperium. If he does this, all the virtues will flourish among his subjects, and he will be prospered in his actions ...

This ecclesiastical administration is performed chiefly through two duties. The first is the introduction of orthodox religious doctrine and practice in the realm. The other is the conservation, defence, and transmission to posterity of this doctrine and practice ...

By a religious covenant (*pactum religiosum*) the magistrate, together with the members of the realm commonly and solemnly consenting in councils of the realm, promise to God the performance of this twofold duty. They agree assiduously to perform this service by which God may be constantly and truly known and worshipped by each and all in the entire realm. And in this agreement they recognize their realm to be under God, and they promise to him fidelity and obedience as subjects and vassals. 'For the earth and the fulness thereof are God's.' 'He is the Lord of lords, and the King of kings.' He is the proprietory lord of all creatures, and concedes their administration to him whom he wills. But he does not thereby lose his own authority ...

The debtors in this religious covenant are those who make the promise, or the supreme magistrate of the realm and its ephors together with the entire people. The creditor is God to whom the promise is made ... The supreme magistrate of the realm and the ephors representing the people are the debtors in such a manner that the fulfillment of their promise can be entirely and continuously demanded of both magistrate and ephors as if each were the principal obligant. For God does not will that the church, or the responsibility for acknowledging and worshipping him, be committed to one person alone, but to the entire people represented by its ministers, ephors, and supreme magistrate. These administrators represent the people as if they corporately sustain the church as one person, and yet as if anyone from among them were obligated for the entire responsibility ...

God makes a promise to the magistrate and people in this religious covenant concerning those who perform these things, as well as a threat to those who neglect or violate this compact (*fedus*). He promises to those who perform them that he will be to them a benevolent God and a merciful protector. He threatens those who disobey and violate this compact that he will be a just and severe exactor of punishments ...

God is the vindicator of this covenant when it is violated by the magistrate or by the ephors representing the people. One debtor is held responsible for the fault of the other, and shares his sins if he does not hold the violator of this covenant to his duty, and resist and impede him so far as he is able. 'He will cast Israel down because of the sins of Jeroboam.' For this reason the ephors are expected to remind a deviating magistrate of his duty, and to resist him. Therefore, if the ephors do not do this, but by remaining silent, defaulting, dissembling, permitting, or submitting they do not obstruct the violation of this covenant by the supreme magistrate, they are deservedly punished by God for this fault and surrender, as many examples indicate ...

TYRANNY AND ITS REMEDIES
*(Chapter 38)*

The nature of just and upright administration should be sufficiently clear from the things that we have said. We will now throw light on the opposite of these things, which is tyranny, and will add to this the remedies of tyranny by which the commonwealth is liberated and preserved from so much evil. Tyranny is the contrary of just and upright administration. By it the foundations and bonds of universal association are obstinately, persistently, and insanely destroyed and overthrown by the supreme magistrate against his pledged word and declared oath ... A tyrant is therefore one who, violating both word and oath, begins to shake the foundations and unloosen the bonds of the associated body of the commonwealth.

This tyranny, or tyrannical administration of a commonwealth, is twofold. One type of it is concerned with the overthrow and destruction of the fundamental laws of the realm. The other consists in the administration of functions and things of the associated body in a manner that is contrary to piety and justice. The first type of tyranny has two species. One species occurs when the supreme magistrate violates, changes, or overthrows the fundamental laws of the realm, especially those that concern true religion. Such a tyrant was Athaliah. Such also was Philip, king of Spain, who established an administration in Belgium by force and arms against the fundamental laws and hereditary ways of the commonwealth ... The other occurs when he does not maintain faith with the associated body, despises his oath, and breaks up the orders and estates, or impedes them in the performance of their offices ...

Having become acquainted with the nature of tyranny, we are now to look for the remedy by which it may be opportunely removed. This consists in resistance to and deposition of the tyrant, which remedy has been entrusted to the optimates alone. This resistance is the process by which the ephors impede the tyranny of the supreme magistrate by word and deed. And when he is incurable, or the laws of the associated body cannot otherwise be kept sound, well-protected, and in good condition, or the commonwealth free from evil, they depose him and cast him out of their midst ...

Special ephors are obligated to defend only that part of the realm whose care and safety have been entrusted to them. ... What is to be done collectively by the estates or ephors of the realm is not permitted to one of them when the others do not consent. ... However, it shall be permitted one part of the realm, or individual ephors or estates of the realm, to withdraw from subjection to the tyranny of their magistrate and to defend themselves ...

Even one ephor is required to drive from the entire realm the tyranny of an enemy and someone without title (*tyrannus absque titulo*) who wishes to force himself into the position of a legitimate magistrate when he is not one. A single ephor is expected to defend the associated body of which he is a member against force and injury ... So Holland, Zeeland, Frisia, Gelderland, and other confederates defended the remaining estates and orders of the Belgian provinces against the force and tyranny of Spain. But those writers are wrong who assign to the Roman pontiff the power of deposing kings and emperors ...

A tyrant is to be resisted so long as tyranny endures, and so far as he assails or acts contrary to the declared covenant. He should be resisted until the commonwealth is restored to its original condition. And to this end the optimates can remove such a person from office, deprive him of his entrusted administration, and, if they cannot defend themselves against force by any other means, even kill him, and substitute another in his place ...

The position we have thus far taken about the ephors applies only to public persons. It plainly does not apply to private persons when the magistrate is a tyrant by practice because they do not have the use and right of the sword, nor may they employ this right ... This is to be understood, however, in such a manner that these private persons are not forced to be servants of tyranny, or to do anything that is contrary to God. Under these circumstances they should flee to another place so that they avoid obedience not by resisting, but by fleeing ...

Accordingly, such private persons may do nothing by their private authority against their supreme magistrate, but rather shall await the command of one of the optimates before they come forth with support and arms to correct a tyrant by practice. But when a tyrant without title invades the realm, each and every optimate and private person who loves his fatherland can and should resist, even by his private authority without awaiting the command of another ...

One of the estates, or one part of the realm, can abandon the remaining body to which it belonged and choose for itself a separate ruler or a new form of commonwealth when the public and manifest welfare of this entire part altogether requires it, or when fundamental laws of the country are not observed by the magistrate but are obstinately and outrageously violated, or when the true worship and disclosed command of God clearly require and demand that this be done. And then this part of the realm can defend by force and arms its new form and status against the other parts of the realm from which it withdrew. Thus the Israelites broke loose from the house and imperium of David and founded their own realm ...

### NOTES

1   in Latin *symbiotici*: those who live together.
2   *symbiosis*: living together.
3   private: family and collegium (see n. 6).
4   public: city, province, and commonwealth.
5   the family and the collegium respectively (see n. 6).
6   *collegium* (pl. *collegia*): guild; corporation; voluntary association.
7   *optimates*: the chief men of the realm.

# 2

# War, Peace and Sovereignty

## THOMAS HOBBES

### Leviathan

#### THE INTRODUCTION

Nature (the art whereby God hath made and governs the world) is by the art of man, as in many other things, so in this also imitated, that it can make an artificial animal ... Art goes yet further ... For by art is created that great LEVIATHAN called a COMMON-WEALTH, or STATE, (in Latin CIVITAS) which is but an artificial man; though of greater stature and strength than the natural, for whose protection and defence it was intended; and in which, the sovereignty is an artificial soul, as giving life and motion to the whole body ... The pacts and covenants, by which the parts of this body politic were at first made, set together, and united, resemble that *Fiat*, or the *Let us make man*, pronounced by God in the creation.

To describe the nature of this artificial man, I will consider:

First, the matter thereof, and the artificer; both which is man.
Secondly, how, and by what covenants it is made; what are the rights and just power or authority of a sovereign; and what it is that preserveth and dissolveth it ...

*Source:* Thomas Hobbes, *Leviathan* (1651). The text is based on ed. M. Oakeshott (Oxford: Basil Blackwell, 1946). For ease of reading, use of italics has been greatly reduced. Hobbes's 'propriety' has throughout been altered to the modern 'property'. Extracts reprinted by permission.

OF THE INTERIOR BEGINNINGS OF VOLUNTARY MOTIONS: COMMONLY
CALLED THE PASSIONS. AND THE SPEECHES BY WHICH THEY
ARE EXPRESSED

*(Part I, chapter 6)*

There be in animals, two sorts of motions peculiar to them: one called *vital*; begun in generation, and continued without interruption through their whole life; such as are the course of the blood, the pulse, the breathing, the concoction, nutrition, excretion etc.; to which motions there needs no help of imagination. The other is *animal* motion, otherwise called *voluntary* motion; as to go, to speak, to move any of our limbs, in such manner as is first fancied in our minds ... And because going, speaking, and the like voluntary motions, depend always upon a precedent thought of whither, which way, and what: it is evident, that the imagination is the first internal beginning of all voluntary motion. And although unstudied men, do not conceive any motion at all to be there, where the thing moved is invisible; or the space it is moved in, is (for the shortness of it) insensible; yet that doth not hinder, but that such motions are. For let a space be never so little, that which is moved over a greater space, whereof that little one is part, must first be moved over that. These small beginnings of motion, within the body of man, before they appear in walking, speaking, striking, and other visible actions, are commonly called ENDEAVOUR.

This endeavour, when it is toward something which causes it, is called APPETITE, or DESIRE; the latter being the general name ... And when the endeavour is fromward something, it is generally called AVERSION ...

But whatsoever is the object of any man's appetite or desire; that is it, which he for his part calleth *good*: and the object of his hate and aversion, *evil* ... For these words of good, evil [etc.] are ever used with relation to the person that useth them: there being nothing simply and absolutely so; nor any common rule of good and evil, to be taken from the nature of the objects themselves; but from the person of the man (where there is no Commonwealth;) or, (in a Commonwealth,) from the person that representeth it; or from an arbitrator or judge, whom men disagreeing shall by consent set up, and make his sentence the rule thereof ...

OF POWER ...
### (Part I, chapter 10)

The power of a man, (to take it universally,) is his present means, to obtain some future apparent good ...

OF THE DIFFERENCE OF MANNERS
### (Part I, chapter 11)

... The felicity of this life, consisteth not in the repose of a mind satisfied. For there is no such *Finis ultimus* (utmost aim,) nor *Summum Bonum*, (greatest good,) as is spoken of in the books of the old moral philosophers. Nor can a man any more live, whose desires are at an end, than he, whose senses and imaginations are at a stand. Felicity is a continual progress of the desire, from one object to another; the attaining of the former, being still but the way to the latter. The cause whereof is, that the object of man's desire, is not to enjoy once only, and at one instant of time; but to assure for ever, the way of his future desire. And therefore the voluntary actions, and inclinations of all men, tend, not only to the procuring, but also to the assuring of a contended life; and differ only in the way; which ariseth partly from the diversity of passions, in divers men; and partly from the difference of the knowledge, or opinion each one has of the causes, which produce the effect desired.

So that in the first place, I put for a general inclination of all mankind, a perpetual and restless desire of power after power, that ceaseth only in death. And the cause of this, is not always that a man hopes for a more intensive delight, than he has already attained to; or that he cannot be content with a moderate power: but because he cannot assure the power and means to live well, which he hath present, without the acquisition of more ...

Competition of riches, honour, command or other power, inclineth to contention, enmity and war; because the way of one competitor, to the attaining of his desire, is to kill, subdue, supplant or repel the other ...

OF THE NATURAL CONDITION OF MANKIND, AS CONCERNING THEIR
FELICITY, AND MISERY
*(Part I, chapter 13)*

NATURE hath made men so equal, in the faculties of the body, and mind; as that though there be found one man sometimes manifestly stronger in body, or of quicker mind than another; yet when all is reckoned together, the difference between man, and man, is not so considerable, as that one man can thereupon claim to himself any benefit, to which another may not pretend, as well as he. For as to the strength of body, the weakest has strength enough to kill the strongest, either by secret machination, or by confederacy with others, that are in the same danger with himself.

And as to the faculties of the mind, ... I find yet a greater equality amongst men, than that of strength ... That which may perhaps make such equality incredible, is but a vain conceit of one's own wisdom, which almost all men think they have in a greater degree, than the vulgar; that is, than all men but themselves, and a few others, whom by fame, or for concurring with themselves, they approve ... But this proveth rather that men are in that point equal than unequal. For there is not ordinarily a greater sign of the equal distribution of any thing, than that every man is contented with his share.

From this equality of ability, ariseth equality of hope in the attaining of our ends. And therefore if any two men desire the same thing, which nevertheless they cannot both enjoy, they become enemies; and in the way to their end, which is principally their own conservation, and sometimes their delectation only, endeavour to destroy, or subdue one another. And from hence it comes to pass, that where an invader hath no more to fear, than another man's single power; if one plant, sow, build, or possess a convenient seat, others may probably be expected to come prepared with forces united, to dispossess, and deprive him, not only of the fruit of his labour, but also of his life, or liberty. And the invader again is in the like danger of another.

And from this diffidence of one another, there is no way for any man to secure himself, so reasonable, as anticipation; that is, by force, or wiles, to master the persons of all men he can, so long, till he see no other power great enough to endanger him: and this is no more than his own conservation requireth, and is generally allowed. Also because there be some, that taking pleasure in contemplating their own power in the acts of conquest, which they pursue farther than their security requires; if others, that otherwise would be glad to be at ease within modest bounds, should not by invasion increase their power, they would not be able, long time, by standing only on their defence, to subsist. And by consequence, such augmentation of dominion over men being necessary to a man's conservation, it ought to be allowed him.

Again, men have no pleasure, but on the contrary a great deal of grief, in keeping company, where there is no power able to over-awe them all. For every man looketh that his companion should value him, at the same rate he sets upon himself: and upon all signs of contempt, or undervaluing, naturally endeavours, as far as he dares, (which amongst them that have no common power to keep them in quiet, is far enough to make them destroy each other), to extort a greater value from his contemners, by damage; and from others, by the example.

So that in the nature of man, we find three principal causes of quarrel. First, competition; secondly, diffidence; thirdly, glory.

The first, maketh men invade for gain; the second, for safety; and the third, for reputation. The first use violence, to make themselves masters of other men's persons, wives, children, and cattle; the second, to defend them; the third, for trifles, as a word, a smile, a different opinion, and any other sign of undervalue . . .

Hereby it is manifest, that during the time men live without a common power to keep them all in awe, they are in that condition which is called war; and such a war, as is of every man, against every man. For WAR, consisteth not in battle only, or the act of fighting; but in a tract of time, wherein the will to contend by battle is sufficiently known . . .

Whatsoever therefore is consequent to a time of war, where every man is enemy to every man; the same is consequent to the time, wherein men live without other security, than what their own strength, and their own invention shall furnish them withal. In such condition, there is no place for industry; because the fruit thereof is uncertain: and consequently no culture of the earth; no navigation, nor use of the commodities that may be imported by sea; no commodious building; no instruments of moving, and removing, such things as require much force; no knowledge of the face of the earth; no account of time; no arts; no letters; no society; and which is worst of all, continual fear, and danger of violent death; and the life of man, solitary, poor, nasty, brutish, and short.

It may seem strange to some man, that has not well weighed these things; that nature should thus dissociate, and render men apt to invade, and destroy one another: and he may therefore, not trusting to this inference, made from the passions, desire perhaps to have the same confirmed by experience. Let him therefore consider with himself, when taking a journey, he arms himself, and seeks to go well accompanied; when going to sleep, he locks his doors; when even in his house he locks his chests; and this when he knows there be laws, and public officers, armed, to revenge all injuries shall be done him; what opinion he has of his fellow subjects, when he rides armed; of his fellow citizens, when he locks his doors; and of his children, and servants, when he locks his chests. Does he not there as much accuse mankind by his actions, as I do by my words? ...

It may peradventure be thought, there was never such a time, nor condition of war as this; and I believe it was never generally so, over all the world: but there are many places, where they live so now. For the savage people in many places of America, except the government of small families, the concord whereof dependeth on natural lust, have no government at all; and live at this day in that brutish manner, as I said before. Howsoever, it may be perceived what manner of life there would be, where there were no common power to fear, by the manner of life, which men that have formerly lived under a peaceful government, use to degenerate into, in a civil war ...

To this war of every man, against every man, this also is consequent; that nothing can be unjust. The notions of right and wrong, justice and injustice have there no place. Where there is no common power, there is no law: where no law, no injustice. Force, and fraud, are in war the two cardinal virtues ... It is consequent also to the same condition, that there be no property, no domination, no mine and thine distinct; but only that to be every man's, that he can get: and for so long, as he can keep it. And thus much for the ill condition, which man by mere nature is actually placed in; though with a possibility to come out of it, consisting partly in the passions, partly in his reason.

The passions that incline men to peace, are fear of death; desire of such things as are necessary to commodious living; and a hope by their industry to obtain them. And reason suggesteth convenient articles of peace, upon which men may be drawn to agreement. These articles, are they, which otherwise are called the Laws of Nature ...

OF THE FIRST AND SECOND NATURAL LAWS, AND OF CONTRACTS
*(Part I, chapter 14)*

The RIGHT OF NATURE, which writers commonly call *jus naturale*, is the liberty each man hath, to use his own power, as he will himself, for the preservation of his own nature; that is to say, of his own life; and consequently, of doing any thing, which in his own judgment, and reason, he shall conceive to be the aptest means thereunto . . .

A LAW OF NATURE, *lex naturalis*, is a precept or general rule, found out by reason, by which a man is forbidden to do that, which is destructive of his life, or taketh away the means of preserving the same; and to omit that, by which he thinketh it may be best preserved. For though they that speak of this subject, use to confound *jus*, and *lex*, right and law: yet they ought to be distinguished; because RIGHT, consisteth in liberty to do, or to forbear: whereas LAW, determineth, and bindeth to one of them: so that law, and right, differ as much, as obligation, and liberty . . .

And because the condition of man, as hath been declared in the precedent chapter, is a condition of war of every one against every one; in which case every one is governed by his own reason; and there is nothing he can make use of, that may not be a help unto him, in preserving his life against his enemies; it followeth, that in such a condition, every man has a right to every thing; even to one another's body. And therefore, as long as this natural right of every man to every thing endureth, there can be no security to any man, how strong or wise soever he be, of living out the time, which nature ordinarily alloweth men to live. And consequently it is a precept, or general rule of reason, *that every man, ought to endeavour peace, as far as he has hope of obtaining it; and when he cannot obtain it, that he may seek, and use, all helps, and advantages of war.* The first branch of which rule, containeth the first, and fundamental law of nature; which is, *to seek peace, and follow it.* The second, the sum of the right of nature; which is, *by all means we can, to defend ourselves.*

From this fundamental law of nature, by which men are commanded to endeavour peace, is derived this second law; *that a man be willing, when others are so too, as far-forth, as for peace, and defence of himself he shall think it necessary, to lay down this right to all things; and be contented with so much liberty against other men, as he would allow other men against himself.* For as long as every man holdeth this right, of doing any thing he liketh; so long are all men in the condition of war. But if other men will not lay down their right, as well as he; then there is no reason for any one, to divest himself of his: for that were to expose himself to prey, which no man is bound to, rather than to dispose himself to peace ...

Right is laid aside, either by simply renouncing it; or by transferring it to another. By simply RENOUNCING; when he cares not to whom the benefit thereof redoundeth. By TRANSFERRING; when he intendeth the benefit thereof to some certain person, or persons. And when a man hath in either manner abandoned, or granted away his right; then he is said to be OBLIGED, or BOUND, not to hinder those, to whom such right is granted, or abandoned, from the benefit of it: and that he ought, and it is his DUTY, not to make void that voluntary act of his own: and that such hindrance is INJUSTICE, and INJURY, as being *sine jure*; the right being before renounced, or transferred ... The way by which a man either simply renounceth, or transferreth his right, is a declaration, or signification, by some voluntary and sufficient sign, or signs, that he doth so ... And these signs are either words only, or actions only; or, as it happeneth most often, both words, and actions. And the same are the BONDS, by which men are bound, and obliged: bonds, that have their strength, not from their own nature, for nothing is more easily broken than a man's word, but from fear of some evil consequence upon the rupture.

Whensoever a man transferreth his right, or renounceth it; it is either in consideration of some right reciprocally transferred to himself; or for some other good he hopeth for thereby. For it is a voluntary act: and of the voluntary acts of every man, the object is some good to himself. And therefore there be some rights, which no man can be understood by any words, or other signs, to have abandoned, or transferred. As first a man cannot lay down the right of resisting them, that assault him by force, to take away his life; because he cannot be understood to aim thereby, at any good to himself. The same may be said of wounds, and chains, and imprisonment ...

The mutual transferring of right, is that which men call CONTRACT.

There is difference between transferring of right to the thing; and transferring, or ... delivery of the thing itself. For the thing may be delivered together with the translation of the right; as in buying and selling with ready-money; or exchange of goods, or lands: and it may be delivered some time after.

Again, one of the contractors, may deliver the thing contracted for on his part, and leave the other to perform his part at some determinate time after, and in the mean time be trusted; and then the contract on his part, is called PACT, or COVENANT: or both parts may contract now, to perform hereafter: in which cases, he that is to perform in time to come, being trusted, his performance is called keeping of promise, or faith; and the failing of performance, if it be voluntary, violation of faith ...

## OF OTHER LAWS OF NATURE
### *(Part I, chapter 15)*

From that law of nature, by which we are obliged to transfer to another, such rights, as being retained, hinder the peace of mankind, there followeth a third; which is this, *that men perform their covenants made*: without which, covenants are in vain, and but empty words; and the right of all men to all things remaining, we are still in the condition of war.

And in this law of nature, consisteth the fountain and original of JUSTICE. For where no covenant hath preceded, there hath no right been transferred, and every man has right to every thing; and consequently, no action can be unjust. But when a covenant is made, then to break it is unjust: and the definition of INJUSTICE, is no other than the not performance of covenant. And whatsoever is not unjust, is just.

But because covenants of mutual trust, where there is a fear of not performance on either part, ... are invalid; though the original of justice be the making of covenants; yet injustice actually there can be none, till the cause of such fear be taken away; which while men are in the natural condition of war, cannot be done. Therefore before the names of just, and unjust can have place, there must be some coercive power, to compel men equally to the performance of their covenants, by the terror of some punishment, greater than the benefit they expect by the breach of their covenant; and to make good that property, which by mutual contract men acquire, in recompense of the universal right they abandon: and such power there is none before the erection of a commonwealth ... Where there is no commonwealth, there is no property; all men having right to all things: therefore where there is no commonwealth, there nothing is unjust ...

The laws of nature oblige *in foro interno*; that is to say, they oblige to a desire they should take place: but *in foro externo*; that is, to the putting of them in act, not always. For he that should be modest, and tractable, and perform all he promises, in such time and place, where no man else should do so, should but make himself a prey to others, and procure his own certain ruin, contrary to the ground of all laws of nature, which tend to nature's preservation. And again, he that having sufficient security, that others shall observe the same laws towards him, observes them not himself, seeketh not peace, but war; and consequently the destruction of his nature by violence ...

The laws of nature are immutable and eternal; ... and the science of them, is the true and only moral philosophy. For moral philosophy is nothing else but the science of what is good, and evil, in the conversation, and society of mankind. *Good*, and *evil*, are names that signify our appetites, and aversions; which in different tempers, customs, and doctrines of men, are different: ... from whence arise disputes, controversies, and at last war. And therefore so long a man is in the condition of mere nature, which is a condition of war, as private appetite is the measure of good, and evil: and consequently all men agree on this, that peace is good, and therefore also the way, or means of peace, (which ... are justice ... and the rest of the laws of nature) are good; that is to say; moral virtues; and their contrary vices, evil ...

These dictates of reason, men use to call by the name of laws, but improperly: for they are but conclusions, or theorems concerning what conduceth to the conservation and defence of themselves; whereas law, properly, is the word of him, that by right hath command over others. But yet if we consider the same theorems, as delivered in the word of God, that by right commandeth all things; then are they properly called laws ...

### OF THE CAUSES, GENERATION, AND DEFINITION OF A COMMONWEALTH
*(Part II, chapter 17)*

The final cause, end, or design of men, who naturally love liberty, and dominion over others, in the introduction of that restraint upon themselves, in which we see them live in commonwealths, is the foresight of their own preservation, and of a more contented life thereby; that is to say, of getting themselves out from that miserable condition of war, which is necessarily consequent, as hath been shown [Part I, chapter 13], to the natural passions of men, when there is no visible power to keep them in awe, and tie them by fear of punishment to the performance of their covenants, and observation of laws of nature.

For the laws of nature, as justice, equity, modesty, mercy, and, in sum, doing to others, as we would be done to, of themselves, without the terror of some power to cause them to be observed, are contrary to our natural passions, that carry us to partiality, pride, revenge, and the like. And covenants, without the sword, are but words, and of no strength to secure a man at all. Therefore notwithstanding the laws of nature (which every one hath then kept, when he has the will to keep them, when he can do it safely) if there be no power erected, or not great enough for our security; every man will, and may lawfully rely on his own strength and art, for caution against all other men ...

Nor is it the joining together of a small number of men, that gives them this security; because in small numbers, small additions on the one side or the other, make the advantage of strength so great, as is sufficient to carry the victory; and therefore gives encouragement to an invasion. The multitude sufficient to confide in for our security, is not determined by any certain number, but by comparison with the enemy we fear; and is then sufficient, when the odds of the enemy is not of so visible and conspicuous moment, to determine the event of war, as to move him to attempt.

And be there never so great a multitude; yet if their actions be directed according to their particular judgments, and particular appetites, they can expect thereby no defence, nor protection, neither against a common enemy, nor against the injuries of one another. For being distracted in opinions concerning the best use and application of their strength, they do not help but hinder one another; and reduce their strength by mutual opposition to nothing: whereby they are easily, not only subdued by a very few that agree together; but also when there is no common enemy, they make war upon each other, for their particular interests ...

It is true, that certain living creatures, as bees, and ants, live sociably one with another, which are therefore by Aristotle numbered amongst political creatures; and yet have no other direction, than their particular judgments and appetites; nor speech, whereby one of them can signify to another, what he thinks expedient for the common benefit: and therefore some man may perhaps desire to know, why mankind cannot do the same. To which I answer.

First, that men are continually in competition for honour and dignity, which these creatures are not; and consequently amongst men there ariseth on that ground, envy and hatred, and finally war; but amongst these not so.

Secondly, that amongst these creatures, the common good differeth not from the private; and being by nature inclined to their private, they procure thereby the common benefit. But man, whose joy consisteth in comparing himself with other men, can relish nothing but what is eminent.

Thirdly, that these creatures, having not, as man, the use of reason, do not see, nor think they see any fault, in the administration of their common business; whereas amongst men, there are very many, that think themselves wiser, and abler to govern the public, better than the rest; and these strive to reform and innovate, one this way, another that way; and thereby bring it into distraction and civil war ...

Lastly, the agreement of these creatures is natural; that of men, is by covenant only, which is artificial: and therefore it is no wonder if there be somewhat else required, besides covenant, to make their agreement constant and lasting; which is a common power, to keep them in awe, and to direct their actions to the common benefit.

The only way to erect such a common power, as may be able to defend them from the invasion of foreigners, and the injuries of one another, and thereby to secure them in such sort, as that by their own industry, and by the fruits of the earth, they may nourish themselves and live contentedly; is, to confer all their power and strength upon one man, or upon one assembly of men, that may reduce all their wills, by plurality of voices, unto one will: which is as much as to say, to appoint one man, or assembly of men, to bear their person; and every one to own, and acknowledge himself to be author of whatsoever he that so beareth their person, shall act, or cause to be acted, in those things which concern the common peace and safety; and therein to submit their wills, every one to his will, and their judgments, to his judgment. This is more than consent, or concord; it is a real unity of them all, in one and the same person, made by covenant of every man with every man, in such manner, as if every man should say to every man, *I authorize and give up my right of governing myself, to this man, or to this assembly of men, on this condition, that thou give up thy right to him, and authorize all his actions in like manner.* This done, the multitude so united in one person, is called a COMMONWEALTH, in Latin CIVITAS. This is the generation of that great LEVIATHAN, or rather, to speak more reverently, of that mortal god, to which we owe under the immortal God, our peace and defence. For by this authority, given him by every particular man in the commonwealth, he hath the use of so much power and strength conferred on him, that by terror thereof, he is enabled to form the wills of them all, to peace at home, and mutual aid against their enemies abroad. And in him consisteth the essence of the commonwealth; which, to define it, is one person, of whose acts a great multitude, by mutual covenants one with another, have made themselves every one the author, to the end he may use the strength and means of them all, as he shall think expedient, for their peace and common defence.

And he that carrieth this person, is called SOVEREIGN, and said to have sovereign power; and every one besides, his SUBJECT.

The attaining to this sovereign power, is by two ways. One, by natural force; as when a man maketh his children, to submit themselves, and their children to his government, as being able to destroy them if they refuse; or by war subdueth his enemies to his will, giving them their lives on that condition. The other, is when men agree amongst themselves, to submit to some man, or assembly of men, voluntarily, on confidence to be protected by him against all others. This latter, may be called a political commonwealth, or commonwealth by institution; and the former, a commonwealth by acquisition. And first, I shall speak of a commonwealth by institution.

OF THE RIGHTS OF SOVEREIGNS BY INSTITUTION
*(Part II, chapter 18)*

From [the] institution of a commonwealth are derived all the rights, and faculties of him, or them, on whom the sovereign power is conferred by the consent of the people assembled. . . .

[Thus] because the right of bearing the person of them all, is given to him they make sovereign, by covenant only of one to another, and not of him to any of them; there can happen no breach of covenant on the part of the sovereign; and consequently none of his subjects, by any pretence of forfeiture, can be freed from his subjection . . . The opinion that any monarch receiveth his power by covenant, that is to say, on condition, proceedeth from want of understanding this easy truth, that covenants being but words and breath, have no force to oblige, contain, constrain, or protect any man, but what it has from the public sword . . .

[Further], because every subject is by this institution author of all the actions, and judgments of the sovereign instituted; it follows, that whatsoever he doth, it can be no injury to any of his subjects; nor ought he to be by any of them accused of injustice. For he that doth anything by authority from another, doth therein no injury to him by whose authority he acteth: but by this institution of a commonwealth, every particular man is author of all the sovereign doth: and consequently he that complaineth of injury from his sovereign, complaineth of what whereof he himself is author ...

Consequently to that which was said last, no man that hath sovereign power can justly be put to death, or otherwise in any manner by his subjects punished ...

And because the end of this institution, is the peace and defence of them all; and whosoever has right to the end, has right to the means; it belongeth of right, to whatsoever man, or assembly that hath the sovereignty, to be judge both of the means of peace and defence, and also of the hindrances, and disturbances of the same; and to do whatsoever he shall think necessary to be done, both beforehand, for the preserving of peace and security, by prevention of discord at home, and hostility from abroad; and, when peace and security are lost, for the recovery of the same.

And therefore ... it is annexed to the sovereignty, to be judge of what opinions and doctrines are averse, and what conducing to peace; and consequently, on what occasions, how far, and what men are to be trusted withal, in speaking to multitudes of people; and who shall examine the doctrines of all books before they be published. For the actions of men proceed from their opinions; and in the well-governing of opinions, consisteth the well-governing of men's actions, in order to their peace, and concord. And though in matter of doctrine, nothing ought to be regarded but the truth; yet this is not repugnant to regulating the same by peace. For doctrine repugnant to peace, can no more be true, than peace and concord can be against the law of nature ...

[Also] is annexed to the sovereignty, the whole power of pre-scribing the rules, whereby every man may know, what goods he may enjoy, and what actions he may do, without being molested by any of his fellow subjects; and this is it men call property. For before constitution of sovereign power, as hath already been shown, all men had right to all things; which necessarily causeth war: and therefore this property, being necessary to peace, and depending on sovereign power, is the act of that power, in order to the public peace ...

[Also] annexed to the sovereignty, [is] the right of judicature; that is to say, of hearing and deciding all controversies, which may arise concerning law, either civil, or natural; or concerning fact. For without the decision of controversies, there is no protection of one subject, against the injuries of another; the laws concerning *meum* and *tuum* are in vain ...

[Also] annexed to the sovereignty, [is] the right of making war and peace with other nations, and commonwealths; that is to say, of judging when it is for the public good, and how great forces are to be assembled, armed, and paid for that end; and to levy money upon the subjects, to defray the expenses thereof. For the power by which the people are to be defended, consisteth in their armies; and the strength of an army, in the union of their strength under one command; which command the sovereign instituted, therefore hath ...

### OF DOMINION PATERNAL AND DESPOTICAL
*(Part II, chapter 10)*

A commonwealth by acquisition, is that, where the sovereign power is acquired by force; and it is acquired by force, when men simply, or many together by plurality of voices, for fear of death, or bonds, do authorise all the actions of that man, or assembly, that hath their lives and liberty in his power.

And this kind of dominion, or sovereignty, differeth from sovereignty by institution, only in this, that men who choose their sovereign, do it for fear of one another, and not of him whom they institute: but in this case, they subject themselves, to him they are afraid of. In both cases they do it for fear ...

But the rights and consequences of sovereignty, are the same in both ... [The sovereign] cannot be accused by any of his subjects, of injury; he cannot be punished by them; he is judge of what is necessary for peace; and judge of doctrines; he is sole legislator; and supreme judge of controversies; and of the times, and occasions of war, and peace; to him it belongeth to choose magistrates, counsellors, commanders, and all other officers, and ministers; and to determine of rewards, and punishment, honour and order. The reasons whereof, are the same which are alleged in the precedent chapter, for the same rights, and consequences of sovereignty by institution ...

So that it appeareth plainly, to my understanding, ... that the sovereign power, whether placed in one man, as in monarchy, or in one assembly of men, as in popular and aristocratical commonwealths, is as great, as possibly men can be imagined to make it. And though of so unlimited a power, men may fancy many evil consequences, yet the consequences of the want of it, which is perpetual war of every man against his neighbour, are much worse. The condition of man in this life shall never be without incovenience; but there happeneth in no commonwealth any great inconvenience, but what proceeds from the subjects' disobedience, and breach of those covenants, from which the commonwealth hath its being ...

## OF THE LIBERTY OF SUBJECTS
### (Part II, chapter 21)

... To come now to the particulars of the true liberty of a subject; that is to say, what are the things, which though commanded by the sovereign, he may nevertheless, without injustice, refuse to do; we are to consider, what rights we pass away, when we make a commonwealth; or, which is all one, what liberty we deny ourselves, by owning all the actions, without exception, of the man, or assembly we make our sovereign. For in the act of our submission, consisteth both our obligation, and our liberty; which must therefore be inferred by arguments taken from thence; there being no obligation on any man, which ariseth not from some act of his own; for all men equally, are by nature free ...

First therefore, ... it is manifest, that every subject has liberty in all those things, the right whereof cannot by covenant be transferred. I have shown before in the 14th chapter, that covenants, not to defend a man's own body, are void. Therefore,

If the sovereign command a man, though justly condemned, to kill, wound, or maim himself; or not to resist those that assault him; or to abstain from the use of food, air, medicine or any other thing, without which he cannot live; yet hath that man the liberty to disobey.

If a man be interrogated by the sovereign, or his authority, concerning a crime done by himself, he is not bound, without assurance of pardon, to confess it; because no man, as I have shown in the same chapter, can be obliged by covenant to accuse himself ... The obligation a man may sometimes have, upon the command of the sovereign to execute any dangerous, or dishonourable office, dependeth not on the words of our submission; but on the intention, which is to be understood by the end thereof. When therefore our refusal to obey, frustrates the end for which the sovereignty was ordained; then there is no liberty to refuse: otherwise there is.

Upon this ground, a man that is commanded as a soldier to fight against the enemy, though his sovereign have right enough to punish his refusal with death, may nevertheless in many cases refuse, without injustice; as when he substituteth a sufficient soldier in his place; for in this case he deserteth not the service of the commonwealth. And there is allowance to be made for natural timorousness; not only to women, of whom no such dangerous duty is expected, but also to men of feminine courage. When armies fight, there is on one side, or both, a running away; yet when they do it not out of treachery, but fear, they are not esteemed to do it unjustly, but dishonourably . . . [But] when the defence of the commonwealth, requireth at once the help of all that are able to bear arms, every one is obliged; because otherwise the institution of the commonwealth, which they have not the purpose, or courage to preserve, was in vain.

To resist the sword of the commonwealth, in defence of another man, guilty, or innocent, no man hath liberty; because such liberty, takes away from the sovereign, the means of protecting us; and is therefore destructive of the very essence of government. But in case a great many men together, have already resisted the sovereign power unjustly, or committed some capital crime, for which every one of them expecteth death, whether have they not the liberty then to join together, and assist, and defend one another? Certainly they have: for they but defend their lives, which the guilty man may as well do, as the innocent. There was indeed injustice in the first breach of their duty; their bearing of arms subsequent to it, though it be to maintain what they have done, is no new unjust act. And if it be only to defend their persons, it is not unjust at all. But the offer of pardon taketh from them, to whom it is offered, the plea of self-defence, and maketh their perseverance in assisting, or defending the rest, unlawful.

As for other liberties, they depend on the silence of the law . . .

The obligation of subjects to the sovereign, is understood to last as long, and no longer, than the power lasteth, by which he is able to protect them. For the right men have by nature to protect themselves, when none else can protect them, can by no covenant be relinquished . . . The end of obedience is protection; which, wheresoever a man seeth it, either in his own, or in another's sword, nature applieth his obedience to it, and his endeavour to maintain it. And though sovereignty, in the intention of them that make it, be immortal; yet it is in its own nature, not only subject to violent death, by foreign war; but also through the ignorance, and passions of men, it hath in it, from the very institution, many seeds of a natural mortality, by intestine discord . . .

## OF CIVIL LAWS
### (Part II, *chapter* 26)

The law of nature, and the civil law, contain each other, and are of equal extent . . . The civil law is a part of the dictates of nature. For justice, that is to say, performance of covenant, and giving to every man his own, is a dictate of the law of nature. But every subject in a commonwealth, hath covenanted to obey the civil law, (either one with another, as when they assemble to make a common representative, or with the representative itself one by one, when subdued by the sword they promise obedience, that they may receive life,) and therefore obedience to the civil law is also part of the law of nature.

### OF THOSE THINGS THAT WEAKEN, OR TEND TO THE DISSOLUTION OF A COMMONWEALTH
#### (Part II, chapter 29)

... [There are] diseases of a commonwealth, [that] proceed from the poison of seditious doctrines; whereof one is, That every private man is judge of good and evil actions. This is true in the condition of mere nature, where there are no civil laws; and also under civil government, in such cases as are not determined by the law. But otherwise, it is manifest, that the measure of good and evil actions, is the civil law ...

[Another] opinion, repugnant to the nature of a commonwealth, is this, That he that hath sovereign power, is subject to the civil laws. It is true, that sovereigns are all subject to the laws of nature ... But to those laws which the sovereign himself, that is, which the commonwealth maketh, he is not subject ...

[Another] doctrine, that tendeth to the dissolution of a commonwealth, is, That every man has absolute property in his goods; such as excludeth the right of the sovereign. Every man has indeed a property that excludes the right of every other subject: and he has it only from the sovereign power; without the protection whereof, every other man should have equal right to the same. But if the right of the sovereign also be excluded, he cannot perform the office they have put him into; ... and consequently there is no longer a commonwealth ...

Lastly, when in a war (foreign or intestine), the enemies get a final victory; so as (the forces of the commonwealth keeping the field no longer) there is no further protection of subjects in their loyalty; then is the commonwealth DISSOLVED, and every man at liberty to protect himself by such courses as his own discretion shall suggest unto him. For the sovereign, is the public soul, giving life and motion to the commonwealth; which expiring, the members of it are governed by it no more, than the carcass of a man, by his departed (though immortal) soul ...

# 3

# The State as the Outcome of Two Contracts

## SAMUEL PUFENDORF

### On the Duty of Man and Citizen

ON NATURAL LAW
*(Book I, chapter 3)*

What is the character of the natural law, what its necessity, and of what precepts it consists in the present state of mankind, are most clearly seen, after one has thoroughly examined the nature and disposition of man . . .

Now man shares with all the animals that have consciousness the fact that he holds nothing dearer than himself, and is eager in every way to preserve himself; that he strives to gain what seem to him good things, and to reject the evil. This feeling is regularly so strong that all the others give way to it. And one cannot but resent it, if any man make an attack upon one's life, so much so that, even after the threatened danger has been averted, hatred usually still remains, and a desire for vengeance.

But in one respect man seems to be in a worse state even than the brutes — that scarcely any other animal is attended from birth by such weakness. Hence it would be a miracle, if anyone reached mature years, if he have not the aid of other men, since, as it is, among all the helps which have been invented for human needs,

*Source:* Extracts from S. Pufendorf, *De Officio Hominis et Civis*, translated by F. G. Moore as *On the Duty of Man and Citizen* (New York: Oxford UP, 1927); and *De Jure Naturae et Gentium*, translated by C. H. and W. A. Oldfather as *On the Law of Nature and Nations* (Oxford: Clarendon Press, 1934). Reprinted here by permission of the Carnegie Endowment for International Peace. The bulk of this chapter comes from *De Officio*, which is much the more accessible of the two books.

careful training for a number of years is required, to enable a man to gain his food and clothing by his own efforts. Let us imagine a man brought to maturity without any care and training bestowed upon him by others, having no knowledge except what sprang up of itself in his own mind, and in a desert, deprived of all help and society of other men. Certainly a more miserable animal it will be hard to find. Speechless and naked, he has nothing left him but to pluck herbs and roots, or gather wild fruits, to slake his thirst from spring or river, or the first marsh he encountered, to seek shelter in a cave from the violence of the weather, or to cover his body somehow with moss or grass, to pass his time most tediously in idleness, to shudder at any noise or the encounter with another creature, finally to perish by hunger or cold or some wild beast. On the other hand, whatever advantages now attend human life have flowed entirely from the mutual help of men. It follows that, after God, there is nothing in this world from which greater advantage can come to man than from man himself.

Yet this animal, though so useful to his kind, suffers from not a few faults, and is endowed with no less power to injure; which facts make contact with him rather uncertain, and call for great caution, that one may not receive evil from him instead of good. First of all, there is generally a greater tendency to injure found in man than in any of the brutes. For the brutes are usually excited by the desire for food and for love, both of which, however, they can themselves easily satisfy. But having stilled that craving, they are not readily roused to anger or to injure people, unless someone provokes them. But man is an animal at no time disinclined to lust, and by its goad he is excited much more frequently than would seem necessary for the conservation of the race. And his belly desires not merely to be satisfied, but also to be tickled, and often craves more than nature is able to digest. That the brutes should not need clothing nature has provided. But man delights to clothe himself, not for necessity only, but also for display. Many more passions and desires unknown to the brutes are found in man, as the desire to have superfluities, avarice, the love of glory and eminence, envy, emulation, and rivalry of wits. Witness the fact that most wars, in which men clash with men, are waged for reasons unknown to the brutes. And all these things can, and usually do, incite men to desire to injure one another. Then too there is in many a notable insolence and passion for insulting their fellows, at which the rest, modest though they be by nature, cannot fail to take offense, and gird themselves to resist, from the desire to maintain and defend themselves and their freedom. At times also men are driven to mutual injury by want, and the fact that their present resources are insufficient for their desires or their need.

Moreover men have in them great power for the infliction of mutual injuries. For though not formidable because of teeth or claws or horns, as are many of the brutes, still manual dexterity can prove a most effective means of injury; and shrewdness gives a man the opportunity to attack by cunning and in ambush, where the enemy cannot be reached by open force. Hence it is very easy for man to inflict upon man the worst of natural evils, namely death.

Finally, we must also consider in mankind such a remarkable variety of gifts as is not observed in single species of animals, which, in fact, generally have like inclinations, and are led by the same passion and desire ... And there is no less variety in the tastes and habits, the inclinations to exert mental powers — a variety which we see now in the almost countless modes of life. That men may not thus be brought into collision, there is need of careful regulation and control.

Thus then man is indeed an animal most bent upon self-preservation, helpless in himself, unable to save himself without the aid of his fellows, highly adapted to promote mutual interests; but on the other hand no less malicious, insolent, and easily provoked, also as able as he is prone to inflict injury upon another. Whence it follows that, in order to be safe, he must be sociable, that is, must be united with men like himself, and so conduct himself toward them that they may have no good cause to injure him, but rather may be ready to maintain and promote his interests.

The laws then of this sociability, or those which teach how a man should conduct himself, to become a good member of human society, are called natural laws.

So much settled, it is clear that the fundamental natural law is this: that every man must cherish and maintain sociability, so far as in him lies. From this it follows that, as he who wishes an end, wishes also the means, without which the end cannot be obtained, all things which necessarily and universally make for that sociability are understood to be ordained by natural law, and all that confuse or destroy it forbidden. The remaining precepts are mere corollaries, so to speak, under this general law, and the natural light given to mankind declares that they are evident.

Again, although those precepts have manifest utility, still, if they are to have the force of law, it is necessary to presuppose that God exists, and by His providence rules all things; also that He has enjoined upon the human race that they observe those dictates of the reason, as laws promulgated by Himself by means of our natural light. For otherwise they might, to be sure, be observed perhaps, in view of their utility, like the prescriptions of physicians for the regimen of health, but not as laws; since these of necessity presuppose a superior, and in fact one who has actually undertaken the direction of another.

But that God is the author of the natural law, is proved by the natural reason, if only we limit ourselves strictly to the present condition of humanity, disregarding the question whether his primitive condition was different from the present, or whence that change has come about. The nature of man is so constituted that the race cannot be preserved without the social life, and man's mind is found to be capable of all the notions which serve that end. And it is in fact clear, not only that the human race owes its origin, as do the other creatures, to God, but also that, whatever be its present state, God includes the race in the government of His providence. It follows from these arguments that God wills that man use for the conservation of his own nature those special powers which he knows are peculiarly his own, as compared with the brutes, and thus that man's life be distinguished from the lawless life of the brutes. And as this cannot be secured except by observing the natural law, we understand too that man has been obliged by God to keep the same, as a means not devised by will of men, and changeable at their discretion, but expressly ordained by God Himself, in order to insure this end . . .

### ON RECOGNITION OF THE NATURAL EQUALITY OF MEN
#### (Book I, chapter 7)

Man is an animal not only most devoted to self-preservation, but one in which has been implanted a sensitive self-esteem. And if this be in any way slighted, he is in general no less perturbed, than if an injury has been inflicted upon his person or property. Even the word *man* is thought to contain a certain dignity, so that the last and most effective argument in repelling the insolent contempt of others is this: 'I am certainly not a dog, but a man as well as you.' Inasmuch then as human nature is the same for all alike, and no one is perfectly willing or able to be associated with another, who does not esteem him as at least equally a man and a sharer in the common nature; therefore, among the mutual duties . . . is . . . this: that each esteem and treat the other as naturally his equal, that is, as a man just as much as himself.

But this equality of men consists not only in the fact that adult men are about equal in strength, in so far as the weaker can inflict death upon the stronger by ambush, or with the help of dexterity, or an effective weapon; but also in this, that, although one has been fitted out by nature with various gifts of mind and body beyond the other, he must none the less practice the precepts of natural law toward other men, and himself expects the same treatment from others; and in the fact that no more freedom is given the man to injure others on that account ... For the obligation to cultivate the social life with others binds all men equally, and one is no more permitted than another to violate the natural laws in their dealings with each other ...

### ON THE DUTIES OF CONTRACTING PARTIES IN GENERAL
*(Book I, chapter 9)*

From the absolute duties we pass to the conditional, by way of agreements as a transition .... We have then to treat here of the nature of agreements, and what is to be observed by those who enter into them.

Now it is sufficiently clear that it was necessary for men to enter into agreements. For, although the duties of humanity are widely diffused throughout human life, it is still impossible to deduce from that one source all that men were entitled to receive to advantage from one another. For not all have such natural goodness, that they are willing, out of mere humanity, to do all the things by means of which they may benefit others, without an assured hope of receiving the like in return. Often, too, favors which can come to us from others, are of a sort to make us unable to demand without a blush that they be done for us for nothing ... Therefore, in order that the mutual duties of men (the fruit, that is, of sociability) may be discharged more frequently and according to certain rules, it was necessary for men to agree among themselves, as to the mutual performance of all that they could not certainly promise themselves from others, on the basis of the law of humanity alone. And indeed it was necessary to determine in advance, what one was bound to perform for another, and what the latter should in turn expect and exact as his right from the former. And this is done by promises and agreements.

In regard to these, the general duty which we owe under natural law is, that a man keep his plighted word, that is, fulfill his promises and agreements. For, but for this, we should lose the greatest part of the advantage which is apt to arise for the race from the interchange of services and property ...

ON THE NATURAL STATE OF MEN
*(Book II, chapter 1)*

We have next to inquire about those duties whose performance is incumbent upon a man, in view of the particular state in which we find him living the common life ...

The state of men is either natural or adventitious. The natural state can be considered under three heads ...

Viewed in the first way, the natural state of man is that condition in which he was placed by the Creator, when He willed that man should be an animal superior to all the rest ... Hence this state is contrasted with the life and condition of the brutes.

In the second way we can consider the natural state of man, if we imagine what his condition would be, if one were left entirely to himself, without any added support from other men, assuming indeed that condition of human nature which is found at present. Certainly it would seem to have been more wretched than that of any wild beast, if we take into account with what weakness man goes forth into this world, to perish at once, but for the help of others; and how rude a life each would lead, if he had nothing more than what he owed to his own strength and ingenuity ... And in this sense the natural state is opposed to a life improved by the industry of men.

In the third way we consider the natural state of man according as men are understood to be related to each other, merely from that common kinship which results from similarity of nature, before any agreement or act of man, by which one came to be particularly bound to another. In this sense we speak of men as living together in the natural state, if they have no common master, and one is not subject to the other, and they are not known to each other by kindness or injury. In this sense the natural state is opposed to the civil state.

Again, the character of this natural state can be considered either as it is represented by a figment, or as it really exists. We have the former, if we conceive that from the beginning a multitude of men came into being at once, without any interdependence, as the story of the Cadmean brothers has it; or else, if we imagine the whole human race as now so broken up, that each man would govern himself apart, and none be bound to any by other bond than similarity of nature. But the state of nature which really exists, has this feature, that one is joined to some men by a special alliance, but with all the others has nothing in common except one's humanity, and owes them nothing on any other account.

Such a condition now exists between different states, and between the citizens of different nations, and formerly it obtained among the scattered patriarchs.

For it is clear that the whole human race has never at one and the same time been in the natural state. For those who were born to our first parents, from whom all mortals draw their origin, as the Holy Scriptures relate, were subject to the paternal authority. Later, however, this natural state did appear among some men. For the first men, in order to fill a world still empty, and to seek a roomier habitation for themselves and their flocks, left the paternal homes, separated in different directions, and nearly every male set up a household for himself ... Their descendants ... scattered in the same way. So when at the first mankind separated into different family groups ... such groups lived in a mutual state of nature* ...; until later, when the race had multiplied remarkably, and they had discovered the inconvenience of the isolated life, by degrees the nearest neighbors united to form societies, first smaller, then larger, by the voluntary or enforced union of several of the smaller. Between these communities, as they are joined by no other bond than that of common humanity, the natural state certainly still exists.

Now those who live in the natural state have this particular right, that they are subject and responsible to none but God. From which standpoint that state is called natural liberty ... And from the same standpoint each is accounted equal to every other, and neither is subject to him, nor holds him in subjection to himself. Moreover, since the light of reason has been placed in man, and, by its beams he can guide his actions, it follows that every man living in natural liberty depends upon no one for the regulation of his conduct; but, in accordance with his own judgment and will, has the power of doing everything that agrees with sound reason. And on account of the common inclination, implanted in all creatures, a man can but endeavor by every means to preserve his body and his life, and to banish what seems to destroy life, and must employ the means to that end. For this reason, and because in the natural state no one has another man as his superior, to whom he has submitted his own will and judgment, therefore in that state every one of his own judgment determines the fitness of means, and whether they conduce to self-preservation or not ... But that this self-government be rightly conducted, it is required that it be undertaken according to the dictate of right reason and the natural law.

*The phrase 'So when ... nature' is from *On the Law of Nature and Nations*.

However much the natural state allures by the name of freedom and immunity from all subjection, still, until men have united into communities, it has many added disadvantages, whether we imagine all men as existing singly in that state, or consider the situation of the scattered patriarchs. For if you conceive a man who even in adult age is left alone in this world, and without any of the comforts and supports with which the ingenuity of men has made life more civilized and less hard, you will see an animal, naked, dumb, needy, driving away his hunger as best he can by roots and herbs, his thirst by any water he chances upon, the severity of the weather by caves, an animal exposed to the wild beasts, and alarmed when he meets any of them. A life somewhat more civilized was possible among those who lived in scattered families — a life, however, which could not be compared in any way with civil life, not so much on account of want, which the household, with its limited desires, seems fairly well able to banish, as because security is not fully provided for there. And, to be brief, in the natural state each man is protected by his own powers only, in the community by those of all. In the former no one has a certain reward of his industry; in the latter all have it. In the one there is the rule of passion, war, fear, poverty, ugliness, solitude, barbarism, ignorance, savagery; in the other the rule of reason, peace, security, riches, beauty, society, refinement, knowledge, good will.

Moreover in the natural state, if a man does not willingly perform for another what he ought under an agreement, or if he has injured him, or if some controversy arises otherwise, there is no one who by authority can compel the other to perform what he ought, or repair the injury, and can thus settle the quarrel, as in states, where one may implore the aid of a common judge . . .

Again, although it was the will of Nature herself that there should be a certain kinship between men, and that, by virtue of this, it should be wrong for one to injure another, and — better still — right for every man to spend himself for the advantage of others, nevertheless among those who live together in natural liberty this kinship generally exerts a very feeble force. Hence any man who is not our fellow-citizen, or one with whom we live in the natural state, is to be regarded, not indeed as an enemy, but still as an inconstant friend. The reason for this is that men are not only perfectly able to injure each other, but for various reasons very often willing to do so. For in some cases perversity of nature, or the passion for ruling and possessing superfluities, spurs men on to injure others. Other men, though of modest temper, rush to arms in the desire to preserve themselves, and not to be anticipated by others. Many are matched against each other by desire for the same thing, others by a rivalry of talent. Hence in this state suspicions all but perpetual are rife, as are distrust, the desire to undermine the strength of others, the passion for getting ahead of others, or of strengthening one's self by the ruin of others ...

### ON THE DUTIES OF PARENTS AND CHILDREN
#### *(Book II, chapter 3)*

From marriage, spring children, over whom paternal authority has been established — the most ancient and at the same time the most sacred kind of rule, under which children are bound to respect the commands and recognize the superiority of parents ...

But although the mother contributes no less than the father, to the production of children, and a child naturally owes its mother respect and gratitude, it is nevertheless not bound by the commands of the mother — those at least which conflict with the just instructions of the father ...

In adult years, when the children have indeed mature judgment, but are still a part of the paternal household, we can distinguish the authority which the father has as father, from that which he has as head of the household ... He who wishes to be supported out of the paternal property, and in turn to succeed to it, must adjust himself to the circumstances of the father's household, for the control of the latter is unquestionably in the hands of the father.

But the patriarchs, who had not yet entered into communities, wielded in their homes an authority like that of princes. Hence their children too, still remaining in the household, were bound to respect their authority as the highest ...

### ON THE IMPELLING CAUSE FOR THE ESTABLISHMENT OF A STATE
#### *(Book II, chapter 5)*

It remains for us to investigate the question, why men ..., not content with those little first societies, have established the great societies which go by the names of states. For it is from these foundations that we must deduce the reason for the duties which attend the civil status of men.

Here then it is not enough to say that man is by Nature herself drawn into civil society, so that without it he cannot and will not live. For surely it is evident that man is an animal of the kind that loves itself and its interest to the utmost degree. When, therefore, he voluntarily seeks civil society, it must be that he has had regard to some utility which he will derive from it for himself. And though, outside of society with his kind, man would have been much the most miserable of creatures, still the natural desires and necessities of man could have been abundantly satisfied through the first communities, and the duties performed out of humanity or by agreement. Hence it cannot at once be inferred from man's sociability that his nature does tend exactly to civil society.

This will be clearer, if we consider what condition arises among men from the establishment of states; what is required, if one is to be truly called a political animal, that is, a good citizen; and finally what in man's nature is found to conflict with the character of the civil life.

The man who becomes a citizen suffers a loss of natural liberty, and subjects himself to an authority which includes the right of life and death — an authority at whose command one must do many things from which one would otherwise shrink, and must leave undone many things which one greatly desired to do. And then many actions must be referred to the good of society, which often conflicts with the good of individuals. And yet, by tendencies already inborn, man does not incline to be subject to anyone, but to do everything at his own pleasure, and to favor his own interest in all things.

We call a man a truly political animal, that is, a good citizen, if he promptly obeys the commands of the rulers, if he strives with all his might for the public good, and willingly subordinates thereto his private good, or rather if he thinks nothing good for himself, unless it is likewise good for the state too; and finally if he shows himself accommodating to the other citizens. Yet few men's natures are found to be of themselves adapted to this end. The majority are restrained somehow by the fear of punishment. Many remain all their lives bad citizens and non-political animals.

Finally, no animal is fiercer or more untameable than man, and more prone to vices capable of disturbing the peace of society . . .

Therefore the genuine and principal reason why the patriarchs, abandoning their natural liberty, took to founding states, was that they might fortify themselves against the evils which threaten man from man. For, after God, man can most help man, and has no less power for harm. And they are right in their judgment of the malice of men and its remedy, who have accepted as a proverb the saying, that, if there were no courts, one man would devour another. But after men had been brought through their communities into such order that they could be safe from mutual injuries, the natural result was that they enjoyed more richly those advantages which can come to men from other men; for example, that they were imbued from childhood with more friendly habits, and discovered and cultivated various arts, by which human life was made rich and comfortable.

The reason for founding a state will become still clearer, if we consider that other means of restraining the malice of men would not have sufficed. For although the natural law commands men to abstain from inflicting any injury, still respect for that law cannot insure to men the ability to live quite safely in natural liberty. For although there may be men of so quiet a temper that, even with impunity assured, they would not injure others; and also other men who somehow check their desires from the fear of an evil that will result; still there is, on the other hand, a great multitude of those to whom every right is worthless, whenever the hope of gain has enticed them, or confidence in their own strength or shrewdness, by which they hope to be able to repel or elude those whom they have injured. There is no one who does not strive to protect himself against such persons, if he loves his own safety; and that protection cannot be had more conveniently than by the help of states. For in spite of the fact that some may have given a mutual pledge to help each other, still, unless there be something to unite their judgments, and firmly bind their wills to carry out the pledge, it is vain for one to promise himself unfailing aid from the others . . .

### ON THE INTERNAL STRUCTURE OF STATES [I]
*(Book II, chapter 6)*

Our next task is to investigate the manner in which states have been erected, and how their internal structure is held together. . . .

It is . . . certain that the agreement of two or three cannot afford . . . security against other men. For it is easy for so many to conspire to overpower these few, that they can insure for themselves a perfectly certain victory over the others; and the hope of success and impunity will give them confidence for the attack. Therefore, to this end it is necessary for a considerable mass of men to join together, that the addition of a few to the numbers of the enemy may not be of appreciable moment in helping them to victory.

Among the many who unite with this end in view, there must be agreement in regard to the employment of means suited to that same end. For even many will accomplish nothing, if they are not agreed among themselves, but are divided in opinion and have different aims ... And although they promise by general agreement that they will employ their powers for the common defense, still, even in this way, the multitude is not sufficiently safeguarded for any length of time. But something further must be added, that those who have once consented together for peace and mutual aid in the interest of the common good, may be prevented from disagreeing again later, when their own private good seems to clash with the public ... Diversity of inclinations and of judgment is counteracted if there is constituted some authority, which can inflict upon those who resist the common advantage, some immediate and sensible punishment.

The wills of many men can be united in no other way, than if each subjects his will to the will of one man, or one council, so that henceforth, whatever such an one shall will concerning things necessary to the common security, must be accounted the will of all, collectively and singly.

Moreover, a power, such as must be feared by all, can likewise be constituted among a multitude of men in no other way than if all, collectively and singly, have bound themselves to employ their powers in the way he shall prescribe, to whom they have all resigned the direction of their powers. But when a union both of wills and powers has been brought about, then at last a multitude of men is quickened into the strongest of bodies, a state.

Again, for a state to coalesce regularly, two compacts and one decree are necessary. For first of all, when the many men, who are thought of as established in natural liberty, gather to form a state, they individually enter a joint agreement, that they are ready to enter into a permanent community, and to manage the business of their safety and security by common counsel and guidance, in a word, that they mutually desire to become fellow-citizens. They must all together and singly agree to this compact; and a man who shall not do so, remains outside the state that is to be.

After this compact a decree must be made, stating what form of government is to be introduced. For until they have settled this point, nothing that makes for the common safety can be steadily carried out.

After the decree concerning the form of government, another compact is needed, when the person, or persons, upon whom the government of the nascent state is conferred are established in authority. By this compact these bind themselves to take care of the common security and safety, the rest to yield them their obedience; and by it also all subject their own wills to the will of that person or persons, and at the same time make over to him, or to them, the use and employment of their powers for the common defense. And only when this compact has been duly executed, does a perfect and regular state come into being.

A state thus constituted is conceived as a single person, and distinguished and differentiated from all individual men by a single name; and it has its own peculiar rights and its possessions, which neither individuals, nor many persons, nor in fact all together, can claim for themselves, except him who has the highest authority, that is, to whom the rule of the state has been entrusted. Hence a state is defined as a composite moral person, whose will, intertwined and united by virtue of the compacts of the many, is regarded as the will of all, so that it can use the powers and resources of all for the common peace and security.

But the will of a state, as the source of public acts, declares itself either through one man, or one council, according as the chief authority has been conferred upon him or them. Where the government of the state is in the hands of one man, the state is understood to will whatever that man shall please (it is presupposed that he is in his right mind), in regard to matters concerning the end for which states exist.

But where the government of a state has been conferred upon a council, consisting of a number of men, each one of whom retains his natural will, the will of the state is regularly understood to be that upon which a majority of the men composing the council have agreed; unless it has been expressly determined what fraction of the council must be in agreement, in order to represent the will of the whole body.

The state being thus constituted, the central authority, according as it is one man, or one council of the few, or of all, is called a monarch, a senate, or a free people. The rest are styled subjects, or citizens ...

However, what has been laid down with regard to the origin of states does not prevent us from saying with good reason, that civil authority is from God. For it is His will that the natural law be observed by all men; and in fact, after the race had multiplied, life would have come to be so barbarous, as to leave scarcely any place for the natural law, whereas its observance is greatly promoted by the establishment of states ...

## On the Law of Nature and Nations

ON THE INTERNAL STRUCTURE OF STATES [II]
*(Book VII, chapter 2)*

Now we would not have it thought that these remarks on the pacts which give rise to a state, are a creation of our imagination, because the origins of most states are unknown, or at least it is not entirely certain that they were established in that manner. For one thing is sure, namely, that every state had at some time its beginning. And yet it was necessary that those who compose a state be not held together before its establishment by the same bond as they are afterwards; and that they be not subject to the same persons to whom they are afterwards. Yet since it is impossible to understand that union and subjection without the above-mentioned pacts, they must have interposed, tacitly at least, in the formation of states. Nor is there anything to prevent men from being able to reason out the origin of a thing, despite the fact that there remain no written records upon them.

It may be worth while in this connexion to present a little more in detail the opinion of Hobbes, who recognizes in the formation of states but a single pact between individuals, and everywhere maintains that none passes between a king, or nobles, and citizens. And the reason that has led him to make such statements is clear enough from the scheme of his works on politics, as it is clearly set forth in his *Leviathan*. He attacked first of all those seditious men who in former years endeavored to circumscribe the royal power, and to place it under the control of subjects, or even to do away with it altogether. To take from them their excuse for rebellion, namely, that the pledge between a king and citizen is reciprocal, and that when the former does not keep the promises he made by a pact, the latter are freed from obedience; and to prevent turbulent citizens from making a case of broken faith out of any actions of a king which do not suit them, he undertook to deny that there was any pact between a king and his subjects ...

But although it be the highest interest of mankind that the royal power be held sacred and free from the cavils of churlish men, yet that does not necessitate our denying matters as clear as daylight, and refusing to recognize a pact, when there exists a mutual promise about performing that which was not due before. When I subject myself to a prince, I promise him obedience, and stipulate for myself defence, while the prince in accepting me as a citizen promises me defence and stipulates from me obedience. Before that promise, neither of us was under an obligation, at least not a perfect one, I to obey him, or he to defend me. Who now would undertake to exclude such an act from the class of pacts? Nor is such a pact rendered superfluous because it appears that there was a prior agreement among those who voluntarily establish a king over themselves, to elevate this or that man to the throne. For . . . those who voluntarily confer upon another power over themselves wish that in its exercise he strive toward the end set for that power . . .

Therefore, in the case of those who offer sovereignty to another, just as they promise what the nature of their subjection requires, so they also, on the other hand, bargain to secure from him the things for which civil sovereignties are established. What else is this than to enter into a pact?

Nor, indeed, when we admit the existence of a pact between king and citizens, do those inconveniences necessarily follow, which Hobbes seems to have had before his eyes. All pacts, for that matter, have this feature, namely, that they imply a necessity to do some particular thing. But there is the greatest difference possible between those pacts by which a man subjects himself to another, and those by which neither accepts any sovereignty over the other. The right of a master over a slave, at least over one who voluntarily accepts slavery, is established by a pact, as also the power of a father over him who offers himself for adoption, and the command of a general over mercenaries. And yet that does not prevent the former from having the faculty to command, and the latter from being under necessity to obey, nor can the latter throw off the restraint when the orders of their superiors do not suit them . . .

Finally, it seems highly dangerous to derive the obligation to a king from a pact of this kind with every other citizen: 'Out of favor to you I transfer my right to the king, so that you as well, out of favor to me, may transfer your right to him.' For by this device every citizen will appear to have made his necessity to obey depend upon the obedience of every citizen, and as a result, when any one of them does not render obedience, all the rest would be free from theirs. And yet for this reason alone it is necessary that every citizen be obligated to the supreme power for himself, and unconditioned by another's obedience, so that even if one or another chafe at their restraint, the sovereign can avail himself of the strength of the rest in reducing the refractory one to his place . . .

We must observe that a man may become a member of any state in two ways: by an expressed or by a tacit pact. For those who establish states in the first place are surely not held to have done so with the thought that they would cease with the death of their founders, but they had before their eyes the obtaining in this way of advantages which would be lasting and perpetual, and would be a source of gratification to their children and all their posterity. Therefore, it is held that they also had in mind that their children and descendants should upon birth enjoy the common advantages and rewards of the state; and since these cannot be secured without sovereignty, which is, as it were, the soul of a state, all who are born in a state are also understood to have subjected themselves to that sovereignty. Hence it is that those who have once accepted the sovereignty in a state are under no necessity of requiring anew an express subjection from each newly-born child, although all of those who first conferred sovereignty upon them may be dead . . .

## On the Duty of Man and Citizen

### THE CHARACTERISTICS OF CIVIL AUTHORITY
*(Book II, Chapter 9)*

Every authority by which an entire state is ruled, in any form of government, has this quality, that it is supreme, that is, not dependent in its exercise upon any man as a superior, but operating according to its own judgment and discretion, so that its acts cannot be nullified by any man as a superior.

It follows then that the same supreme authority is ἀνυπεύθυνος [unaccountable], in other words, not bound so to render account to any human being, that, if that person did not approve the account, it would for that reason be liable to human penalties or constraint, proceeding as it were from a superior.

Connected with this is the fact that the same supreme authority is superior to human and civil laws as such, and thus not directly bound by them. For those laws are dependent upon the supreme authority in origin as well as in duration. Hence it is impossible for it to be bound by them, since it would otherwise be superior to itself . . .

Lastly, the supreme authority has a special sanctity, so that not only is it wrong to resist its legitimate commands, but also the citizens must patiently bear with its severity, just as the peevishness of parents is borne by good children. And even when it has threatened the most cruel injuries, individuals will seek their safety in flight, or endure any amount of misfortune, rather than draw the sword against one who is indeed harsh, but still the father of his country . . .

ON THE DUTY OF RULERS
*(Book II, chapter 11)*

What precepts make up the duty of rulers, is clearly deduced from the character and end of states, and from a consideration of the functions of the supreme authority ...

The general law of rulers is this: the welfare of the people is the supreme law. For authority was conferred upon them, with the intention that the end for which states have been established, should thereby be insured. Hence they ought also to believe that nothing is to their private advantage, if it is not also to the advantage of the state.

For the internal tranquility of states it is necessary that the wills of the citizens be controlled and guided, as is expedient for the welfare of the state. Hence it is the duty of rulers not only to prescribe laws suited to that end, but also so to confirm the public education, that the citizens shall accept legal prescription not so much from fear of punishment as by habit. It contributes to this end also, to take care that Christian doctrine, in its pure and unmixed form, shall flourish in the state, and that in the public schools such teachings be imparted, as are in conformity with the purpose of states ...

Moreover, inasmuch as the purpose with which men united to form a community was to insure security from injuries inflicted by others, it is the duty of rulers to prevent citizens from injuring each other, and this with a severity proportioned to the increased opportunities for injury afforded by their living constantly together ...

ON THE DUTIES OF CITIZENS
*(Book II, Chapter 18)*

To the rulers of the state a citizen owes respect, loyalty and obedience. This implies that one acquiesce in the present régime, and have no thoughts of revolution; that one refrain from attaching himself to any other, or admiring and respecting him; that one have a good and honorable opinion of the rulers and their acts, and express himself accordingly.

A good citizen's duty towards the whole state is to have nothing dearer than its welfare and safety, to offer his life, property, and fortunes freely for its preservation; to exert all the strength of his mind and industry to add to its fame and promote its interests.

# 4

# Natural Rights and Civil Society

JOHN LOCKE

SECOND TREATISE OF GOVERNMENT
*(Chapter 1)*

Political power I take to be a right of making laws with penalties of death, and consequently all less penalties, for the regulating and preserving of property, and of employing the force of the community in the execution of such laws, and in the defence of the commonwealth from foreign injury; and all this only for the public good.

OF THE STATE OF NATURE
*(Chapter 2)*

To understand political power aright, and derive it from its original, we must consider what state all men are naturally in, and that is a state of perfect freedom to order their actions and dispose of their possessions and persons as they think fit, within the

*Source:* J. Locke, *The Second Treatise of Government*, ed. J. W. Gough (Oxford: Blackwell, 1956). Extracts reprinted by permission.

bounds of the law of nature, without asking leave, or depending upon the will of any other man.

A state also of equality, wherein all the power and jurisdiction is reciprocal, no one having more than another; there being nothing more evident than that creatures of the same species and rank, promiscuously born to all the same advantages of nature, and the use of the same faculties, should also be equal one amongst another without subordination or subjection, unless the Lord and Master of them all should by any manifest declaration of his will set one above another, and confer on him, by an evident and clear appointment, an undoubted right to dominion and sovereignty . . .

But though this be a state of liberty, yet it is not a state of licence; though man in that state have an uncontrollable liberty to dispose of his person or possessions, yet he has not liberty to destroy himself, or so much as any creature in his possession, but where some nobler use than its bare preservation calls for it. The state of nature has a law of nature to govern it, which obliges every one; and reason, which is that law, teaches all mankind who will but consult it, that, being all equal and independent, no one ought to harm another in his life, health, liberty, or possessions. For men being all the workmanship of one omnipotent and in-finitely wise Maker — all the servants of one sovereign Master, sent into the world by his order, and about his business — they are his property, whose workmanship they are, made to last during his, not one another's pleasure; and being furnished with like faculties, sharing all in one community of nature, there cannot be supposed any such subordination among us, that may authorize us to destroy one another, as if we were made for one another's uses, as the inferior ranks of creatures are for ours. Every one, as he is bound to preserve himself, and not to quit his station wilfully, so, by the like reason, when his own preservation comes not in competition, ought he, as much as he can, to preserve the rest of mankind, and may not, unless it be to do justice on an offender, take away or impair the life, or what tends to the preservation of the life, the liberty, health, limb, or goods of another.

And that all men may be restrained from invading others' rights, and from doing hurt to one another, and the law of nature be observed, which willeth the peace and preservation of all mankind, the execution of the law of nature is in that state put into every

man's hand, whereby every one has a right to punish the trans-
gressors of that law to such a degree as may hinder its violation.
For the law of nature would, as all other laws that concern men in
this world, be in vain if there were nobody that, in the state of
nature, had a power to execute that law, and thereby preserve the
innocent and restrain offenders. And if any one in the state of
nature may punish another for any evil he has done, every one
may do so. For in that state of perfect equality, where naturally
there is no superiority or jurisdiction of one over another, what
any may do in prosecution of that law, every one must needs have
a right to do ...

'Tis not every compact that puts an end to the state of nature
between men, but only this one of agreeing together mutually to
enter into one community, and make one body politic; other
promises and compacts men may make one with another, and yet
still be in the state of nature. The promises and bargains for truck,
etc., between the two men in the desert island, mentioned by
Garcilasso de la Vega in his history of Peru; or between a Swiss
and an Indian, in the woods of America, are binding to them,
though they are perfectly in a state of nature in reference to one
another. For truth and keeping of faith belong to men as men, and
not as members of society.

To those that say there were never any men in the state of
nature, I will not only oppose the authority of the judicious
Hooker, *Ecclesiastical Polity*, lib. i, sect. 10, where he says, 'The
laws which have been hitherto mentioned,' *i.e.*, the laws of nature,
'do bind men absolutely, even as they are men, although they have
never any settled fellowship, and never any solemn agreement
amongst themselves what to do or not to do; but forasmuch as we
are not by ourselves sufficient to furnish ourselves with competent
store of things needful for such a life as our nature doth desire − a
life fit for the dignity of man − therefore to supply those defects
and imperfections which are in us, as living single and solely by
ourselves, we are naturally induced to seek communion and fellowship with others; this was the cause of men's uniting themselves at
first in politic societies,' but I moreover affirm that all men are
naturally in that state, and remain so, till by their own con-
sents they make themselves members of some politic society; and
I doubt not, in the sequel of this discourse, to make it very
clear.

OF THE STATE OF WAR
*(Chapter 3)*

The state of war is a state of enmity and destruction; and therefore declaring by word or action, not a passionate and hasty, but a sedate, settled design upon another man's life, puts him in a state of war with him against whom he has declared such an intention, and so has exposed his life to the other's power to be taken away by him, or any one that joins with him in his defence and espouses his quarrel; it being reasonable and just I should have a right to destroy that which threatens me with destruction. For by the fundamental law of nature, man being to be preserved as much as possible, when all cannot be preserved, the safety of the innocent is to be preferred; and one may destroy a man who makes war upon him, or has discovered an enmity to his being, for the same reason that he may kill a wolf or a lion; because such men are not under the ties of the common law of reason, have no other rule but that of force and violence, and so may be treated as beasts of prey, those dangerous and noxious creatures that will be sure to destroy him whenever he falls into their power.

And hence it is that he who attempts to get another man into his absolute power does thereby put himself into a state of war with him; it being to be understood as a declaration of a design upon his life ... He that in the state of nature would take away the freedom that belongs to any one in that state, must necessarily be supposed to have a design to take away everything else, that freedom being the foundation of all the rest; as he that in the state of society would take away the freedom belonging to those of that society or commonwealth, must be supposed to design to take away from them everything else, and so be looked on as in a state of war ...

And here we have the plain difference between the state of nature and the state of war, which however some men have confounded, are as far distant as a state of peace, good will, mutual assistance, and preservation, and a state of enmity, malice, violence, and mutual destruction, are one from another. Men living together according to reason, without a common superior on earth with authority to judge between them, are properly in the state of nature. But force, or a declared design of force, upon the person of another, where there is no common superior on earth to appeal to for relief, is the state of war; and 'tis the want of such an appeal gives a man the right of war even against an aggressor, though he be in society and a fellow-subject. Thus a thief, whom I cannot harm, but by appeal to the law, for having stolen all that I am worth, I may kill, when he sets on to rob me but of my horse or coat; because the law, which was made for my preservation, where it cannot interpose to secure my life from present force, which if lost is capable of no reparation, permits me my own defence, and the right of war, a liberty to kill the aggressor, because the aggressor allows not time to appeal to our common judge, nor the decision of the law, for remedy in a case where the mischief may be irreparable. Want of a common judge with authority puts all men in a state of nature; force without right upon a man's person makes a state of war, both where is, and is not, a common judge.

But when the actual force is over, the state of war ceases between those that are in society, and are equally on both sides subjected to the fair determination of the law; because then there lies open the remedy of appeal for the past injury, and to prevent future harm. But where no such appeal is, as in the state of nature, for want of positive laws and judges with authority to appeal to, the state of war once begun continues, with a right to the innocent party to destroy the other whenever he can, until the aggressor offers peace, and desires reconciliation on such terms as may repair any wrongs he has already done, and secure the innocent for the future ...

To avoid this state of war (wherein there is no appeal but to heaven, and wherein every the least difference is apt to end, where there is no authority to decide between the contenders) is one great reason of men's putting themselves into society and quitting the state of nature. For where there is an authority, a power on earth, from which relief can be had by appeal, there the continuance of the state of war is excluded, and the controversy is decided by that power.

OF SLAVERY
*(Chapter 4)*

The natural liberty of man is to be free from any superior power on earth, and not to be under the will or legislative authority of man, but to have only the law of nature for his rule. The liberty of man in society is to be under no other legislative power but that established by consent in the commonwealth; nor under the dominion of any will or restraint of any law, but what that legislative shall enact according to the trust put in it. Freedom then is not what Sir Robert Filmer tells us, O. A. 55,[1] 'a liberty for every one to do what he lists, to live as he pleases, and not to be tied by any laws'. But freedom of men under government is to have a standing rule to live by, common to every one of that society, and made by the legislative power erected in it; a liberty to follow my own will in all things, where the rule prescribes not; and not to be subject to the inconstant, uncertain, unknown, arbitrary will of another man; as freedom of nature is to be under no other restraint but the law of nature.

This freedom from absolute, arbitrary power is so necessary to, and closely joined with, a man's preservation, that he cannot part with it but by what forfeits his preservation and life together. For a man not having the power of his own life cannot by compact, or his own consent, enslave himself to any one, nor put himself under the absolute, arbitrary power of another to take away his life when he pleases. Nobody can give more power than he has himself; and he that cannot take away his own life, cannot give another power over it ...

OF PROPERTY
*(Chapter 5)*

Whether we consider natural reason, which tells us that men being once born have a right to their preservation, and consequently to meat and drink and such other things as nature affords for their subsistence; or revelation, which gives us an account of those grants God made of the world to Adam, and to Noah and his sons, 'tis very clear that God, as King David says, Psalm cxv. 16, 'has given the earth to the children of men,' given it to mankind in common. But this being supposed, it seems to some a very great difficulty how any one should ever come to have a property in anything ... But I shall endeavour to shew how men might come to have a property in several parts of that which God gave to mankind in common, and that without any express compact of all the commoners.

God, who hath given the world to men in common, hath also given them reason to make use of it to the best advantage of life and convenience. The earth and all that is therein is given to men for the support and comfort of their being. And though all the fruits it naturally produces, and beasts it feeds, belong to mankind in common, as they are produced by the spontaneous hand of nature; and nobody has originally a private dominion exclusive of the rest of mankind in any of them as they are thus in their natural state; yet being given for the use of men, there must of necessity be a means to appropriate them some way or other before they can be of any use or at all beneficial to any particular man. The fruit or venison which nourishes the wild Indian, who knows no enclosure, and is still a tenant in common, must be his, and so his, *i.e.*, a part of him, that another can no longer have any right to it, before it can do any good for the support of his life.

Though the earth and all inferior creatures be common to all men, yet every man has a property in his own person; this nobody has any right to but himself. The labour of his body and the work of his hands we may say are properly his. Whatsoever, then, he removes out of the state that nature hath provided and left it in, he hath mixed his labour with, and joined to it something that is his own, and thereby makes it his property ... For this labour being the unquestionable property of the labourer, no man but he can have a right to what that is once joined to, at least where there is enough and as good left in common for others.

He that is nourished by the acorns he picked up under an oak, or the apples he gathered from the trees in the wood, has certainly appropriated them to himself ... And will any one say he had no right to those acorns or apples he thus appropriated, because he had not the consent of all mankind to make them his? Was it a robbery thus to assume to himself what belonged to all in common? If such a consent as that was necessary man had starved, notwithstanding the plenty God had given him ...

It will perhaps be objected to this, that if gathering the acorns, or other fruits of the earth, etc., makes a right to them, then any one may engross as much as he will. To which I answer, Not so. The same law of nature, that does by this means give us property, does also bound that property too. 'God has given us all things richly' (1 Tim. vi. 12), is the voice of reason confirmed by inspiration. But how far has he given it us? To enjoy. As much as any one can make use of to any advantage of life before it spoils, so much he may by his labour fix a property in; whatever is beyond this is more than his share, and belongs to others. Nothing was made by God for man to spoil or destroy. And thus considering the plenty of natural provisions there was a long time in the world, and the few spenders, and to how small a part of that provision the industry of one man could extend itself, and engross it to the prejudice of others — especially keeping within the bounds, set by reason, of what might serve for his use — there could be then little room for quarrels or contentions about property so established.

But the chief matter of property being now not the fruits of the earth, and the beasts that subsist on it, but the earth itself, as that which takes in and carries with it all the rest, I think it is plain that property in that, too, is acquired as the former. As much land as a man tills, plants, improves, cultivates, and can use the product of, so much is his property. He by his labour does as it were enclose it from the common. Nor will it invalidate his right to say, everybody else has an equal title to it; and therefore he cannot appropriate, he cannot enclose, without the consent of all his fellow-commoners, all mankind. God, when he gave the world in common to all mankind, commanded man also to labour, and the penury of his condition required it of him. God and his reason commanded him to subdue the earth, *i.e.*, improve it for the benefit of life, and therein lay out something upon it that was his own, his labour. He that, in obedience to this command of God, subdued, tilled, and sowed any part of it, thereby annexed to it something that was his property, which another had no title to, nor could without injury take from him.

Nor was this appropriation of any parcel of land, by improving it, any prejudice to any other man, since there was still enough and as good left; and more than the yet unprovided could use. So that in effect there was never the less left for others because of his enclosure for himself ...

God gave the world to men in common; but since he gave it to them for their benefit, and the greatest conveniences of life they were capable to draw from it, it cannot be supposed he meant it should always remain common and uncultivated. He gave it to the use of the industrious and rational (and labour was to be his title to it), not to the fancy or covetousness of the quarrelsome and contentious. He that had as good left for his improvement as was already taken up, needed not complain, ought not to meddle with what was already improved by another's labour; if he did, 'tis plain he desired the benefit of another's pains, which he had no right to, and not the ground which God had given him in common with others to labour on, and whereof there was as good left as that already possessed, and more than he knew what to do with, or his industry could reach to ...

The measure of property nature has well set by the extent of men's labour and the conveniencies of life. ... This measure did confine every man's possession to a very moderate proportion, and such as he might appropriate to himself without injury to anybody, in the first ages of the world, when men were more in danger to be lost by wandering from their company in the then vast wilderness of the earth than to be straitened for want of room to plant in ... And the same rule of propriety, *viz.*, that every man should have as much as he could make use of, would hold still in the world without straitening anybody, since there is land enough in the world to suffice double the inhabitants, had not the invention of money, and the tacit agreement of men to put a value on it, introduced (by consent) larger possessions and a right to them; which how it has done I shall by and by shew more at large ...

To this let me add, that he who appropriates land to himself by his labour does not lessen but increase the common stock of mankind. For the provisions serving to the support of human life produced by one acre of enclosed and cultivated land are (to speak much within compass) ten times more than those which are yielded by an acre of land of an equal richness lying waste in common. And therefore he that encloses land, and has a greater plenty of the conveniencies of life from ten acres than he could have from an hundred left to nature, may truly be said to give ninety acres to mankind: for his labour now supplies him with provisions out of ten acres, which were but the product of an hundred lying in common. I have here rated the improved land very low, in making its product but as ten to one, when it is much nearer an hundred to one. For I ask, whether in the wild woods and uncultivated waste of America, left to nature without any improvement, tillage, or husbandry, a thousand acres yield the needy and wretched inhabitants as many conveniences of life as ten acres of equally fertile land do in Devonshire, where they are well cultivated? ...

The greatest part of things really useful to the life of man, and such as the necessity of subsisting made the first commoners of the world look after, as it doth the Americans now, are generally things of short duration, such as, if they are not consumed by use, will decay and perish of themselves: gold, silver, and diamonds are things that fancy or agreement have put the value on more than real use and the necessary support of life. Now, of those good things which nature hath provided in common, every one had a right (as hath been said) to as much as he could use, and property in all he could effect with his labour; all that his industry could extend to, to alter from the state nature had put it in, was his ... He was only to look that he used them before they spoiled, else he took more than his share, and robbed others; and, indeed, it was a foolish thing, as well as dishonest, to hoard up more than he could make use of. If he gave away a part to anybody else, so that it perished not uselessly in his possession, these he also made use of; and if he also bartered away plums that would have rotted in a week, for nuts that would last good for his eating a whole year, he did no injury; he wasted not the common stock, destroyed no part of the portion of goods that belonged to others, so long as nothing perished uselessly in his hands. Again, if he would give his nuts for a piece of metal, pleased with its colour; or exchange his sheep for shells, or wool for a sparkling pebble or a diamond, and keep those by him all his life, he invaded not the right of others; he might heap up as much of these durable things as he pleased, the exceeding of the bounds of his just property not lying in the largeness of his possession, but the perishing of anything uselessly in it.

And thus came in the use of money — some lasting thing that men might keep without spoiling, and that, by mutual consent, men would take in exchange for the truly useful but perishable supports of life.

And as different degrees of industry were apt to give men possessions in different proportions, so this invention of money gave them the opportunity to continue and enlarge them; for supposing an island, separate from all possible commerce with the rest of the world, wherein there were but an hundred families — but there were sheep, horses, and cows, with other useful animals, wholesome fruits, and land enough for corn for a hundred thousand times as many, but nothing in the island, either because of its commonness or perishableness, fit to supply the place of money — what reason could any one have there to enlarge his possessions beyond the use of his family and a plentiful supply to its consumption, either in what their own industry produced, or they could barter for like perishable useful commodities with others? . . .

Thus in the beginning all the world was America, and more so than that is now, for no such thing as money was anywhere known. Find out something that hath the use and value of money amongst his neighbours, you shall see the same man will begin presently to enlarge his possessions.

But since gold and silver, being little useful to the life of man in proportion to food, raiment, and carriage, has its value only from the consent of men, whereof labour yet makes, in great part, the measure, it is plain that men have agreed to a disproportionate and unequal possession of the earth; they having, by a tacit and voluntary consent, found out a way how a man may fairly possess more land than he himself can use the product of, by receiving in exchange for the overplus, gold and silver, which may be hoarded up without injury to any one; these metals not spoiling or decaying in the hands of the possessor. This partage of things in an inequality of private possessions men have made practicable, out of the bounds of society, and without compact, only by putting a value on gold and silver, and tacitly agreeing in the use of money. For in governments the laws regulate the right of property, and the possession of land is determined by positive constitutions ...

OF POLITICAL OR CIVIL SOCIETY
*(Chapter 7)*

Man being born, as has been proved, with a title to perfect freedom, and an uncontrolled enjoyment of all the rights and privileges of the law of nature equally with any other man or number of men in the world, hath by nature a power not only to preserve his property — that is, his life, liberty, and estate — against the injuries and attempts of other men, but to judge of and punish the breaches of that law in others as he is persuaded the offence deserves, even with death itself, in crimes where the heinousness of the fact in his opinion requires it. But because no political society can be nor subsist without having in itself the power to preserve the property, and, in order thereunto, punish the offences of all those of that society; there, and there only, is political society, where every one of the members hath quitted this natural power, resigned it up into the hands of the community in all cases that exclude him not from appealing for protection to the law established by it. And thus all private judgment of every particular member being excluded, the community comes to be umpire, by settled, standing rules, indifferent, and the same to all parties; and by men having authority from the community for the execution of those rules, decides all the differences that may happen between any members of that society concerning any matter of right, and punishes those offences which any member hath committed against the society, with such penalties as the law has established; whereby it is easy to discern who are and who are not in political society together. Those who are united into one body, and have a common established law and judicature to appeal to, with authority to decide controversies between them and punish offenders, are in civil society one with another; but those who have no such common appeal — I mean on earth — are still in the state of nature, each being, where there is no other, judge for himself and executioner, which is, as I have before shewn it, the perfect state of nature ...

Wherever, therefore, any number of men are so united into one society, as to quit every one his executive power of the law of nature, and to resign it to the public, there, and there only, is a political, or civil society. And this is done wherever any number of men, in the state of nature, enter into society to make one people, one body politic, under one supreme government, or else when any one joins himself to, and incorporates with, any government already made. For hereby he authorizes the society, or, which is all one, the legislative thereof, to make laws for him, as the public good of the society shall require, to the execution whereof his own assistance (as to his own decrees) is due. And this puts men out of a state of nature into that of a commonwealth, by setting up a judge on earth with authority to determine all the controversies and redress the injuries that may happen to any member of the commonwealth; which judge is the legislative, or magistrates appointed by it ...

Hence it is evident that absolute monarchy, which by some men is counted the only government in the world, is indeed inconsistent with civil society, and so can be no form of civil government at all. For the end of civil society being to avoid and remedy those inconveniences of the state of nature which necessarily follow from every man's being judge in his own case, by setting up a known authority to which every one of that society may appeal upon any injury received or controversy that may arise, and which every one of the society ought to obey; wherever any persons are, who have not such an authority to appeal to and decide any difference between them, there those persons are still in the state of nature. And so is every absolute prince, in respect of those who are under his dominion.

For he being supposed to have all, both legislative and executive, power in himself alone, there is no judge to be found; no appeal lies open to any one who may fairly and indifferently and with authority decide, and from whose decision relief and address may be expected of any injury or inconvenience that may be suffered from the prince or by his order; so that such a man, however entitled − Czar, or Grand Seignior, or how you please − is as much in the state of nature, with all under his dominion, as he is with the rest of mankind. For wherever any two men are, who have no standing rule and common judge to appeal to on earth for the determination of controversies of right betwixt them, there they are still in the state of nature, and under all the inconveniences of it, with only this woeful difference to the subject, or rather slave, of an absolute prince: that, whereas in the ordinary state of nature he has a liberty to judge of his right, and according to the best of his power to maintain it; now, whenever his property is invaded by the will and order of his monarch, he has not only no appeal, as those in society ought to have, but, as if he were degraded from the common state of rational creatures, is denied a liberty to judge of or to defend his right; and so is exposed to all the misery and inconveniencies that a man can fear from one who, being in the unrestrained state of nature, is yet corrupted with flattery, and armed with power ... As if when men quitting the state of nature entered into society, they agreed that all of them but one should be under the restraint of laws, but that he should still retain all the liberty of the state of nature, increased with power, and made licentious by impunity. This is to think that men are so foolish that they take care to avoid what mischiefs may be done them by polecats or foxes, but are content, nay, think it safety, to be devoured by lions ...

### OF THE BEGINNING OF POLITICAL SOCIETIES
*(Chapter 8)*

Men being, as has been said, by nature all free, equal, and independent, no one can be put out of this estate, and subjected to the political power of another, without his own consent. The only way whereby any one divests himself of his natural liberty and puts on the bonds of civil society is by agreeing with other men to join and unite into a community for their comfortable, safe, and peaceable living one amongst another, in a secure enjoyment of their properties, and a greater security against any that are not of it. This any number of men may do, because it injures not the freedom of the rest; they are left as they were in the liberty of the state of nature. When any number of men have so consented to make one community or government, they are thereby presently incorporated, and make one body politic, wherein the majority have a right to act and conclude the rest ...

To this I find two objections made.

First: That there are no instances to be found in story of a company of men, independent and equal one amongst another, that met together, and in this way began and set up a government.

Secondly: 'Tis impossible of right that men should do so, because all men being born under government, they are to submit to that, and are not at liberty to begin a new one.

To the first there is this to answer: That it is not at all to be wondered that history gives us but a very little account of men that lived together in the state of nature. The inconveniencies of that condition, and the love and want of society, no sooner brought any number of them together, but they presently united and incorporated if they designed to continue together. And if we may not suppose men ever to have been in the state of nature, because we hear not much of them in such a state, we may as well suppose that armies of Salmanasser or Xerxes were never children, because we hear little of them till they were men, and embodied in armies. Government is everywhere antecedent to records, and letters seldom come in amongst a people, till a long continuation of civil society has, by other more necessary arts, provided for their safety, ease, and plenty . . .

I will not deny, that if we look back as far as history will direct us, towards the original of commonwealths, we shall generally find them under the government and administration of one man. And I am also apt to believe that where a family was numerous enough to subsist by itself, and continued entire together, without mixing with others, as it often happens where there is much land and few people, the government commonly began in the father . . . But when either the father died, and left his next heir, for want of age, wisdom, courage, or any other qualities, less fit for rule; or where several families met and consented to continue together, there 'tis not to be doubted but they used their natural freedom to set up him whom they judged the ablest and most likely to rule well over them. Conformable hereunto we find the people of America, who (living out of the reach of the conquering swords and spreading domination of the two great empires of Peru and Mexico) enjoyed their own natural freedom, though, *cæteris paribus*, they commonly prefer the heir of their deceased king; yet if they find him any way weak or uncapable, they pass him by and set up the stoutest and bravest man for their ruler.

Thus, though looking back as far as records give us any account of peopling the world, and the history of nations, we commonly find the government to be in one hand; yet it destroys not that which I affirm, *viz.*, that the beginning of politic society depends upon the consent of the individuals to join into and make one society; who, when they are thus incorporated, might set up what form of government they thought fit . . .

Every man being, as has been shewn, naturally free, and nothing being able to put him into subjection to any earthly power but only his own consent, it is to be considered what shall be understood to be a sufficient declaration of a man's consent to make him subject to the laws of any government. There is a common distinction of an express and a tacit consent, which will concern our present case. Nobody doubts but an express consent of any man entering into any society makes him a perfect member of that society, a subject of that government. The difficulty is, what ought to be looked upon as a tacit consent, and how far it binds, *i.e.*, how far any one shall be looked on to have consented, and thereby submitted to any government, where he has made no expressions of it at all. And to this I say that every man that hath any possessions, or enjoyment of any part of the dominions of any government, doth thereby give his tacit consent, and is as far forth obliged to obedience to the laws of that government during such enjoyment as any one under it; whether this his possession be of land to him and his heirs for ever, or a lodging only for a week; or whether it be barely travelling freely on the highway; and in effect it reaches as far as the very being of any one within the territories of that government.

To understand this the better, it is fit to consider that every man when he at first incorporates himself into any commonwealth, he, by his uniting himself thereunto, annexes also, and submits to the community, those possessions which he has or shall acquire that do not already belong to any other government; for it would be a direct contradiction for any one to enter into society with others for the securing and regulating of property, and yet to suppose his land, whose property is to be regulated by the laws of the society, should be exempt from the jurisdiction of that government to which he himself, the proprietor of the land, is a subject. ... Whoever therefore from thenceforth by inheritance, purchases, permission, or otherwise, enjoys any part of the land so annexed to, and under the government of that commonwealth, must take it with the condition it is under, that is, of submitting to the government of the commonwealth under whose jurisdiction it is, as far forth as any subject of it.

The obligation any one is under, by virtue of such enjoyment, to submit to the government, begins and ends with the enjoyment; so that whenever the owner, who has given nothing but such a tacit consent to the government, will by donation, sale, or otherwise, quit the said possession, he is at liberty to go and incorporate himself into any other commonwealth, or to agree with others to begin a new one, *in vacuis locis*, in any part of the world they can find free and unpossessed. Whereas he that has once by actual agreement and any express declaration given his consent to be of any commonwealth is perpetually and indispensably obliged to be and remain unalterably a subject to it, and can never be again in the liberty of the state of nature; unless, by any calamity, the government he was under comes to be dissolved, or else by some public acts cuts him off from being any longer a member of it.

But submitting to the laws of any country, living quietly and enjoying privileges and protection under them, makes not a man a member of that society. This is only a local protection and homage due to and from all those who, not being in the state of war, come within the territories belonging to any government, to all parts whereof the force of its law extends. But this no more makes a man a member of that society, a perpetual subject of that common-wealth, than it would make a man a subject to another in whose family he found it convenient to abide for some time; though whilst he continued in it he were obliged to comply with the laws, and submit to the government he found there. And thus we see, that foreigners by living all their lives under another government, and enjoying the privileges and protection of it, though they are bound even in conscience to submit to its administration as far forth as any denizen, yet do not thereby come to be subjects or members of that commonwealth. Nothing can make any man so, but his actually entering into it by positive engagement, and express promise and compact. This is that which I think concerning the beginning of political societies, and that consent which makes any one a member of any commonwealth.

OF THE ENDS OF POLITICAL SOCIETY AND GOVERNMENT
*(Chapter 9)*

If man in the state of nature be so free, as has been said; if he be absolute lord of his own person and possessions, equal to the greatest, and subject to nobody, why will he part with his freedom? Why will he give up this empire, and subject himself to the dominion and control of any other power? To which 'tis obvious to answer, that though in the state of nature he hath such a right, yet the enjoyment of it is very uncertain, and constantly exposed to the invasion of others. For all being kings as much as he, every man his equal, and the greater part no strict observers of equity and justice, the enjoyment of the property he has in this state is very unsafe, very unsecure. This makes him willing to quit a condition, which, however free, is full of fears and continual dangers; and 'tis not without reason that he seeks out and is willing to join in society with others, who are already united, or have a mind to unite, for the mutual preservation of their lives, liberties, and estates, which I call by the general name, property.

The great and chief end, therefore, of men's uniting into commonwealths, and putting themselves under government, is the preservation of their property; to which in the state of nature there are many things wanting.

First, There wants an established, settled, known law, received and allowed by common consent to be the standard of right and wrong, and the common measure to decide all controversies between them. For though the law of nature be plain and intelligible to all rational creatures; yet men, being biased by their interest, as well as ignorant for want of study of it, are not apt to allow of it as a law binding to them in the application of it to their particular cases.

Secondly, In the state of nature there wants a known and indifferent judge, with authority to determine all differences according to the established law. For every one in that state, being both judge and executioner of the law of nature, men being partial to themselves, passion and revenge is very apt to carry them too far, and with too much heat in their own cases, as well as negligence and unconcernedness, to make them too remiss in other men's.

Thirdly, In the state of nature there often wants power to back and support the sentence when right, and to give it due execution. They who by any injustice offended will seldom fail, where they are able, by force to make good their injustice; such resistance many times makes the punishment dangerous, and frequently destructive to those who attempt it.

Thus mankind, notwithstanding all the privileges of the state of nature, being but in an ill condition while they remain in it, are quickly driven into society ... And in this we have the original right and rise of both the legislative and executive power, as well as of the governments and societies themselves.

For in the state of nature, to omit the liberty he has of innocent delights, a man has two powers.

The first is to do whatsoever he thinks fit for the preservation of himself and others within the permission of the laws of nature, by which law, common to them all, he and all the rest of mankind are of one community, make up one society, distinct from all other creatures. And were it not for the corruption and viciousness of degenerate men there would be no need of any other, no necessity that men should separate from this great and natural community, and by positive agreements combine into smaller and divided associations.

The other power a man has in the state of nature is the power to punish the crimes committed against that law. Both these he gives up when he joins in a private, if I may so call it, or particular political society, and incorporates into any commonwealth separate from the rest of mankind.

The first power, *viz.*, of doing whatsoever he thought fit for the preservation of himself and the rest of mankind, he gives up to be regulated by laws made by the society, so far forth as the preservation of himself and the rest of that society shall require; which laws of the society in many things confine the liberty he had by the law of nature.

Secondly, The power of punishing he wholly gives up, and engages his natural force (which he might before employ in the execution of the law of nature, by his own single authority as he thought fit), to assist the executive power of the society, as the law thereof shall require. For being now in a new state, wherein he is to enjoy many conveniencies, from the labour, assistance, and society of others in the same community, as well as protection from its whole strength; he has to part also with as much of his natural liberty, in providing for himself, as the good, prosperity, and safety of the society shall require; which is not only necessary but just, since the other members of the society do the like.

But though men when they enter into society give up the equality, liberty, and executive power they had in the state of nature into the hands of the society, to be so far disposed of by the legislative as the good of the society shall require; yet it being only with an intention in every one the better to preserve himself, his liberty, and property (for no rational creature can be supposed to change his condition with an intention to be worse), the power of the society, or legislative constituted by them, can never be supposed to extend farther than the common good, but is obliged to secure every one's property by providing against those three defects above-mentioned that made the state of nature so unsafe and uneasy. And so whoever has the legislative or supreme power of any commonwealth is bound to govern by established standing laws, promulgated and known to the people, and not by extemporary decrees; by indifferent and upright judges, who are to decide controversies by those laws; and to employ the force of the community at home only in the execution of such laws, or abroad to prevent or redress foreign injuries, and secure the community from inroads and invasion. And all this to be directed to no other end but the peace, safety, and public good of the people . . .

OF THE EXTENT OF THE LEGISLATIVE POWER
*(Chapter 11)*

Though the legislative, whether placed in one or more, whether it be always in being, or only by intervals, though it be the supreme power in every commonwealth, yet,

First, It is not nor can possibly be absolutely arbitrary over the lives and fortunes of the people. For it being but the joint power of every member of the society given up to that person, or assembly, which is legislator; it can be no more than those persons had in a state of nature before they entered into society, and gave it up to the community. For nobody can transfer to another more power than he has in himself; and nobody has an absolute arbitrary power over himself, or over any other, to destroy his own life, or take away the life or property of another. A man, as has been proved, cannot subject himself to the arbitrary power of another; and having in the state of nature no arbitrary power over the life, liberty, or possession of another, but only so much as the law of nature gave him for the preservation of himself, and the rest of mankind; this is all he doth, or can give up to the commonwealth, and by it to the legislative power, so that the legislative can have no more than this. Their power, in the utmost bounds of it, is limited to the public good of the society. It is a power that hath no other end but preservation, and therefore can never have a right to destroy, enslave, or designedly to impoverish the subjects. The obligations of the law of nature cease not in society, but only in many cases are drawn closer, and have by human laws known penalties annexed to them to enforce their observation. Thus the law of nature stands as an eternal rule to all men, legislators as well as others. The rules that they make for other men's actions must, as well as their own and other men's acions, be conformable to the law of nature, *i.e.*, to the will of God, of which that is a declaration, and the fundamental law of nature being the preservation of mankind, no human sanction can be good or valid against it . . .

OF THE SUBORDINATION OF THE POWERS OF THE COMMONWEALTH
*(Chapter 13)*

Though in a constituted commonwealth, standing upon its own basis, and acting according to its own nature, that is, acting for the preservation of the community, there can be but one supreme power, which is the legislative, to which all the rest are and must be subordinate, yet the legislative being only a fiduciary power to act for certain ends, there remains still in the people a supreme power to remove or alter the legislative, when they find the legislative act contrary to the trust reposed in them; for all power given with trust for the attaining an end being limited by that end, whenever that end is manifestly neglected or opposed, the trust must necessarily be forfeited, and the power devolve into the hands of those that gave it, who may place it anew where they shall think best for their safety and security. And thus the community perpetually retains a supreme power of saving themselves from the attempts and designs of any body, even of their legislators, whenever they shall be so foolish or so wicked as to lay and carry on designs against the liberties and properties of the subject; for no man or society of men, having a power to deliver up their preservation, or consequently the means of it, to the absolute will and arbitrary dominion of another, whenever any one shall go about to bring them into such a slavish condition, they will always have a right to preserve what they have not a power to part with; and to rid themselves of those who invade this fundamental, sacred, and unalterable law of self-preservation for which they entered into society. And thus the community may be said in this respect to be always the supreme power, but not as considered under any form of government, because this power of the people can never take place till the government be dissolved ...

OF CONQUEST
*(Chapter 16)*

Though governments can originally have no other rise than that before-mentioned, nor polities be founded on anything but the consent of the people, yet such has been the disorders ambition has filled the world with, that, in the noise of war, which makes so great a part of the history of mankind, this consent is little taken notice of; and therefore many have mistaken the force of arms for the consent of the people, and reckon conquest as one of the originals of government. But conquest is as far from setting up any government as demolishing a house is from building a new one in the place. Indeed, it often makes way for a new frame of a commonwealth, by destroying the former; but, without consent of the people, can never erect a new one ...

The conqueror, 'tis true, usually, by the force he has over them, compels them, with a sword at their breasts, to stoop to his conditions, and submit to such a government as he pleases to afford them; but the enquiry is: What right he has to do so? If it be said they submit by their own consent, then this allows their own consent to be necessary to give the conqueror a title to rule over them. It remains only to be considered whether promises extorted by force, without right, can be thought consent, and how far they bind. To which I shall say, they bind not at all ...

OF TYRANNY
*(Chapter 18)*

As usurpation is the exercise of power which another hath a right to, so tyranny is the exercise of power beyond right, which nobody can have a right to. And this is making use of the power any one has in his hands, not for the good of those who are under it, but for his own private separate advantage. When the governor, however entitled, makes not the law but his will the rule, and his commands and actions are not directed to the preservation of the properties of his people, but the satisfaction of his own ambition, revenge, covetousness, or any other irregular passion ...

May the commands then of a prince by opposed? May he be resisted as often as any one shall find himself aggrieved, and but imagine he has not right done him? This will unhinge and overturn all polities, and, instead of government and order, leave nothing but anarchy and confusion.

To this I answer, that force is to be opposed to nothing but to unjust and unlawful force; whoever makes any opposition in any other case draws on himself a just condemnation both from God and man and so no such danger or confusion will follow, as is often suggested ...

OF THE DISSOLUTION OF GOVERNMENT
*(Chapter 19)*

He that will with any clearness speak of the dissolution of government ought, in the first place, to distinguish between the dissolution of the society and the dissolution of the government. That which makes the community, and brings men out of the loose state of nature into one politic society, is the agreement which every one has with the rest to incorporate and act as one body, and so be one distinct commonwealth. The usual, and almost only way whereby this union is dissolved, is the inroad of foreign force making a conquest upon them. For in that case (not being able to maintain and support themselves as one entire and independent body) the union belonging to that body which consisted therein must necessarily cease, and so every one return to the state he was in before, with a liberty to shift for himself and provide for his own safety as he thinks fit in some other society. Whenever the society is dissolved, it is certain the government of that society cannot remain ...

There is ... another way whereby governments are dissolved, and that is when the legislative or the prince, either of them, act contrary to their trust ...

The legislative acts against the trust reposed in them when they endeavour to invade the property of the subject, and to make themselves or any part of the community masters or arbitrary disposers of the lives, liberties, or fortunes of the people ...

The end of government is the good of mankind; and which is best for mankind, that the people should be always exposed to the boundless will of tyranny, or that the rulers should be sometimes liable to be opposed when they grow exorbitant in the use of their power, and employ it for the destruction and not the preservation of the properties of their people? ...

Whosoever uses force without right, as every one does in society who does it without law, puts himself into a state of war with those against whom he so uses it; and in that state all former ties are cancelled, all other rights cease, and every one has a right to defend himself and to resist the aggressor ...

Here, 'tis like, the common question will be made: Who shall be judge whether the prince or legislative act contrary to their trust? This, perhaps, ill-affected and factious men may spread amongst the people, when the prince only makes use of his due prerogative. To this I reply: The people shall be judge; for who shall be judge whether his trustee or deputy acts well, and according to the trust reposed in him, but he who deputes him, and must, by having deputed him, have still a power to discard him when he fails in his trust? If this be reasonable in particular cases of private men, why should it be otherwise in that of the greatest moment, where the welfare of millions is concerned, and also where the evil, if not prevented, is greater, and the redress very difficult, dear, and dangerous?

But farther, this question, who shall be judge, cannot mean that there is no judge at all; for where there is no judicature on earth to decide controversies amongst men, God in heaven is judge. He alone, 'tis true, is judge of the right; but every man is judge for himself, as in all other cases, so in this, whether another hath put himself into a state of war with him, and whether he should appeal to the Supreme Judge, as Jephtha did.

If a controversy arise betwixt a prince and some of the people, in a matter where the law is silent or doubtful, and the thing be of great consequence, I should think the proper umpire in such a case should be the body of the people; for in cases where the prince hath a trust reposed in him, and is dispensed from the common ordinary rules of the law; there, if any men find themselves aggrieved, and think the prince acts contrary to or beyond that trust, who so proper to judge as the body of the people (who at first lodged that trust in him) how far they meant it should extend? But if the prince, or whoever they be in the administration, decline that way of determination, the appeal then lies nowhere but to heaven; force between either persons who have no known superior on earth, or which permits no appeal to a judge on earth, being properly a state of war, wherein the appeal lies only to heaven; and in that state the injured party must judge for himself when he will think fit to make use of that appeal and put himself upon it.

To conclude, the power that every individual gave the society, when he entered into it, can never revert to the individuals again as long as the society lasts, but will always remain in the community; because without this there can be no community, no commonwealth, which is contrary to the original agreeement; so also when the society hath placed the legislative in any assembly of men, to continue in them and their successors, with direction and authority for providing such successors, the legislative can never revert to the people whilst that government lasts; because having provided a legislative with power to continue for ever, they have given up their political power to the legislative and cannot resume it. But if they have set limits to the duration of their legislative, and made this supreme power in any person or assembly only temporary; or else, when by the miscarriages of those in authority it is forfeited; upon the forfeiture, or at the determination of the time set, it reverts to the society, and the people have a right to act as supreme, and continue the legislative in themselves; or erect a new form, or under the old form place it in new hands, as they think good.

NOTES

1   i.e. *Observations upon Aristotle's Politics.*

# 5

# The Social Contract and the General Will

## JEAN-JACQUES ROUSSEAU

## The Social Contract

### I

I mean to inquire if, in the civil order, there can be any sure and legitimate rule of administration, men being taken as they are and laws as they might be. In this inquiry I shall endeavour always to unite what right sanctions with what is prescribed by interest in order that justice and utility may in no case be divided ...

### SUBJECT OF THE FIRST BOOK
### (Chapter 1)

Man was born free; and everywhere he is in chains. One thinks himself the master of others, and still remains a greater slave than they. How did this change come about? I do not know. What can make it legitimate? That question I think I can answer ...

### SLAVERY
### (Chapter 4)

Since no man has a natural authority over his fellow, and force creates no right, we must conclude that conventions form the basis of all legitimate authority among men.

If an individual, says Grotius, can alienate his liberty and make

*Source:* Extracts, reprinted by permission, from J.-J. Rousseau, *The Social Contract*, translated by G. D. H. Cole, Everyman edition (London: J. M. Dent & Sons Ltd, 1913).

himself the slave of a master, why could not a whole people do the same and make itself subject to a king? There are in this passage plenty of ambiguous words which would need explaining; but let us confine ourselves to the word *alienate*. To alienate is to give or to sell. Now, a man who becomes the slave of another does not give himself; he sells himself, at the least for his subsistence: but for what does a people sell itself? A king is so far from furnishing his subjects with their subsistence that he gets his own only from them; and, according to Rabelais, kings do not live on nothing. Do subjects then give their persons on condition that the king takes their goods also? I fail to see what they have left to preserve.

It will be said that the despot assures his subjects civil tranquillity. Granted; but what do they gain, if the wars his ambition brings down upon them, his insatiable avidity, and the vexatious conduct of his ministers press harder on them than their own dissensions would have done? What do they gain, if the very tranquillity they enjoy is one of their miseries? Tranquillity is found also in dungeons; but is that enough to make them desirable places to live in? The Greeks imprisoned in the cave of the Cyclops lived there very tranquilly, while they were awaiting their turn to be devoured.

To say that a man gives himself gratuitously, is to say what is absurd and inconceivable; such an act is null and illegitimate, from the mere fact that he who does it is out of his mind. To say the same of a whole people is to suppose a people of madmen; and madness creates no right.

Even if each man could alienate himself, he could not alienate his children: they are born men and free; their liberty belongs to them, and no one but they has the right to dispose of it. Before they come to years of discretion, the father can, in their name, lay down conditions for their preservation and well-being, but he cannot give them irrevocably and without conditions: such a gift is contrary to the ends of nature, and exceeds the rights of paternity. It would therefore be necessary, in order to legitimize an arbitrary government, that in every generation the people should be in a position to accept to reject it; but, were this so, the government would be no longer arbitrary.

To renounce liberty is to renounce being a man, to surrender the rights of humanity and even its duties. For him who renounces everything no indemnity is possible. Such a renunciation is incompatible with man's nature; to remove all liberty from his will is to remove all morality from his acts. Finally, it is an empty and contradictory convention that sets up, on the one side, absolute authority, and, on the other, unlimited obedience. Is it not clear that we can be under no obligation to a person from whom we have the right to exact everything? Does not this condition alone, in the absence of equivalence or exchange, in itself involve the nullity of the act? For what right can my slave have against me, when all that he has belongs to me, and, his right being mine, this right of mine against myself is a phrase devoid of meaning? ...

### THAT WE MUST ALWAYS GO BACK TO A FIRST CONVENTION
*(Chapter 5)*

Even if I granted all that I have been refuting, the friends of despotism would be no better off. There will always be a great difference between subduing a multitude and ruling a society. Even if scattered individuals were successively enslaved by one man, however numerous they might be, I still see no more than a master and his slaves, and certainly not a people and its ruler; I see what may be termed an aggregation, but not an association; there is as yet neither public good nor body politic. The man in question, even if he has enslaved half the world, is still only an individual; his interest, apart from that of others, is still a purely private interest. If this same man comes to die, his empire, after him, remains scattered and without unity, as an oak falls and dissolves into a heap of ashes when the fire has consumed it.

A people, says Grotius, can give itself to a king. Then, according to Grotius, a people is a people before it gives itself. The gift is itself a civil act, and implies public deliberation. It would be better, before examining the act by which a people gives itself to a king, to examine that by which it has become a people: for this act, being necessarily prior to the other, is the true foundation of society.

Indeed, if there were no prior convention, where, unless the election were unanimous, would be the obligation on the minority to submit to the choice of the majority? How have a hundred men who wish for a master the right to vote on behalf of ten who do not? The law of majority voting is itself something established by convention, and presupposes unanimity, on one occasion at least.

### THE SOCIAL COMPACT
*(Chapter 6)*

I suppose men to have reached the point at which the obstacles in the way of their preservation in the state of nature show their power of resistance to be greater than the resources at the disposal of each individual for his maintenance in that state. That primitive condition can then subsist no longer; and the human race would perish unless it changed its manner of existence.

But, as men cannot engender new forces, but only unite and direct existing ones, they have no other means of preserving themselves than the formation, by aggregation, of a sum of forces great enough to overcome the resistance. These they have to bring into play by means of a single motive power, and cause to act in concert.

This sum of forces can arise only where several persons come together: but, as the force and liberty of each man are the chief instruments of his self-preservation, how can he pledge them without harming his own interests, and neglecting the care he owes to himself? This difficulty, in its bearing on my present subject, may be stated in the following terms:

'The problem is to find a form of association which will defend and protect with the whole common force the person and goods of each associate, and in which each, while uniting himself with all, may still obey himself alone, and remain as free as before.' This is the fundamental problem of which the social contract provides the solution.

The clauses of this contract are so determined by the nature of the act that the slightest modification would make them vain and ineffective; so that, although they have perhaps never been formally set forth, they are everywhere the same and everywhere tacitly admitted and recognized, until, on the violation of the social compact, each regains his original rights and resumes his natural liberty, while losing the conventional liberty in favour of which he renounced it.

These clauses, properly understood, may be reduced to one — the total alienation of each associate, together with all his rights, to the whole community; for, in the first place, as each gives himself absolutely, the conditions are the same for all; and, this being so, no one has any interest in making them burdensome to others.

Moreover, the alienation being without reserve, the union is as perfect as it can be, and no associate has anything more to demand: for, if the individuals retained certain rights, as there would be no common superior to decide between them and the public, each, being on one point his own judge, would ask to be so on all; the state of nature would thus continue, and the association would necessarily become inoperative or tyrannical.

Finally, each man, in giving himself to all, gives himself to nobody; and as there is no associate over which he does not acquire the same right as he yields others over himself, he gains an equivalent for everything he loses, and an increase of force for the preservation of what he has.

If then we discard from the social compact what is not of its essence, we shall find that it reduces itself to the following terms:

'*Each of us puts his person and all his power in common under the supreme direction of the general will, and, in our corporate capacity, we receive each member as an indivisible part of the whole.*'

At once, in place of the individual personality of each contracting party, this act of association creates a moral and collective body, composed of as many members as the assembly contains voters, and receiving from this act its unity, its common identity, its life, and its will. This public person, so formed by the union of all other persons, formerly took the name of *city*, and now takes that of *Republic* or *body politic*; it is called by its members *State* when passive, *Sovereign* when active, and *Power* when compared with others like itself. Those who are associated in it take collectively the name of *people*, and severally are called *citizens*, as sharing in the sovereign authority and *subjects*, as being under the laws of the State. But these terms are often confused and taken one for another: it is enough to know how to distinguish them when they are being used with precision.

THE SOVEREIGN
*(Chapter 7)*

This formula shows us that the act of association comprises a mutual undertaking between the public and the individuals, and that each individual, in making a contract, as we may say, with himself, is bound in a double relation; as a member of the Sovereign he is bound to the individuals, and as a member of the State to the Sovereign ...

Attention must further be called to the fact that public deliberation, while competent to bind all the subjects to the Sovereign, because of the two different capacities in which each of them may be regarded, cannot, for the opposite reason, bind the Sovereign to itself; and that it is consequently against the nature of the body politic for the Sovereign to impose on itself a law which it cannot infringe. Being able to regard itself in only one capacity, it is in the position of an individual who makes a contract with himself; and this makes it clear that there neither is nor can be any kind of fundamental law binding on the body of the people — not even the social contract itself . . .

As soon as this multitude is so united in one body, it is impossible to offend against one of the members without attacking the body, and still more to offend against the body without the members resenting it. Duty and interest therefore equally oblige the two contracting parties to give each other help; and the same men should seek to combine, in their double capacity, all the advantages dependent upon that capacity.

Again, the Sovereign, being formed wholly of the individuals who compose it, neither has nor can have any interest contrary to theirs; and consequently the sovereign power need give no guarantee to its subjects, because it is impossible for the body to wish to hurt all its members. We shall also see later on that it cannot hurt any in particular. The Sovereign, merely by virtue of what it is, is always what it should be.

This, however, is not the case with the relation of the subjects to the Sovereign, which, despite the common interest, would have no security that they would fulfil their undertakings, unless it found means to assure itself of their fidelity.

In fact, each individual, as a man, may have a particular will contrary or dissimilar to the general will which he has as a citizen. His particular interest may speak to him quite differently from the common interest: his absolute and naturally independent existence may make him look upon what he owes to the common cause as a gratuitous contribution, the loss of which will do less harm to others than the payment of it is burdensome to himself; and, regarding the moral person which constitutes the State as a *persona ficta*, because not a man, he may wish to enjoy the rights of citizenship without being ready to fulfil the duties of a subject. The continuance of such an injustice could not but prove the undoing of the body politic.

In order then that the social compact may not be an empty formula, it tacitly includes the undertaking, which alone can give force to the rest, that whoever refuses to obey the general will shall be compelled to do so by the whole body. This means nothing less than that he will be forced to be free; for this is the condition which, by giving each citizen to his country, secures him against all personal dependence. In this lies the key to the working of the political machine; this alone legitimizes civil undertakings, which, without it, would be absurd, tyrannical and liable to the most frightful abuses.

THE CIVIL STATE
*(Chapter 8)*

The passage from the state of nature to the civil state produces a very remarkable change in man, by substituting justice for instinct in his conduct, and giving his actions the morality they had formerly lacked. Then only, when the voice of duty takes the place of physical impulses and right of appetite, does man, who so far had considered only himself, find that he is forced to act on different principles, and to consult his reason before listening to his inclinations. Although, in this state, he deprives himself of some advantages which he got from nature, he gains in return others so great, his faculties are so stimulated and developed, his ideas so extended, his feelings so ennobled, and his whole soul so uplifted, that, did not the abuses of this new condition often degrade him below that which he left, he would be bound to bless continually the happy moment which took him from it for ever, and, instead of a stupid and unimaginative animal, made him an intelligent being and a man.

Let us draw up the whole account in terms easily commensurable. What man loses by the social contract is his natural liberty and an unlimited right to everything he tries to get and succeeds in getting; what he gains is civil liberty and the proprietorship of all he possesses. If we are to avoid mistake in weighing one against the other, we must clearly distinguish natural liberty, which is bounded only by the strength of the individual, from civil liberty, which is limited by the general will; and possession, which is merely the effect of force or the right of the first occupier, from property, which can be founded only on a positive title.

We might, over and above all this, add, to what man acquires in the civil state, moral liberty, which alone makes him truly master of himself; for the mere impulse of appetite is slavery, while obedience to a law which we prescribe to ourselves is liberty ...

REAL PROPERTY
*(Chapter 9)*

Each member of the community gives himself to it, at the moment of its foundation, just as he is, with all the resources at his command, including the goods he possesses. This act does not make possession, in changing hands, change its nature, and become property in the hands of the Sovereign; but, as the forces of the city are incomparably greater than those of an individual, public possession is also, in fact, stronger and more irrevocable, without being any more legitimate, at any rate from the point of view of foreigners. For the State, in relation to its members, is master of all their goods by the social contract, which, within the State, is the basis of all rights; but, in relation to other powers, it is so only by the right of the first occupier, which it holds from its members . . .

The peculiar fact about this alienation is that, in taking over the goods of individuals, the community, so far from despoiling them, only assures them legitimate possession, and changes usurpation into a true right and enjoyment into proprietorship. Thus the possessors, being regarded as depositaries of the public good, and having their rights respected by all the members of the State and maintained against foreign aggression by all its forces, have, by a cession which benefits both the public and still more themselves, acquired, so to speak, all that they gave up. This paradox may easily be explained by the distinction between the rights which the Sovereign and the proprietor have over the same estate, as we shall see later on.

It may also happen that men begin to unite one with another before they possess anything, and that, subsequently occupying a tract of country which is enough for all, they enjoy it in common, or share it out among themselves, either equally or according to a scale fixed by the Sovereign. However the acquisition be made, the right which each individual has to his own estate is always subordinate to the right which the community has over all: without this, there would be neither stability in the social tie, nor real force in the exercise of Sovereignty.

I shall end this chapter and this book by remarking on a fact on which the whole social system should rest: i.e. that, instead of destroying natural inequality, the fundamental compact substitutes, for such physical inequality as nature may have set up between men, an equality that is moral and legitimate, and that men, who may be unequal in strength or intelligence, become every one equal by convention and legal right . . .

## II

### THE LIMITS OF THE SOVEREIGN POWER
### *(Chapter 4)*

If the State is a moral person whose life is in the union of its members, and if the most important of its cares is the care for its own preservation, it must have a universal and compelling force, in order to move and dispose each part as may be most advantageous to the whole. As nature gives each man absolute power over all his members, the social compact gives the body politic absolute power over all its members also; and it is this power which, under the direction of the general will, bears, as I have said, the name of Sovereignty.

But, besides the public person, we have to consider the private persons composing it, whose life and liberty are naturally independent of it. We are bound then to distinguish clearly between the respective rights of the citizens and the Sovereign, and between the duties the former have to fulfil as subjects, and the natural rights they should enjoy as men.

Each man alienates, I admit, by the social compact, only such part of his powers, goods, and liberty as it is important for the community to control; but it must also be granted that the Sovereign is sole judge of what is important.

Every service a citizen can render the State he ought to render as soon as the Sovereign demands it; but the Sovereign, for its part, cannot impose upon its subjects any fetters that are useless to the community, nor can it even wish to do so; for no more by the law of reason than by the law of nature can anything occur without a cause.

The undertakings which bind us to the social body are obligatory only because they are mutual; and their nature is such that in fulfilling them we cannot work for others without working for ourselves. Why is it that the general will is always just and that all continually will the happiness of each one, unless it is because there is not a man who does not think of 'each' as meaning him, and consider himself in voting for all? This proves that equality of rights and the idea of justice which such equality creates originate in the preference each man gives to himself, and accordingly in the very nature of man. It proves that the general will, to be really such, must be general in its object as well as its essence; that it must both come from all and apply to all; and that it loses its natural rectitude when it is directed to some particular and determinate object, because in such a case we are judging of something foreign to us, and have no true principle of equity to guide us.

Indeed, as soon as a question of particular fact or right arises on a point not previously regulated by a general convention, the matter becomes contentious. It is a case in which the individuals concerned are one party, and the public the other, but in which I can see neither the law that ought to be followed nor the judge

who ought to give the decision. In such a case, it would be absurd
to propose to refer the question to an express decision of the
general will, which can be only the conclusion reached by one of
the parties and in consequence will be, for the other party, merely
an external and particular will, inclined on this occasion to injustice
and subject to error. Thus, just as a particular will cannot stand
for the general will, the general will, in turn, changes its nature,
when its object is particular, and, as general, cannot pronounce on
a man or a fact. When, for instance, the people of Athens nominated
or displaced its rulers, decreed honours to one, and imposed
penalties on another, and, by a multitude of particular decrees,
exercised all the functions government indiscriminately, it had in
such cases no longer a general will in the strict sense; it was acting
no longer as Sovereign, but as magistrate . . .

It should be seen from the foregoing that what makes the will
general is less the number of voters than the common interest
uniting them; for, under this system, each necessarily submits to
the conditions he imposes on others: and this admirable agreement
between interest and justice gives to the common deliberations an
equitable character which at once vanishes when any particular
question is discussed, in the absence of a common interest to unite
and identify the ruling of the judge with that of the party.

From whatever side we approach our principle, we reach the
same conclusion, that the social compact sets up among the citizens
an equality of such a kind, that they all bind themselves to observe
the same conditions and should therefore all enjoy the same rights.
Thus, from the very nature of the compact, every act of Sovereignty,
i.e. every authentic act of the general will, binds or favours all the
citizens equally; so that the Sovereign recognizes only the body of
the nation, and draws no distinctions between those of whom it is
made up. What, then, strictly speaking, is an act of Sovereignty? It
is not a convention between a superior and an inferior, but a
convention between the body and each of its members. It is legitimate, because based on the social contract, and equitable, because
common to all; useful, because it can have no other object than
the general good, and stable, because guaranteed by the public
force and the supreme power. So long as the subjects have to
submit only to conventions of this sort, they obey no one but their
own will; and to ask how far the respective rights of the Sovereign
and the citizens extend, is to ask up to what point the latter can
enter into undertakings with themselves, each with all, and all
with each.

We can see from this that the sovereign power, absolute, sacred, and inviolable as it is, does not and cannot exceed the limits of general conventions, and that every man may dispose at will of such goods and liberty as these conventions leave him; so that the Sovereign never has a right to lay more charges on one subject than on another, because, in that case, the question becomes particular, and ceases to be within its competency.

When these distinctions have once been admitted, it is seen to be so untrue that there is, in the social contract, any real renunciation on the part of the individuals, that the position in which they find themselves as a result of the contract is really preferable to that in which they were before. Instead of a renunciation, they have made an advantageous exchange: instead of an uncertain and precarious way of living they have got one that is better and more secure; instead of natural independence they have got liberty, instead of the power to harm others security for themselves, and instead of their strength, which others might overcome, a right which social union makes invincible. Their very life, which they have devoted to the State, is by it constantly protected; and when they risk it in the State's defence, what more are they doing than giving back what they have received from it? What are they doing that they would not do more often and with greater danger in the state of nature, in which they would inevitably have to fight battles at the peril of their lives in defence of that which is the means of their preservation? All have indeed to fight when their country needs them; but then no one has ever to fight for himself. Do we not gain something by running, on behalf of what gives us our security, only some of the risks we should have to run for ourselves, as soon as we lost it?

## LAW
### (Chapter 6)

By the social compact we have given the body politic existence and life; we have now by legislation to give it movement and will. For the original act by which the body is formed and united still in no respect determines what it ought to do for its preservation. . . .

But what, after all, is a law? As long as we remain satisfied with attaching purely metaphysical ideas to the word, we shall go on arguing without arriving at an understanding; and when we have defined a law of nature, we shall be no nearer the definition of a law of the State.

I have already said that there can be no general will directed to a particular object . . . But when the whole people decrees for the whole people, it is considering only itself ... In that case the matter about which the decree is made is, like the decreeing will, general. This act is what I call a law.

When I say that the object of laws is always general, I mean that law considers subjects *en masse* and actions in the abstract, and never a particular person or action. Thus the law may indeed decree that there shall be privileges, but cannot confer them on anybody by name. It may set up several classes of citizens, and even lay down the qualifications for membership of these classes, but it cannot nominate such and such persons as belonging to them; it may establish a monarchical government and hereditary succession, but it cannot choose a king, or nominate a royal family. In a word, no function which has a particular object belongs to the legislative power.

On this view, we at once see that it can no longer be asked whose business it is to make laws, since they are acts of the general will; nor whether the prince is above the law, since he is a member of the State; nor whether the law can be unjust, since no one is unjust to himself; nor how we can be both free and subject to the laws, since they are but registers of our wills.

We see further that, as the law unites universality of will with universality of object, what a man, whoever he be, commands of his own motion cannot be a law; and even what the Sovereign commands with regard to a particular matter is no nearer being a law, but is a decree, an act, not of sovereignty, but of magistracy.

I therefore give the name 'Republic' to every State that is governed by laws, no matter what the form of its administration may be: for only in such a case does the public interest govern, and the *res publica* rank as a *reality*. Every legitimate government is republican; what government is I will explain later on.

Laws are, properly speaking, only the conditions of civil association. The people, being subject to the laws, ought to be their author: the conditions of the society ought to be regulated solely by those who come together to form it. But how are they to regulate them? Is it to be by common agreement, by a sudden inspiration? Has the body politic an organ to declare its will? Who can give it the foresight to formulate and announce its acts in advance? Or how is it to announce them in the hour of need? How can a blind multitude, which often does not know what it wills, because it rarely knows what is good for it, carry out for itself so great and difficult an enterprise as a system of legislation? Of itself the people wills always the good, but of itself it by no means always sees it. The general will is always a just will, but the judgment which guides it is not always enlightened. It must be got to see objects as they are, and sometimes as they ought to appear to it; it must be shown the good road it is in search of, secured from the seductive influences of individual wills, taught to see the bearing of time and place, and made to weigh the attractions of present and sensible advantages against the danger of distant and hidden evils. The individuals see the good they reject; the public wills the good it does not see. All stand equally in need of guidance. The former must be compelled to bring their wills into conformity with their reason; the latter must be taught to know what it wills. If that is done, public enlightenment leads to the union of understanding and will in the social body: the parts are made to work exactly together, and the whole is raised to its highest power. This makes a legislator necessary.

### THE LEGISLATOR
### *(Chapter 7)*

The legislator occupies in every respect an extraordinary position in the State. If he should do so by reason of his genius, he does so no less by reason of his office, which is neither magistracy, nor Sovereignty. This office, which sets up the Republic, nowhere enters into its constitution; it is an individual and superior function, which has nothing in common with human empire; for if he who holds command over men ought not to have command over the laws, he who has command over the laws ought not any more to have it over men; or else his laws would be the ministers of his passions and would often merely serve to perpetuate his injustices: his private aims would inevitably mar the sanctity of his work. . . .

He, therefore, who draws up the laws has, or should have, no right of legislation, and the people cannot, even if it wishes, deprive itself of this incommunicable right, because according to the fundamental compact, only the general will can bind the individuals, and there can be no assurance that a particular will is in conformity with the general will, until it has been put to the free vote of the people. This I have said already; but it is worth while to repeat it . . .

### THE PEOPLE
### *(Chapter 8)*

What people, then, is a fit subject for legislation? One which, already bound by some unity of origin, interest, or convention, has never yet felt the real yoke of law; one that has neither customs nor superstitions deeply ingrained, one which stands in no fear of being overwhelmed by sudden invasion; one which, without entering into its neighbours' quarrels, can resist each of them single-handed, or get the help of one to repel another; one in which every member may be known by every other, and there is no need to lay on any man burdens too heavy for a man to bear; one which can do without other peoples, and without which all others can do; one which is neither rich nor poor, but self-sufficient; and lastly, one which unites the consistency of an ancient people with the docility of a new one. Legislation is made difficult less by what it is necessary to build up than by what has to be destroyed; and what makes success so rare is the impossibility of finding natural simplicity together with social requirements. All these conditions are indeed rarely found united, and therefore few States have good constitutions.

There is still in Europe one country capable of being given laws — Corsica. The valour and persistency with which that brave people has regained and defended its liberty well deserves that some wise man should teach it how to preserve what it has won. I have a feeling that some day that little island will astonish Europe . . .

### III

#### THAT THE INSTITUTION OF GOVERNMENT IS NOT A CONTRACT
#### *(Chapter 16)*

The legislative power once well established, the next thing is to establish similarly the executive power; for this latter, which operates only by particular acts, not being of the essence of the former, is naturally separate from it. Were it possible for the Sovereign, as such, to possess the executive power, right and fact would be so confounded that no one could tell what was law and what was not; and the body politic, thus disfigured, would soon fall a prey to the violence it was instituted to prevent.

As the citizens, by the social contract, are all equal, all can prescribe what all should do, but no one has a right to demand that another shall do what he does not do himself. It is strictly this right, which is indispensable for giving the body politic life and movement, that the Sovereign, in instituting the government, confers upon the prince.

It has been held that this act of establishment was a contract between the people and the rulers it sets over itself — a contract in which conditions were laid down between the two parties binding the one to command and the other to obey. It will be admitted, I am sure, that this is an odd kind of contract to enter into. But let us see if this view can be upheld.

First, the supreme authority can no more be modified than it can be alienated; to limit it is to destroy it. It is absurd and contradictory for the Sovereign to set a superior over itself; to bind itself to obey a master would be to return to absolute liberty.

Moreover, it is clear that this contract between the people and such and such persons would be a particular act; and from this it follows that it can be neither a law nor an act of Sovereignty, and that consequently it would be illegitimate ...

### THE INSTITUTION OF GOVERNMENT
#### (Chapter 17)

Under what general idea then should the act by which government is instituted be conceived as falling? I will begin by stating that the act is complex, as being composed of two others — the establishment of the law and its execution.

By the former, the Sovereign decrees that there shall be a governing body established in this or that form; this act is clearly a law. .

By the latter, the people nominates the rulers who are to be entrusted with the government that has been established. This nomination, being a particular act, is clearly not a second law, but merely a consequence of the first and a function of government ...

## IV

### VOTING
#### (Chapter 2)

There is but one law which, from its nature, needs unanimous consent. This is the social compact; for civil association is the most voluntary of all acts. Every man being born free and his own master, no one, under any pretext whatsoever, can make any man subject without his consent. To decide that the son of a slave is born a slave is to decide that he is not born a man.

If then there are opponents when the social compact is made, their opposition does not invalidate the contract, but merely prevents them from being included in it. They are foreigners among citizens. When the State is instituted, residence constitutes consent; to dwell within its territory [if one is free to leave it] is to submit to the Sovereign.

Apart from this primitive contract, the vote of the majority always binds all the rest. This follows from the contract itself. But it is asked how a man can be both free and forced to conform to wills that are not his own. How are the opponents at once free and subject to laws they have not agreed to?

I retort that the question is wrongly put. The citizen gives his consent to all the laws, including those which are passed in spite of his opposition, and even those which punish him when he dares to break any of them. The constant will of all the members of the State is the general will; by virtue of it they are citizens and free. When in the popular assembly a law is proposed, what the people is asked is not exactly whether it approves or rejects the proposal, but whether it is in conformity with the general will, which is their will. Each man, in giving his vote, states his opinion on that point; and the general will is found by counting votes. When therefore the opinion that is contrary to my own prevails, this proves neither more nor less than that I was mistaken, and that what I thought to be the general will was not so. If my particular opinion had carried the day I should have achieved the opposite of what was my will; and it is in that case that I should not have been free.

This presupposes, indeed, that all the qualities of the general will still reside in the majority: when they cease to do so, whatever side a man may take, liberty is no longer possible . . .

# 6

# Social Contract as an Idea of Reason

IMMANUEL KANT

## I

## The Metaphysics of Morals: Political Right

*Public right* is the sum total of those laws which require to be made universally public in order to produce a state of right. It is therefore a system of laws for a people, i.e. an aggregate of human beings, or for an aggregate of peoples. Since these individuals or peoples must influence one another, they need to live in a state of right under a unifying will: that is, they require a *constitution* in order to enjoy their rights.

A condition in which the individual members of a people are related to each other in this way is said to be a *civil* one (*status civilis*), and when considered as a whole in relation to its own members, it is called a *state* (*civitas*) ...

Experience teaches us the maxim that human beings act in a violent and malevolent manner, and that they tend to fight among themselves until an external coercive legislation supervenes. But it is not experience or any kind of factual knowledge which makes public legal coercion necessary. On the contrary, even if we imagine men to be as benevolent and law-abiding as we please, the *a priori* rational idea of a non-lawful state will still tell us that before a public and legal state is established, individual men, peoples and

*Source:* Extracts, reprinted by permission of Cambridge University Press, from H. Reiss (ed.), *Kant's Political Writings* (Cambridge University Press, 1977). Sections I and III are taken from *Foundations of the Metaphysics of Morals* (1785), 'The Theory of Public Right'; Section II is taken from *Theory and Practice* (1793). This arrangement was adopted as affording the most logical structure for the material.

states can never be secure against acts of violence from one another, since each will have his own right to do *what seems right and good to him*, independently of the opinion of others. Thus the first decision the individual is obliged to make, if he does not wish to renounce all concepts of right, will be to adopt the principle that one must abandon the state of nature in which everyone follows his own desires, and unite with everyone else (with whom he cannot avoid having intercourse) in order to submit to external, public and lawful coercion. He must accordingly enter into a state wherein that which is to be recognised as belonging to each person is allotted to him *by law* and guaranteed to him by an adequate power (which is not his own, but external to him). In other words, he should at all costs enter into a state of civil society.

The state of nature need not necessarily be a *state of injustice* (*iniustus*) merely because those who live in it treat one another solely in terms of the amount of power they possess. But it is a *state devoid of justice* (*status iustitia vacuus*), for if a *dispute* over rights (*ius controversum*) occurs in it, there is no competent judge to pronounce legally valid decisions. Anyone may thus use force to impel the others to abandon this state for a state of right ...

Every state contains three powers, i.e. the universally united will is made up of three separate persons (*trias politica*). These are the *ruling power* (or sovereignty) in the person of the legislator, the *executive power* in the person of the individual who governs in accordance with the law, and the *judicial power* (which allots to everyone what is his by law) in the person of the judge (*potestas legislatoria, rectoria et iudiciaria*) ...

The legislative power can belong only to the united will of the people. For since all right is supposed to emanate from this power, the laws it gives must be absolutely *incapable* of doing anyone an injustice. Now if someone makes dispositions for *another* person, it is always possible that he may thereby do him an injustice, although this is never possible in the case of decisions he makes for himself (for *volenti non fit iniuria*). Thus only the unanimous and combined will of everyone whereby each decides the same for all and all decide the same for each — in other words, the general united will of the people — can legislate.

The members of such a society (*societas civilis*) or state who unite for the purpose of legislating are known as *citizens* (*cives*) ... Fitness to vote is the necessary qualification which every citizen must possess. To be fit to vote, a person must have an independent position among the people. He must therefore be not just a part of the commonwealth, but a member of it, i.e. he must by his own free will actively participate in a community of other people. But this latter quality makes it necessary to distinguish between the *active* and the *passive* citizen, although the latter concept seems to contradict the definition of the concept of a citizen altogether. The following examples may serve to overcome this difficulty. Apprentices to merchants or tradesmen, servants who are not employed by the state, minors, women in general and all those who are obliged to depend for their living (i.e. for food and protection) on the offices of others (excluding the state) — all of these people have no civil personality, and their existence is, so to speak, purely inherent. The woodcutter whom I employ on my premises; the blacksmith in India who goes from house to house with his hammer, anvil and bellows to do work with iron, as opposed to the European carpenter or smith who can put the products of his work up for public sale; the domestic tutor as opposed to the academic, the tithe-holder as opposed to the farmer; and so on — they are all mere auxiliaries to the commonwealth, for they have to receive orders or protection from other individuals, so that they do not possess civil independence.

This dependence upon the will of others and consequent inequality does not, however, in any way conflict with the freedom and equality of all men as *human beings* who together constitute a people. On the contrary, it is only by accepting these conditions that such a people can become a state and enter into a civil constitution. But all are not equally qualified within this constitution to possess the right to vote, i.e. to be citizens and not just subjects among other subjects. For from the fact that as passive members of the state, they can demand to be treated by all others in accordance with laws of natural freedom and equality, it does not follow that they also have a right to influence or organise the state itself as *active* members, or to co-operate in introducing particular laws. Instead, it only means that the positive laws to which the voters agree, of whatever sort they may be, must not be at variance with the natural laws of freedom and with the corresponding equality of all members of the people whereby they are allowed to work their way up from their passive condition to an active one ...

The act by which the people constitutes a state for itself, or more precisely, the mere idea of such an act (which alone enables us to consider it valid in terms of right), is the *original contract*. By this contract, all members of the people (*omnes et singuli*) give up their external freedom in order to receive it back at once as members of a commonwealth, i.e. of the people regarded as a state (*universi*). And we cannot say that men within a state have sacrificed a *part* of their inborn external freedom for a specific purpose; they have in fact completely abandoned their wild and lawless freedom, in order to find again their entire and undiminished freedom in a state of lawful dependence (i.e. in a state of right), for this dependence is created by their own legislative will ...

It is futile to hunt for *historical documentation* of the origins of this mechanism. That is, we cannot reach back to the time at which civil society first emerged (for savages do not set up any formal instruments in submitting themselves to the law, and it can easily be gathered from the nature of uncivilised man that they must have initially used violent means). But it would be quite culpable to undertake such researches with a view to forcibly changing the constitution at present in existence. For this sort of change could only be effected by the people by means of revolutionary conspiracy, and not by the legislature. But revolution under an already existing constitution means the destruction of all relationships governed by civil right, and thus of right altogether. And this is not a change but a dissolution of the civil constitution ...

But the *spirit* of the original contract (*anima pacti originarii*) contains an obligation on the part of the constitutive power to make the *mode of government* conform to the original idea, and thus to alter the mode of government by a gradual and continuous process (if it cannot be done at once) until it accords *in its effects* with the only rightful constitution, that of a pure republic. The old empirical (and statutory) forms, which serve only to effect the *subjection* of the people, should accordingly resolve themselves into the original (rational) form which alone makes *freedom* the principle and indeed the condition of all *coercion* ...

Any true republic, however, is and cannot be anything other than a *representative system* of the people whereby the people's rights are looked after on their behalf by deputies who represent the united will of the citizens ...

For the supreme power originally rests with the people, and all the rights of individuals as mere subjects (and particularly as state officials) must be derived from this supreme power ...

II

### Theory and Practice in Political Right
### (Against Hobbes)

Among all the contracts by which a large group of men unites to form a society (*pactum sociale*), the contract establishing a *civil constitution* (*pactum unionis civilis*) is of an exceptional nature.

For while, so far as its execution is concerned, it has much in common with all others that are likewise directed towards a chosen end to be pursued by joint effort, it is essentially different from all others in the principle of its constitution (*constitutionis civilis*). In all social contracts, we find a union of many individuals for some common end which they all *share*. But a union as an end in itself which they all *ought to share* and which is thus an absolute and primary duty in all external relationships whatsoever among human beings (who cannot avoid mutually influencing one another), is only found in a society in so far as it constitutes a civil state, i.e. a commonwealth. And the end which is a duty in itself in such external relationships, and which is indeed the highest formal condition (*conditio sine qua non*) of all other external duties, is the *right* of men *under coercive public laws* by which each can be given what is due to him and secured against attack from any others. But the whole concept of an external right is derived entirely from the concept of *freedom* in the mutual external relationships of human beings, and has nothing to do with the end which all men have by nature (i.e. the aim of achieving happiness) or with the recognised means of attaining this end. And thus the latter end must on no account interfere as a determinant with the laws governing external right. *Right* is the restriction of each individual's freedom so that it harmonises with the freedom of everyone else (in so far as this is possible within the terms of a general law). And *public right* is the distinctive quality of the *external laws* which make this constant harmony possible. Since every restriction of freedom through the arbitrary will of another party is termed *coercion*, it follows that a civil constitution is a relationship among *free* men who are subject to coercive laws, while they retain their freedom within the general union with their fellows. Such is the requirement of pure reason, which legislates *a priori*, regardless of all empirical ends (which can all be summed up under the general heading of happiness). Men have different views on the empirical end of happiness and what it consists of, so that as far as happiness is concerned, their will cannot be brought under any common principle nor thus under any external law harmonising with the freedom of everyone.

The civil state, regarded purely as a lawful state, is based on the following *a priori* principles:

1    The *freedom* of every member of society as a *human being*.
2    The *equality* of each with all the others as a *subject*.
3    The *independence* of each member of a commonwealth as a *citizen*.

These principles are not so much laws given by an already established state, as laws by which a state can alone be established in accordance with pure rational principles of external human right. Thus:

1 Man's *freedom* as a human being, as a principle for the constitution of a commonwealth, can be expressed in the following formula. No-one can compel me to be happy in accordance with his conception of the welfare of others, for each may seek his happiness in whatever way he sees fit, so long as he does not infringe upon the freedom of others to pursue a similar end which can be reconciled with the freedom of everyone else within a workable general law — i.e. he must accord to others the same right as he enjoys himself. A government might be established on the principle of benevolence towards the people, like that of a father towards his children. Under such a *paternal government* (*imperium paternale*), the subjects, as immature children who cannot distinguish what is truly useful or harmful to themselves, would be obliged to behave purely passively and to rely upon the judgement of the head of state as to how they *ought* to be happy, and upon his kindness in willing their happiness at all. Such a government is the greatest conceivable *despotism*, i.e. a constitution which suspends the entire freedom of its subjects, who thenceforth have no rights whatsoever.

2 Man's *equality* as a subject might be formulated as follows. Each member of the commonwealth has rights of coercion in relation to all the others, except in relation to the head of state. For he alone is not a member of the commonwealth, but its creator or preserver, and he alone is authorised to coerce others without being subject to any coercive law himself. But all who are subject to laws are the subjects of a state, and are thus subject to the right of coercion along with all other members of the commonwealth. ...

This uniform equality of human beings as subjects of a state is, however, perfectly consistent with the utmost inequality of the mass in the degree of its possessions, whether these take the form of physical or mental superiority over others, or of fortuitous external property and of particular rights (of which there may be many) with respect to others. Thus the welfare of the one depends very much on the will of the other (the poor depending on the rich), the one must obey the other (as the child its parents or the wife her husband), the one serves (the labourer) while the other pays, etc. Nevertheless, they are all equal as subjects *before the law*, which, as the pronouncement of the general will, can only be single in form, and which concerns the form of right and not the material or object in relation to which I possess rights ...

From this idea of the equality of men as subjects in a commonwealth, there emerges this further formula: every member of the commonwealth must be entitled to reach any degree of rank which a subject can earn through his talent, his industry and his good fortune. And his fellow-subjects may not stand in his way by *hereditary* prerogatives or privileges of rank and thereby hold him and his descendants back indefinitely ... The *birthright* of each individual in such a state (i.e. before he has performed any acts which can be judged in relation to right) is absolutely *equal* as regards his authority to coerce others to use their freedom in a way which harmonises with his freedom. Since birth is not an act on the part of the one who is born, it cannot create any inequality in his legal position and cannot make him submit to any coercive laws except in so far as he is a subject, along with all the others, of the one supreme legislative power. Thus no member of the commonwealth can have a hereditary privilege as against his fellow-subjects; and no-one can hand down to his descendants the privileges attached to the rank he occupies in the commonwealth, nor act as if he were qualified as a ruler by birth and forcibly prevent others from reaching the higher levels of the hierarchy (which are *superior* and *inferior*, but never *imperans* and *subiectus*) through their own merit. He may hand down everything else, so long as it is material and not pertaining to his person, for it may be acquired and disposed of as property and may over a series of generations create considerable inequalities in wealth among the members of the commonwealth (the employee and the employer, the landowner and the agricultural servants, etc.). But he may not prevent his subordinates from raising themselves to his own level if they are able and entitled to do so by their talent, industry and good fortune. If this were not so, he would be allowed to practise coercion without himself being subject to coercive counter-measures from others, and would thus be more than their fellow-subject ...

3   The *independence* (*sibisufficientia*) of a member of the commonwealth as a *citizen*, i.e. as a co-legislator, may be defined as follows. In the question of actual legislation, all who are free and equal under existing public laws may be considered equal, but not as regards the right to make these laws. These who are not entitled to this right are nonetheless obliged, as members of the commonwealth, to comply with these laws, and they thus likewise enjoy their protection (not as *citizens* but as co-beneficiaries of this

protection). For all right depends on laws. But a public law which defines for everyone that which is permitted and prohibited by right, is the act of a public will, from which all right proceeds and which must not therefore itself be able to do an injustice to any one. And this requires no less than the will of the entire people (since all men decide for all men and each decides for himself) ... The basic law, which can come only from the general, united will of the people, is called the *original contract*.

Anyone who has the right to vote on this legislation is a *citizen* ... The only qualification required by a citizen (apart, of course, from being an adult male) is that he must be his *own master* (*sui iuris*), and must have some *property* (which can include any skill, trade, fine art or science) to support himself. In cases where he must earn his living from others, he must earn it only by *selling* that which is his, and not by allowing others to make use of him. He who does a piece of work (*opus*) can sell it to someone else, just as if it were his own property. But guaranteeing one's labour (*praestatio operae*) is not the same as selling a commodity. The domestic servant, the shop assistant, the labourer, or even the barber, are merely labourers (*operarii*), not masters of an art (*artifices*, in the wider sense) or members of the state, and are thus unqualified to be citizens. A citizen must in the true sense of the word *serve* no-one but the commonwealth. In this respect, artisans and large or small landowners are all equal, and each is entitled to one vote only ... The number of those entitled to vote on matters of legislation must be calculated purely from the number of property owners, not from the size of their properties.

Those who possess this right to vote must agree *unanimously* to the law of public justice, or else a legal contention would arise between those who agree and those who disagree, and it would require yet another higher legal principle to resolve it. An entire people cannot, however, be expected to reach unanimity, but only to show a majority of votes (and not even of direct votes, but simply of the votes of those delegated in a large nation to represent the people). Thus the actual principle of being content with majority decisions must be accepted unanimously and embodied in a contract; and this itself must be the ultimate basis on which a civil constitution is established.

### CONCLUSION

This, then, is an *original contract* by means of which a civil and thus completely lawful constitution and commonwealth can alone be established. But we need by no means assume that this contract (*contractus originarius* or *pactum sociale*), based on a coalition of the wills of all private individuals in a nation to form a common, public will for the purposes of rightful legislation, actually exists as a *fact*, for it cannot possibly be so. Such an assumption would mean that we would first have to prove from history that some nation, whose rights and obligations have been passed down to us, did in fact perform such on act, and handed down some authentic record or legal instrument, orally or in writing, before we could regard ourselves as bound by a pre-existing civil constitution. It is in fact merely an *idea* of reason, which nonetheless has undoubted practical reality; for it can oblige every legislator to frame his laws in such a way that they could have been produced by the united will of a whole nation, and to regard each subject, in so far as he can claim citizenship, as if he had consented within the general will. This is the test of the rightfulness of every public law. For if the law is such that a whole people could not *possibly* agree to it (for example, if it stated that a certain class of *subjects* must be privileged as a hereditary *ruling class*), it is unjust; but if it is at least *possible* that a people could agree to it, it is our duty to consider the law as just, even if the people is at present in such a position or attitude of mind that it would probably refuse its consent if it were consulted. If, for example, a war tax were proportionately imposed on all subjects, they could not claim, simply because it is oppressive, that it is unjust because the war is in their opinion unnecessary. For they are not entitled to judge this issue, since it is at least *possible* that the war is inevitable and the tax indispensable, so that the tax must be deemed rightful in the judgement of the subjects. But if certain estate owners were oppressed with levies for such a war, while others of the same class were exempted, it is easily seen that a whole people could never agree to a law of this kind, and it is entitled at least to make representations against it, since an unequal distribution of burdens can never be considered just. But this restriction obviously applies only to the judgement of the legislator, not to that of the subject. Thus if a people, under some existing legislation, were asked to make a judgement which in all probability would prejudice its happiness, what should it do? Should the people not oppose the measure? The only possible answer is that they can do nothing but obey. For we are not concerned here with any happiness which the subject might expect to derive from the institutions or administration of the commonwealth, but primarily with the rights which would thereby be secured for everyone ... No generally valid principle of legislation can be based on happiness. For both the

current circumstances and the highly conflicting and variable il-
lusions as to what happiness is (and no-one can prescribe to others
how they should attain it) make all fixed principles impossible,
so that happiness alone can never be a suitable principle of legislation ... So long as it is not self-contradictory to say that an
entire people could agree to such a law, however painful it might
seem, then the law is in harmony with right. But if a public law is
beyond reproach (*i.e. irreprehensible*) with respect to right, it
carries with it the authority to coerce those to whom it applies,
and conversely, it forbids them to resist the will of the legislator
by violent means. In other words, the power of the state to put the
law into effect is also *irresistible*, and no rightfully established
commonwealth can exist without a force of this kind to suppress
all internal resistance. For such resistance would be dictated by a
maxim which, if it became general, would destroy the whole civil
constitution and put an end to the only state in which men can
possess rights.

It thus follows that all resistance against the supreme legislative
power, all incitement of the subjects to violent expressions of
discontent, all defiance which breaks out into rebellion, is the
greatest and most punishable crime in a commonwealth, for it
destroys its very foundations. This prohibition is *absolute*. And
even if the power of the state or its agent, the head of state, has
violated the original contract by authorising the government to act
tyrannically, and has thereby, in the eyes of the subject, forfeited
the right to legislate, the subject is still not entitled to offer counter-
resistance. The reason for this is that the people, under an
existing civil constitution, has no longer any right to judge how
the constitution should be administered. For if we suppose that it
does have this right to judge and that it disagrees with the judgement of the actual head of state, who is to decide which side is
right? Neither can act as judge of his own cause. Thus there would
have to be another head above the head of state to mediate
between the latter and the people, which is self-contradictory ...

Nonetheless, estimable men have declared that the subject is
justified, under certain circumstances, in using force against his
superiors. I need name only Achenwall, who is extremely cautious,
precise and restrained in his theories of natural right. He says: 'If
the danger which threatens the commonwealth as a result of long
endurance of injustices from the head of state is greater than the
danger to be feared from taking up arms against him, the people
may then resist him. It may use this right to abrogate its contract
of subjection and to dethrone him as a tyrant.' And he concludes:

'The people, in dethroning its ruler, thus returns to the state of nature.'

I well believe that neither Achenwall nor any others of the worthy men who have speculated along the same lines as he would ever have given their advice or agreement to such hazardous projects if the case had arisen. And it can scarcely be doubted that if the revolutions whereby Switzerland, the United Netherlands or even Great Britain won their much admired constitutions had failed, the readers of their history would regard the execution of their celebrated founders as no more than the deserved punishment of great political criminals. For the result usually affects our judgement of the rightfulness of an action, although the result is uncertain, whereas the principles of right are constant. But it is clear that these peoples have done the greatest degree of wrong in seeking their rights in this way, even if we admit that such a revolution did no injustice to a ruler who had violated a specific basic agreement with the people, such as the *Joyeuse Entrée*. For such procedures, if made into a maxim, make all lawful constitutions insecure and produce a state of complete lawlessness (*status naturalis*) where all rights cease at least to be effectual. In view of this tendency of so many right-thinking authors to plead on behalf of the people (and to its own detriment), I will only remark that such errors arise in part . . . because these writers have assumed that the idea of an original contract (a basic postulate of reason) is something which must have taken place *in reality*, even where there is no document to show that any contract was actually submitted to the commonwealth, accepted by the head of state, and sanctioned by both parties. Such writers thus believe that the people retains the right to abrogate the original contract at its own discretion, if, in the opinion of the people, the contract has been severely violated
. . .

If they had first of all asked what is lawful (in terms of *a priori* certainty, which no empiricist can upset), the idea of a social contract would retain its authority undiminished. But it would not exist as a fact (as Danton would have it, declaring that since it does not actually exist, all property and all rights under the existing civil constitution are null and void), but only as a rational principle for judging any lawful public constitution whatsoever. And it would then be seen that, until the general will is there, the people has no coercive right against its ruler, since it can apply coercion legally only through him . . . Thus the people can never possess a right of coercion against the head of state, or be entitled to oppose him in word or deed . . .

While I trust that no-one will accuse me of flattering monarchs too much by declaring them inviolable, I likewise hope that I shall be spared the reproach of claiming too much for the people if I maintain that the people too have inalienable rights against the head of state, even if these cannot be rights of coercion.

Hobbes is of the opposite opinion. According to him (*De Cive*, Chap. 7, § 14), the head of state has no contractual obligations towards the people; he can do no injustice to a citizen, but may act towards him as he pleases. This proposition would be perfectly correct if injustice were taken to mean any injury which gave the injured party a *coercive right*, against the one who has done him injustice. But in its general form, the proposition is quite terrifying.

The non-resisting subject must be able to assume that his ruler has no *wish* to do him injustice. And everyone has his inalienable rights, which he cannot give up even if he wishes to, and about which he is entitled to make his own judgements. But if he assumes that the ruler's attitude is one of good will, any injustice which he believes he has suffered can only have resulted through error, or through ignorance of certain possible consequences of the laws which the supreme authority has made. Thus the citizen must, with the approval of the ruler, be entitled to make public his opinion on whatever of the ruler's measures seem to him to constitute an injustice against the commonwealth. For to assume that the head of state can neither make mistakes nor be ignorant of anything would be to imply that he receives divine inspiration and is more than a human being. Thus *freedom of the pen* is the only safeguard of the rights of the people, although it must not transcend the bounds of respect and devotion towards the existing constitution, which should itself create a liberal attitude of mind among the subjects. To try to deny the citizen this freedom does not only mean, as Hobbes maintains, that the subject can claim no rights against the supreme ruler. It also means withholding from the ruler all knowledge of those matters which, if he knew about them, he would himself rectify ...

### III

### The Metaphysics of Morals: International Right

What we are now about to consider under the name of international right or the right of nations is the right of *states* in relation to one another ... The situation in question is that in which one state, as a moral person, is considered as existing in a state of nature in relation to another state, hence in a condition of constant war. International right is thus concerned partly with the right to make war, partly with the right of war itself, and partly with questions of right after a war, i.e. with the right of states to compel each other to abandon their warlike condition and to create a constitution which will establish an enduring peace. A state of nature among individuals or families (in their relations with one another) is different from a state of nature among entire nations, because international right involves not only the relationship between one state and another within a larger whole, but also the relationship between individual persons in one state and individuals in the other or between such individuals and the other state as a whole ...

The elements of international right are as follows. Firstly, in their external relationships with one another, states, like lawless savages, exist in a condition devoid of right. Secondly, this *condition* is one of war (the right of the stronger), even if there is no actual war or continuous active fighting (i.e. hostilities). But even although neither of two states is done any injustice by the other in this condition, it is nevertheless in the highest degree unjust in itself, for it implies that neither wishes to experience anything better. Adjacent states are thus bound to abandon such a condition. Thirdly, it is necessary to establish a federation of peoples in accordance with the idea of an original social contract, so that states will protect one another against external aggression while refraining from interference in one another's internal disagreements. And fourthly, this association must not embody a sovereign power as in a civil constitution, but only a partnership or *confederation*. It must therefore be an alliance which can be terminated at any time, so that it has to renewed periodically. This right is derived *in subsidium* from another original right, that of preventing oneself from lapsing into a state of actual war with one's partners in the confederation ...

Since the state of nature among nations (as among individual human beings) is a state which one ought to abandon in order to enter a state governed by law, all international rights, as well as all the external property of states such as can be acquired or preserved by war, are purely *provisional* until the state of nature has been abandoned. Only within a universal *union of states* (analogous to the union through which a nation becomes a state) can such rights and property acquire *peremptory* validity and a true *state of peace* be attained. But if an international state of this kind extends over too wide an area of land, it will eventually become impossible to govern it and thence to protect each of its members, and the multitude of corporations this would require must again lead to a state of war. It naturally follows that *perpetual peace*, the ultimate end of all international right, is an idea incapable of realisation. But the political principles which have this aim, i.e. those principles which encourage the formation of international alliances designed to *approach* the idea itself by a continual process, are not impracticable. For this is a project based upon duty, hence also upon the rights of man and of states, and it can indeed be put into execution.

Such a *union of several states* designed to preserve peace may be called a *permanent congress of states*, and all neighbouring states are free to join it. A congress of this very kind (at least as far as the formalities of international right in relation to the preservation of peace are concerned) found expression in the assembly of the States General at The Hague in the first half of this century. To this assembly, the ministers of most European courts and even of the smallest republics brought their complaints about any aggression suffered by one of their number at the hands of another. They thus thought of all Europe as a single federated state, which they accepted as an arbiter in all their public disputes. Since then, however, international right has disappeared from cabinets, surviving only in books, or it has been consigned to the obscurity of the archives as a form of empty deduction after violent measures have already been employed ...

# 7

# Contractarian Justice

## JOHN RAWLS

## A Theory of Justice

JUSTICE AS FAIRNESS
*(Chapter 1)*

In this introductory chapter I sketch some of the main ideas of the theory of justice I wish to develop. ... I begin by describing the role of justice in social cooperation and with a brief account of the primary subject of justice, the basic structure of society. I then present the main idea of justice as fairness, a theory of justice that generalizes and carries to a higher level of abstraction the traditional conception of the social contract. The compact of society is replaced by an initial situation that incorporates certain procedural constraints on arguments designed to lead to an original agreement on principles of justice ...

### The role of justice

Let us assume, to fix ideas, that a society is a more or less self-sufficient association of persons who in their relations to one another recognize certain rules of conduct as binding and who for the most part act in accordance with them. Suppose further that these rules specify a system of cooperation designed to advance the good of those taking part in it. Then, although a society is a cooperative venture for mutual advantage, it is typically marked

*Source*: Extracts reproduced by permission of Harvard University Press from J. Rawls, *A Theory of Justice* (Cambridge, Mass.: Harvard UP, 1971).

by a conflict as well as by an identity of interests. There is an identity of interests since social cooperation makes possible a better life for all than any would have if each were to live solely by his own efforts. There is a conflict of interests since persons are not indifferent as to how the greater benefits produced by their collaboration are distributed, for in order to pursue their ends they each prefer a larger to a lesser share. A set of principles is required for choosing among the various social arrangements which determine this division of advantages and for underwriting an agreement on the proper distributive shares. These principles are the principles of social justice: they provide a way of assigning rights and duties in the basic institutions of society and they define the appropriate distribution of the benefits and burdens of social cooperation ...

Among individuals with disparate aims and purposes a shared conception of justice establishes the bonds of civic friendship; the general desire for justice limits the pursuit of other ends. One may think of a public conception of justice as constituting the fundamental charter of a well-ordered human association.

Existing societies are of course seldom well-ordered in this sense, for what is just and unjust is usually in dispute. Men disagree about which principles should define the basic terms of their association. Yet we may still say, despite this disagreement, that they each have a conception of justice. That is, they understand the need for, and they are prepared to affirm, a characteristic set of principles for assigning basic rights and duties and for determining what they take to be the proper distribution of the benefits and burdens of social cooperation. Thus it seems natural to think of the concept of justice as distinct from the various conceptions of justice and as being specified by the role which these different sets of principles, these different conceptions, have in common. Those who hold different conceptions of justice can, then, still agree that institutions are just when no arbitrary distinctions are made between persons in the assigning of basic rights and duties and when the rules determine a proper balance between competing claims to the advantages of social life ...

## The subject of justice

Many different kinds of things are said to be just and unjust: ... our topic, however, is that of social justice. For us the primary subject of justice is the basic structure of society, or more exactly, the way in which the major social institutions distribute fundamental rights and duties and determine the division of advantages from social cooperation. By major institutions I understand the political constitution and the principal economic and social arrangements ... The basic structure is the primary subject of justice because its effects are so profound and present from the start. The intuitive notion here is that this structure contains various social positions and that men born into different positions have different expectations of life determined, in part, by the political system as well as by economic and social circumstances. In this way the institutions of society favor certain starting places over others. These are especially deep inequalities. Not only are they pervasive, but they affect men's initial chances in life; yet they cannot possibly be justified by an appeal to the notions of merit or desert. It is these inequalities, presumably inevitable in the basic structure of any society, to which the principles of social justice must in the first instance apply. These principles, then, regulate the choice of a political constitution and the main elements of the economic and social system. The justice of a social scheme depends essentially on how fundamental rights and duties are assigned and on the economic opportunities and social conditions in the various sectors of society ...

## The main idea of the theory of justice

My aim is to present a conception of justice which generalizes and carries to a higher level of abstraction the familiar theory of the social contract as found, say, in Locke, Rousseau, and Kant. In order to do this we are not to think of the original contract as one to enter a particular society or to set up a particular form of government. Rather, the guiding idea is that the principles of justice for the basic structure of society are the object of the original agreement. They are the principles that free and rational persons concerned to further their own interests would accept in an initial position of equality as defining the fundamental terms of their association. These principles are to regulate all further agreements; they specify the kinds of social cooperation that can be entered into and the forms of government that can be established. This way of regarding the principles of justice I shall call justice as fairness.

Thus we are to imagine that those who engage in social cooperation choose together, in one joint act, the principles which are to assign basic rights and duties and to determine the division of social benefits. Men are to decide in advance how they are to regulate their claims against one another and what is to be the foundation charter of their society ... The choice which rational men would make in this hypothetical situation of equal liberty, assuming for the present that this choice problem has a solution, determines the principles of justice.

In justice as fairness the original position of equality corresponds to the state of nature in the traditional theory of the social contract. This original position is not, of course, thought of as an actual historical state of affairs, much less as a primitive condition of culture. It is understood as a purely hypothetical situation characterized so as to lead to a certain conception of justice. Among the essential features of this situation is that no one knows his place in society, his class position or social status, nor does any one know his fortune in the distribution of natural assets and abilities, his intelligence, strength, and the like. I shall even assume that the parties do not know their conceptions of the good or their special psychological propensities. The principles of justice are chosen behind a veil of ignorance. This ensures that no one is advantaged or disadvantaged in the choice of principles by the outcome of natural chance or the contingency of social circumstances. Since all are similarly situated and no one is able to design principles to favor his particular condition, the principles of justice are the result of a fair agreement or bargain. For given circumstances of the original position, the symmetry of everyone's relations to each other, this initial situation is fair between individuals as moral persons, that is, as rational beings with their own ends and capable, I shall assume, of a sense of justice. The original position is, one might say, the appropriate initial status quo, and thus the fundamental agreements reached in it are fair. This explains the propriety of the name 'justice as fairness': it conveys the idea that the principles of justice are agreed to in an initial situation that is fair ...

[A] society satisfying the principles of justice as fairness comes as close as a society can to being a voluntary scheme, for it meets the principles which free and equal persons would assent to under circumstances that are fair. In this sense its members are autonomous and the obligations they recognize self-imposed.

One feature of justice as fairness is to think of the parties in the initial situation as rational and mutually disinterested. This does not mean that the parties are egoists, that is, individuals with only certain kinds of interests, say in wealth, prestige, and domination.

But they are conceived as not taking an interest in one another's interests. They are to presume that even their spiritual aims may be opposed, in the way that the aims of those of different religions may be opposed. Moreover, the concept of rationality must be interpreted as far as possible in the narrow sense, standard in economic theory, of taking the most effective means to given ends. One must try to avoid introducing into it any controversial ethical elements. The initial situation must be characterized by stipulations that are widely accepted ...

### The original position and justification

I have said that the original position is the appropriate initial status quo which insures that the fundamental agreements reached in it are fair. This fact yields the name 'justice as fairness'. It is clear, then, that I want to say that one conception of justice is more reasonable than another, or justifiable with respect to it, if rational persons in the initial situation would choose its principles over those of the other for the role of justice. Conceptions of justice are to be ranked by their acceptability to persons so circumstanced. Understood in this way the question of justification is settled by working out a problem of deliberation: we have to ascertain which principles it would be rational to adopt given the contractual situation. This connects the theory of justice with the theory of rational choice.

If this view of the problem of justification is to succeed, we must, of course, describe in some detail the nature of this choice problem. A problem of rational decision has a definite answer only if we know the beliefs and interests of the parties, their relations with respect to one another, the alternatives between which they are to choose, the procedure whereby they make up their minds, and so on. As the circumstances are presented in different ways, correspondingly different principles are accepted. The concept of the original position, as I shall refer to it, is that of the most philosophically favored interpretation of this initial choice situation for the purposes of a theory of justice.

But how are we to decide what is the most favored interpretation? I assume, for one thing; that there is a broad measure of agreement that principles of justice should be chosen under certain conditions. To justify a particular description of the initial situation one shows that it incorporates these commonly shared presumptions. One argues from widely accepted but weak premises to more specific conclusions. Each of the presumptions should by itself be natural and plausible; some of them may seem innocuous or even trivial. The aim of the contract approach is to establish that taken together they impose significant bounds on acceptable principles of justice. The ideal outcome would be that these conditions determine a unique set of principles; but I shall be satisfied if they suffice to rank the main traditional conceptions of social justice.

One should not be misled, then, by the somewhat unusual conditions which characterize the original position. The idea here is simply to make vivid to ourselves the restrictions that it seems reasonable to impose on arguments for principles of justice, and therefore on these principles themselves. Thus it seems reasonable and generally acceptable that no one should be advantaged or disadvantaged by natural fortune or social circumstances in the choice of principles. It also seems widely agreed that it should be impossible to tailor principles to the circumstances of one's own case. We should insure further that particular inclinations and aspirations, and persons' conceptions of their good do not affect the principles adopted. The aim is to rule out those principles that it would be rational to propose for acceptance, however little the chance of success, only if one knew certain things that are irrelevant from the standpoint of justice. For example, if a man knew that he was wealthy, he might find it rational to advance the principle that various taxes for welfare measures be counted unjust; if he knew that he was poor, he would most likely propose the contrary principle. To represent the desired restrictions one imagines a situation in which everyone is deprived of this sort of information. One excludes the knowledge of those contingencies which sets men at odds and allows them to be guided by their prejudices. In this manner the veil of ignorance is arrived at in a natural way. This concept should cause no difficulty if we keep in mind the constraints on arguments that it is meant to express. At any time we can enter the original position, so to speak, simply by following a certain procedure, namely, by arguing for principles of justice in accordance with these restrictions.

It seems reasonable to suppose that the parties in the original position are equal. That is, all have the same rights in the procedure for choosing principles; each can make proposals, submit reasons for their acceptance, and so on. Obviously the purpose of these conditions is to represent equality between human beings as moral persons, as creatures having a conception of their good and capable of a sense of justice. The basis of equality is taken to be similarity in these two respects. Systems of ends are not ranked in value; and each man is presumed to have the requisite ability to understand and to act upon whatever principles are adopted. Together with the veil of ignorance, these conditions define the principles of justice as those which rational persons concerned to advance their interests would consent to as equals when none are known to be advantaged or disadvantaged by social and natural contingencies.

There is, however, another side to justifying a particular description of the original position. This is to see if the principles which would be chosen match our considered convictions of justice or extend them in an acceptable way. We can note whether applying these principles would lead us to make the same judgments about the basic structure of society which we now make intuitively and in which we have the greatest confidence; or whether, in cases where our present judgments are in doubt and given with hesitation, these principles offer a resolution which we can affirm on reflection. There are questions which we feel sure must be answered in a certain way. For example, we are confident that religious intolerance and racial discrimination are unjust. We think that we have examined these things with care and have reached what we believe is an impartial judgment not likely to be distorted by an excessive attention to our own interests. These convictions are provisional fixed points which we presume any conception of justice must fit. But we have much less assurance as to what is the correct distribution of wealth and authority. Here we may be looking for a way to remove our doubts. We can check an interpretation of the initial situation, then, by the capacity of its principles to accommodate our firmest convictions and to provide guidance where guidance is needed ...

A final comment. We shall want to say that certain principles of justice are justified because they would be agreed to in an initial situation of equality. I have emphasized that this original position is purely hypothetical. It is natural to ask why, if this agreement is never actually entered into, we should take any interest in these principles, moral or otherwise. The answer is that the conditions embodied in the description of the original position are ones that we do in fact accept. Or if we do not, then perhaps we can be persuaded to do so by philosophical reflection. Each aspect of the contractual situation can be given supporting grounds ...

THE PRINCIPLES OF JUSTICE
*(Chapter 2)*

## Two principles of justice

I shall now state in a provisional form the two principles of justice that I believe would be chosen in the original position ... The first statement of the two principles reads as follows.

First: each person is to have an equal right to the most extensive basic liberty compatible with a similar liberty for others.

Second: social and economic inequalities are to be arranged so that they are both (a) reasonably expected to be to everyone's advantage, and (b) attached to positions and offices equally open to all ...

By way of general comment, these principles primarily apply, as I have said, to the basic structure of society. They are to govern the assignment of rights and duties and to regulate the distribution of social and economic advantages. As their formulation suggests, these principles presuppose that the social structure can be divided into two more or less distinct parts, the first principle applying to the one, the second to the other. They distinguish between those aspects of the social system that define and secure the equal liberties of citizenship and those that specify and establish social and economic inequalities. The basic liberties of citizens are, roughly speaking, political liberty (the right to vote and to be eligible for public office) together with freedom of speech and assembly; liberty of conscience and freedom of thought; freedom of the person along with the right to hold (personal) property; and freedom from arbitrary arrest and seizure as defined by the concept of the rule of law. These liberties are all required to be equal by the first principle, since citizens of a just society are to have the same basic rights.

The second principle applies, in the first approximation, to the distribution of income and wealth and to the design of organizations that make use of differences in authority and responsibility, or chains of command. While the distribution of wealth and income need not be equal, it must be to everyone's advantage, and at the same time, positions of authority and offices of command must be accessible to all. One applies the second principle by holding positions open, and then, subject to this constraint, arranges social and economic inequalities so that everyone benefits.

These principles are to be arranged in a serial order with the first principle prior to the second. This ordering means that a departure from the institutions of equal liberty required by the first principle cannot be justified by, or compensated for, by greater social and economic advantages. The distribution of wealth and income, and the hierarchies of authority, must be consistent with both the liberties of equal citizenship and equality of opportunity.

It is clear that these principles are rather specific in their content, and their acceptance rests on certain assumptions that I must eventually try to explain and justify. A theory of justice depends upon a theory of society in ways that will become evident as we proceed. For the present, it should be observed that the two principles (and this holds for all formulations) are a special case of a more general conception of justice that can be expressed as follows.

> All social values — liberty and opportunity, income and wealth, and the bases of self-respect — are to be distributed equally unless an unequal distribution of any, or all, of these values is to everyone's advantage.

Injustice, then, is simply inequalities that are not to the benefit of all. Of course, this conception is extremely vague and requires interpretation.

As a first step, suppose that the basic structure of society distributes certain primary goods, that is, things that every rational man is presumed to want. These goods normally have a use whatever a person's rational plan of life. For simplicity, assume that the chief primary goods at the disposition of society are rights and liberties, powers and opportunities, income and wealth ... These are the social primary goods. Other primary goods such as health and vigor, intelligence and imagination, are natural goods; although their possession is influenced by the basic structure, they are not so directly under its control. Imagine, then, a hypothetical initial arrangement in which all the social primary goods are equally distributed: everyone has similar rights and duties, and income and wealth are evenly shared. This state of affairs provides a benchmark for judging improvements. If certain inequalities of wealth and organizational powers would make everyone better off than in this hypothetical starting situation, then they accord with the general conception.

Now it is possible, at least theoretically, that by giving up some of their fundamental liberties men are sufficiently compensated by the resulting social and economic gains. The general conception of justice imposes no restrictions on what sort of inequalities are permissible; it only requires that everyone's position be improved. We need not suppose anything so drastic as consenting to a condition of slavery. Imagine instead that men forgo certain political rights when the economic returns are significant and their capacity to influence the course of policy by the exercise of these rights would be marginal in any case. It is this kind of exchange which the two principles as stated rule out; being arranged in serial order they do not permit exchanges between basic liberties and economic and social gains. The serial ordering of principles expresses an underlying preference among primary social goods. When this preference is rational so likewise is the choice of these principles in this order ...

When principles mention persons, or require that everyone gain from an inequality, the reference is to representative persons holding the various social positions, or offices, or whatever, established by the basic structure. Thus in applying the second principle I assume that it is possible to assign an expectation of well-being to representative individuals holding these positions. This expectation indicates their life prospects as viewed from their social station. In general, the expectations of representative persons depend upon the distribution of rights and duties throughout the basic structure.

Now the second principle insists that each person benefit from permissible inequalities in the basic structure. This means that it must be reasonable for each relevant representative man defined by this structure, when he views it as a going concern, to prefer his prospects with the inequality to his prospects without it. One is not allowed to justify differences in income or organizational powers on the ground that the disadvantages of those in one position are outweighed by the greater advantages of those in another. Much less can infringements of liberty be counterbalanced in this way ...

### Democratic equality and the difference principle

[Democratic equality] is arrived at by combining the principle of fair equality of opportunity with the *difference principle* ... Assuming the framework of institutions required by equal liberty and fair equality of opportunity, the higher expectations of those better situated are just if and only if they work as part of a scheme which improves the expectations of the least advantaged members of society. The intuitive idea is that the social order is not to establish and secure the more attractive prospects of those better off unless doing so is to the advantage of those less fortunate. ...

To illustrate this difference principle, consider the distribution of income among social classes. Let us suppose that the various income groups correlate with representative individuals by reference to whose expectations we can judge the distribution. Now those starting out as members of the entrepreneurial class in a property-owning democracy, say, have a better prospect than those who begin in the class of unskilled laborers. It seems likely that this will be true even when the social injustices which now exist are removed. What, then can possibly justify this kind of initial inequality in life prospects? According to the difference principle, it is justifiable only if the difference in expectation is to the advantage of the representative man who is worse off, in this case the representative unskilled worker. The inequality in expectation is permissible only if lowering it would make the working class even more worse off. Supposedly, given the rider in the second principle concerning open positions, and the principle of liberty generally, the greater expectations allowed to entrepreneurs encourages them to do things which raise the longterm prospects of the laboring class. Their better prospects act as incentives so that the economic process is more efficient, innovation proceeds at a faster pace, and so on. Eventually the resulting material benefits spread throughout the system and to the least advantaged. I shall not consider how far these things are true. The point is that something of this kind must be argued if these inequalities are to be just by the difference principle ...

A scheme is unjust when the higher expectations, one or more of them, are excessive. If these expectations were decreased, the situation of the least favored would be improved ...

## Fair equality of opportunity and pure procedural justice

I should now like to comment upon the second part of the second principle, [which embodies] the liberal principle of fair equality of opportunity. It must not ... be confused with the notion of careers open to talents ...

The reasons for requiring open positions are not solely, or even primarily, those of efficiency. I have not maintained that offices must be open if in fact everyone is to benefit from an arrangement. For it may be possible to improve everyone's situation by assigning certain powers and benefits to positions despite the fact that certain groups are excluded from them. Although access is restricted, perhaps these offices can still attract superior talent and encourage better performance. But the principle of open positions forbids this. It expresses the conviction that if some places were not open on a basis fair to all, those kept out would be right in feeling unjustly treated even though they benefited from the greater efforts of those who were allowed to hold them. They would be justified in their complaint not only because they were excluded from certain external rewards of office such as wealth and privilege, but because they were debarred from experiencing the realization of self which comes from a skillful and devoted exercise of social duties. They would be deprived of one of the main forms of human good ...

## Primary social goods as the basis of expectations

The assumption is that though men's rational plans do have different final ends, they nevertheless all require for their execution certain primary goods, natural and social. Plans differ since individual abilities, circumstances, and wants differ; rational plans are adjusted to these contingencies. But whatever one's system of ends, primary goods are necessary means. Greater intelligence, wealth and opportunity, for example, allow a person to achieve ends he could not rationally contemplate otherwise. The expectations of representative men are, then, to be defined by the index of primary social goods available to them. While the persons in the original position do not know their conception of the good, they do know, I assume, that they prefer more rather than less primary goods. And this information is sufficient for them to know how to advance their interests in the initial situation ...

## Relevant social positions

In applying the two principles of justice to the basic structure of society one takes the position of certain representative individuals and considers how the social system looks to them. The difference principle, for example, requires that the higher expectations of the more advantaged contribute to the prospects of the least advantaged. Or as I sometimes say more loosely, social and economic inequalities must be in the interest of the representative men in all relevant social positions. The perspective of those in these situations defines a suitably general point of view. But certainly not all social positions are relevant. For not only are there farmers, say, but dairy farmers, wheat farmers, farmers working on large tracts of land, and so on for other occupations and groups indefinitely. We cannot have a coherent and manageable theory if we must take such a multiplicity of positions into account. The assessment of so many competing claims is impossible. Therefore we need to identify certain positions as more basic than the others and as providing an appropriate standpoint for judging the social system. Thus the choice of these positions becomes part of the theory of justice. On what principle, though, are they to be identified?

To answer this question we must keep in mind the fundamental problem of justice and the manner in which the two principles cope with it. The primary subject of justice, as I have emphasized, is the basic structure of society. The reason for this is that its effects are so profound and pervasive, and present from birth. This structure favors some starting places over others in the division of the benefits of social cooperation. It is these inequalities which the two principles are to regulate. Once these principles are satisfied, other inequalities are allowed to arise from men's voluntary actions in accordance with the principle of free association. Thus the relevant social positions are, so to speak, the starting places properly generalized and aggregated. By choosing these positions to specify the general point of view one follows the idea that the two principles attempt to mitigate the arbitrariness of natural contingency and social fortune.

I suppose, then, that for the most part each person holds two relevant positions: that of equal citizenship and that defined by his place in the distribution of income and wealth. The relevant representative men, therefore, are the representative citizen and those who stand for the various levels of well-being. Since I assume that in general other positions are entered into voluntarily, we need not consider the point of view of men in these positions in judging the basic structure . . .

The serious difficulty is how to define the least fortunate group. Here it seems impossible to avoid a certain arbitrariness. One possibility is to choose a particular social position, say that of the unskilled worker, and then to count as the least advantaged all those with the average income and wealth of this group, or less. The expectation of the lowest representative man is defined as the average taken over this whole class. Another alternative is a definition solely in terms of relative income and wealth with no reference to social position. Thus all persons with less than half of the median income and wealth may be taken as the least advantaged segment. This definition depends only upon the lower half of the distribution and has the merit of focusing attention on the social distance between those who have least and the average citizen. Surely this gap is an essential feature of the situation of the less favored members of society. I suppose that either of these definitions, or some combination of them, will serve well enough ...

## The tendency to equality

The difference principle represents, in effect, an agreement to regard the distribution of natural talents as a common asset and to share in the benefits of this distribution whatever it turns out to be. Those who have been favored by nature, whoever they are, may gain from their good fortune only on terms that improve the situation of those who have lost out. The naturally advantaged are not to gain merely because they are more gifted, but only to cover the costs of training and education and for using their endowments in ways that help the less fortunate as well. No one deserves his greater natural capacity nor merits a more favorable starting place in society. But it does not follow that one should eliminate these distinctions. There is another way to deal with them. The basic structure can be arranged so that these contingencies work for the good of the least fortunate. Thus we are led to the difference principle if we wish to set up the social system so that no one gains or loses from his arbitrary place in the distribution of natural assets or his initial position in society without giving or receiving compensating advantages in return ...

## Principles for individuals: the natural duties

From the standpoint of justice as fairness, a fundamental natural duty is the duty of justice. This duty requires us to support and to comply with just institutions that exist and apply to us. It also constrains us to further just arrangements not yet established, at least when this can be done without too much cost to ourselves. Thus if the basic structure of society is just, or as just as it is reasonable to expect in the circumstances, everyone has a natural duty to do his part in the existing scheme. Each is bound to these institutions independent of his voluntary acts, performative or otherwise. Thus even though the principles of natural duty are derived from a contractarian point of view, they do not presuppose an act of consent, express or tacit, or indeed any voluntary act, in order to apply. The principles that hold for individuals, just as the principles for institutions, are those that would be acknowledged in the original position ...

THE ORIGINAL POSITION
(*Chapter 3*)

## The circumstances of justice

The circumstances of justice may be described as the normal conditions under which human cooperation is both possible and necessary. Thus, as I noted at the outset, although a society is a cooperative venture for mutual advantage, it is typically marked by a conflict as well as an identity of interests ...

When it is supposed that the parties are severally disinterested, and are not willing to have their interests sacrificed to the others, the intention is to express men's conduct and motives in cases where questions of justice arise. The spiritual ideals of saints and heroes can be as irreconcilably opposed as any other interests. Conflicts in pursuit of these ideals are the most tragic of all. Thus justice is the virtue of practices where there are competing interests and where persons feel entitled to press their rights on each other. In an association of saints agreeing on a common ideal, if such a community could exist, disputes about justice would not occur. Each would work selflessly for one end as determined by their common religion, and reference to this end (assuming it to be clearly defined) would settle every question of right. But a human society is characterized by the circumstances of justice. The account of these conditions involves no particular theory of human motivation. Rather, its aim is to include in the description of the original position the relations of individuals to one another which set the stage for questions of justice ...

## The veil of ignorance

The idea of the original position is to set up a fair procedure so that any principles agreed to will be just. The aim is to use the notion of pure procedural justice as a basis of theory. Somehow we must nullify the effects of specific contingencies which put men at odds and tempt them to exploit social and natural circumstances to their own advantage. Now in order to do this I assume that the parties are situated behind a veil of ignorance. They do not know how the various alternatives will affect their own particular case and they are obliged to evaluate principles solely on the basis of general considerations. The only particular facts which the parties know is that their society is subject to the circumstances of justice and whatever this implies. It is taken for granted, however, that they know the general facts about human society. They understand political affairs and the principles of economic theory; they know the basis of social organization and the laws of human psychology. Indeed, the parties are presumed to know whatever general facts affect the choice of the principles of justice ...

It may be protested that the condition of the veil of ignorance is irrational. Surely, some may object, principles should be chosen in the light of all the knowledge available. There are various replies to this contention. Here I shall sketch those which emphasize the simplifications that need to be made if one is to have any theory at all. ... To begin with, it is clear that since the differences among the parties are unknown to them, and everyone is equally rational and similarly situated, each is convinced by the same arguments. Therefore, we can view the choice in the original position from the standpoint of one person selected at random. If anyone after due reflection prefers a conception of justice to another, then they all do, and a unanimous agreement can be reached ... Thus there follows the very important consequence that the parties have no basis for bargaining in the usual sense ...

## The rationality of the parties

I have assumed throughout that the persons in the original position are rational. In choosing between principles each tries as best he can to advance his interests. But I have also assumed that the parties do not know their conception of the good. This means that while they know that they have some rational plan of life, they do not know the details of this plan, the particular ends and interests which it is calculated to promote. How, then, can they decide which conceptions of justice are most to their advantage? Or must we suppose that they are reduced to mere guessing? To meet this difficulty, I postulate that they accept the account of the good touched upon in the preceding chapter: they assume that they would prefer more primary social goods rather than less. Of course, it may turn out, once the veil of ignorance is removed, that some of them for religious or other reasons may not, in fact, want more of these goods. But from the standpoint of the original position, it is rational for the parties to suppose that they do want a larger share, since in any case they are not compelled to accept more if they do not wish to, nor does a person suffer from a greater liberty. Thus even though the parties are deprived of information about their particular ends, they have enough knowledge to rank the alternatives. They know that in general they must try to protect their liberties, widen their opportunities, and enlarge their means for promoting their aims whatever these are. ...

The concept of rationality invoked here, with the exception of one essential feature, is the standard one familiar in social theory ... The special assumption I make is that a rational individual does not suffer from envy. He is not ready to accept a loss for himself if only others have less as well. He is not downcast by the knowledge or perception that others have a larger index of primary social goods ...

One reason for this procedure is that envy tends to make everyone worse off. In this sense it is collectively disadvantageous. Presuming its absence amounts to supposing that in the choice of principles men should think of themselves as having their own plan of life which is sufficient for itself. They have a secure sense of their own worth so that they have no desire to abandon any of their aims provided others have less means to further theirs ...

The assumption of mutually disinterested rationality, then, comes to this: the persons in the original position try to acknowledge principles which advance their system of ends as far as possible. They do this by attempting to win for themselves the highest index of primary social goods, since this enables them to promote their conception of the good most effectively whatever it turns out to be. The parties do not seek to confer benefits or to impose injuries on one another; they are not moved by affection or rancor. Nor do they try to gain relative to each other; they are not envious or vain. Put in terms of a game, we might say: they strive for as high an absolute score as possible. They do not wish a high or a low score for their opponents, nor do they seek to maximize or minimize the difference between their successes and those of others ...

Since the persons in the original position are assumed to take no interest in one another's interests (although they may have a concern for third parties), it may be thought that justice as fairness is itself an egoistic theory ... Now this is a misconception. For the fact that in the original position the parties are characterized as not interested in one another's concerns does not entail that persons in ordinary life who hold the principles that would be agreed to are similarly disinterested in one another. Clearly the two principles of justice and the principles of obligation and natural duty require us to consider the rights and claims of others. And the sense of justice is a normally effective desire to comply with these restrictions. The motivation of the persons in the original position must not be confused with the motivation of persons in everyday life who accept the principles that would be chosen and who have the corresponding sense of justice ...

## The reasoning leading to the two principles of justice

It will be recalled that the general conception of justice as fairness requires that all primary social goods be distributed equally unless an unequal distribution would be to everyone's advantage. No restrictions are placed on exchanges of these goods and therefore a lesser liberty can be compensated for by greater social and economic benefits. Now looking at the situation from the standpoint of one person selected arbitrarily, there is no way for him to win special advantages for himself. Nor, on the other hand, are there grounds for his acquiescing in special disadvantages. Since it is not reasonable for him to expect more than an equal share in the division of social goods, and since it is not rational for him to agree to less, the sensible thing for him to do is to acknowledge as the first principle of justice one requiring an equal distribution. Indeed, this principle is so obvious that we would expect it to occur to anyone immediately ...

But there is no reason why this acknowledgment should be final. If there are inequalities in the basic structure that work to make everyone better off in comparison with the benchmark of initial equality, why not permit them? ... A person in the original position would, therefore, concede the justice of these inequalities. Indeed, it would be shortsighted of him not to do so. He would hesitate to agree to these regularities only if he would be dejected by the bare knowledge or perception that others were better situated; and I have assumed that the parties decide as if they are not moved by envy. In order to make the principle regulating inequalities determinate, one looks at the system from the standpoint of the least advantaged representative man. Inequalities are permissible when they maximize, or at least all contribute to, the long-term expectations of the least fortunate group in society.

Now this general conception imposes no constraints on what sorts of inequalities are allowed, whereas the special conception, by putting the two principles in serial order (with the necessary adjustments in meaning) forbids exchanges between basic liberties and economic and social benefits ... Roughly, the idea underlying this ordering is that if the parties assume that their basic liberties can be effectively exercised, they will not exchange a lesser liberty for an improvement in economic well-being. It is only when social conditions do not allow the effective establishment of these rights that one can concede their limitation; and these restrictions can be granted only to the extent that they are necessary to prepare the way for a free society. The denial of equal liberty can be defended only if it is necessary to raise the level of civilization so that in due course these freedoms can be enjoyed. Thus in adopting a serial order we are in effect making a special assumption in the original position, namely, that the parties know that the conditions of their society, whatever they are, admit the effective realization of the equal liberties. The serial ordering of the two principles of justice eventually comes to be reasonable if the general conception is consistently followed. This lexical ranking is the long-run tendency of the general view ...

It is useful as a heuristic device to think of the two principles as the maximin solution to the problem of social justice. There is an analogy between the two principles and the maximin rule for choice under uncertainty. This is evident from the fact that the two principles are those a person would choose for the design of a society in which his enemy is to assign him his place. The maximin rule tells us to rank alternatives by their worst possible outcomes: we are to adopt the alternative the worst outcome of which is superior to the worst outcomes of the others. The persons in the original position do not, course, assume that their initial place in society is decided by a malevolent opponent ... This analogy suggests that if the original position has been described so that it is rational for the parties to adopt the conservative attitude expressed by this rule, a conclusive argument can indeed be constructed for these principles. Clearly the maximin rule is not, in general, a suitable guide for choices under uncertainty. But it is attractive in situations marked by certain special features. My aim, then, is to show that a good case can be made for the two principles based on the fact that the original position manifests these features ...

### The reasoning leading to the principle of average utility

[However, first] I examine the reasoning that favors the principle of average utility ... The principle of average utility directs society to maximize not the total but the average utility (per capita) ... To apply this conception to the basic structure, institutions are set up so as to maximize the percentage weighted sum of the expectations of representative individuals. To compute this sum we multiply expectations by the fraction of society at the corresponding position ...

If the parties are viewed as rational individuals who have no aversion to risk and who follow the principle of insufficient reason in computing likelihoods, ... then the idea of the initial situation leads naturally to the average principle. By choosing it the parties maximize their expected well-being as seen from this point of view. Some form of contract theory provides, then, a way of arguing for the average [utility] view ... The average principle appeals to those in the initial situation once they are conceived as single rational individuals prepared to gamble on the most abstract probabilistic reasoning in all cases. To argue for the two principles of justice I must show that the conditions defining the original position exclude this conception of the parties ...

## The main grounds for the two principles of justice

[A main] confirming ground for the two principles can be explained in terms of ... the strains of commitment. I said that the parties have a capacity for justice in the sense that they can be assured that their undertaking is not in vain ... They cannot enter into agreements that may have consequences they cannot accept. They will avoid those that they can adhere to only with great difficulty. Since the original agreement is final and made in perpetuity, there is no second chance. In view of the serious nature of the possible consequences, the question of the burden of commitment is especially acute. A person is choosing once and for all the standards which are to govern his life prospects. Moreover, when we enter an agreement we must be able to honor it even should the worst possibilities prove to be the case. Otherwise we have not acted in good faith. Thus the parties must weigh with care whether they will be able to stick by their commitment in all circumstances. Of course, in answering this question they have only a general knowledge of human psychology to go on. But this information is enough to tell which conception of justice involves the greater stress.

In this respect the two principles of justice have a definite advantage. Not only do the parties protect their basic rights but they insure themselves against the worst eventualities. They run no chance of having to acquiesce in a loss of freedom over the course of their life for the sake of a greater good enjoyed by others, an undertaking that in actual circumstances they might not be able to keep. Indeed, we might wonder whether such an agreement can be made in good faith at all. Compacts of this sort exceed the capacity of human nature. How can the parties possibly know, or be sufficiently sure, that they can keep such an agreement? ... Should a person gamble with his liberties and substantive interests hoping that the application of the principle of utility might secure him a greater well-being, he may have difficulty abiding by his undertaking ...

Looking at the question from the standpoint of the original position, the parties recognize that it would be highly unwise if not irrational to choose principles which may have consequences so extreme that they could not accept them in practice. They would reject the principle of utility and adopt the more realistic idea of designing the social order on a principle of reciprocal advantage ...

EQUAL LIBERTY
*(Chapter 4)*

*Political justice and the constitution*

I now wish to consider political justice, that is, the justice of the constitution, and to sketch the meaning of equal liberty for this part of the basic structure ...

The principle of equal liberty, when applied to the political procedure defined by the constitution, I shall refer to as the principle of (equal) participation. It requires that all citizens are to have an equal right to take part in, and to determine the outcome of, the constitutional process that establishes the laws with which they are to comply ... For the time being I assume that a constitutional democracy can be arranged so as to satisfy the principle of participation.

We may begin by recalling certain elements of a constitutional regime. All sane adults, with certain generally recognized exceptions, have the right to take part in political affairs, and the precept one elector one vote is honored as far as possible. Elections are fair and free, and regularly held. There are firm constitutional protections for certain liberties, particularly freedom of speech and assembly, and liberty to form political associations ...

The principle of participation also holds that all citizens are to have an equal access, at least in the formal sense, to public office. Each is eligible to join political parties, to run for elective positions, and to hold places of authority. To be sure, there may be qualifications of age, residency, and so on. But these are to be reasonably related to the tasks of office; presumably these restrictions are in the common interest and do not discriminate unfairly among persons or groups in the sense that they fall evenly on everyone in the normal course of life ...

Turning now to the worth of political liberty, the constitution must take steps to enhance the value of the equal rights of participation for all members of society. It must underwrite a fair opportunity to take part in and to influence the political process ... But how is this fair value of these liberties to be secured? ...

The liberties protected by the principle of participation lose much of their value whenever those who have greater private means are permitted to use their advantages to control the course of public debate. For eventually these inequalities will enable those better situated to exercise a larger influence over the development of legislation. In due time they are likely to acquire a preponderant weight in settling social questions, at least in regard to those matters upon which they normally agree, which is to say in regard to those things that support their favored circumstances.

Compensating steps must, then, be taken to preserve the fair value for all of the equal political liberties. A variety of devices can be used. For example, in a society allowing private ownership of the means of production, property and wealth must be kept widely distributed and government monies provided on a regular basis to encourage free public discussion. In addition, political parties are to be made independent from private economic interests by allotting them sufficient tax revenues to play their part in the constitutional scheme ... What is necessary is that political parties be autonomous with respect to private demands, that is, demands not expressed in the public forum and argued for openly by reference to a conception of the public good ...

Historically one of the main defects of constitutional government has been the failure to insure the fair value of political liberty. The necessary corrective steps have not been taken, indeed, they never seem to have been seriously entertained. Disparities in the distribution of property and wealth that far exceed what is compatible with political equality have generally been tolerated by the legal system. Public resources have not been devoted to maintaining the institutions required for the fair value of political liberty ...

Universal suffrage is an insufficient counterpoise; for when parties and elections are financed not by public funds but by private contributions, the political forum is so constrained by the wishes of the dominant interests that the basic measures needed to establish just constitutional rule are seldom seriously presented ...

DISTRIBUTIVE SHARES
*(Chapter 5)*

In this chapter I take up the second principle of justice and describe an arrangement of institutions that fulfills its requirements within the setting of a modern state. I begin by noting that the principles of justice may serve as part of a doctrine of political economy ... Throughout the choice between a private-property economy and socialism is left open; from the standpoint of the theory of justice alone, various basic structures would appear to satisfy its principles ...

I should like to conclude with a few comments about the extent to which economic arrangements may rely upon a system of markets in which prices are freely determined by supply and demand ... It is evident ... that there is no essential tie between the use of free markets and private ownership of the instruments of production ... While the notion that a market economy is in some sense the best scheme has been most carefully investigated by so-called bourgeois economists, this connection is a historical contingency in that, theoretically at least, a socialist regime can avail itself of the advantages of this system. One of these advantages is efficiency. Under certain conditions competitive prices select the goods to be produced and allocate resources to their production in such a manner that there is no way to improve upon either the choice of productive methods by firms, or the distribution of goods that arises from the purchases of households. There exists no rearrangement of the resulting economic configuration that makes one household better off (in view of its preferences) without making another worse off ...

A further and more significant advantage of a market system is that, given the requisite background institutions, it is consistent with equal liberties and fair equality of opportunity. Citizens have a free choice of careers and occupations. There is no reason at all for the forced and central direction of labor. Indeed, in the absence of some differences in earnings as these arise in a competitive scheme, it is hard to see how, under ordinary circumstances anyway, certain aspects of a command society inconsistent with liberty can be avoided ...

In noting the consistency of market arrangements which socialist institutions, it is essential to distinguish between the allocative and the distributive functions of prices. The former is connected with their use to achieve economic efficiency, the latter with their determining the income to be received by individuals in return for what they contribute ... Since under socialism the means of production and natural resources are publicly owned, the distributive function is greatly restricted, whereas a private-property system uses prices in varying degrees for both purposes. Which of these systems and the many intermediate forms most fully answers to the requirements of justice cannot, I think, be determined in advance. There is presumably no general answer to this question, since it depends in large part upon the traditions, institutions, and social forces of each country, and its particular historical circumtances ...

## Background institutions for distributive justice

The main problem of distributive justice is the choice of a social system. The principles of justice apply to the basic structure and regulate how its major institutions are combined into one scheme. Now, as we have seen, the idea of justice as fairness is to use the notion of pure procedural justice to handle the contingencies of particular situations. The social system is to be designed so that the resulting distribution is just however things turn out. To achieve this end it is necessary to set the social and economic process within the surroundings of suitable political and legal institutions. Without the proper arrangement of these background institutions the outcome of the distributive process will not be just. Background fairness is lacking. I shall give a brief description of these background institutions as they might exist in a properly organized democratic state that allows private ownership of capital and natural resources. These arrangements are familiar, but it may be useful to see how they fit the two principles of justice ...

First of all, I assume that the basic structure is regulated by a just constitution that secures the liberties of equal citizenship. Liberty of conscience and freedom of thought are taken for granted, and the fair value of political liberty is maintained. The political process is conducted, as far as circumstances permit, as a just procedure for choosing between governments and for enacting just legislation. I assume also that there is fair (as opposed to formal) equality of opportunity. This means that in addition to maintaining the usual kinds of social overhead capital, the government tries to insure equal chances of eduation and culture for persons similarly endowed and motivated either by subsidizing private schools or by establishing a public school system. It also enforces and underwrites equality of opportunity in economic activities and in the free choice of occupation. This is achieved by policing the conduct of firms and private associations and by preventing the establishment of monopolistic restrictions and barries to the more desirable positions. Finally, the government guarantees a social minimum either by family allowances and special payments for sickness and employment, or more systematically by such devices as a graded income supplement (a so-called negative income tax).

In establishing these background institutions the government may be thought of as divided into four branches. Each branch consists of various agencies, or activities thereof, charged with preserving certain social and economic conditions ... The allocation branch, for example, is to keep the price system workably competitive and to prevent the formation of unreasonable market power ... The allocation branch is also charged with identifying and correcting, say by suitable taxes and subsidies and by changes in the definition of property rights, the more obvious departures from efficiency caused by the failure of prices to measure accurately social benefits and costs ... The stabilization branch, on the other hand, strives to bring about reasonably full employment in the sense that those who want work can find it and the free choice of occupation and the deployment of finance is supported by strong effective demand. These two branches together are to maintain the efficiency of the market economy generally.

The social minimum is the responsibility of the transfer branch ... The essential idea is that the workings of this branch takes needs into account and assigns them an appropriate weight with respect to other claims. A competitive price system gives no consideration to needs and therefore it cannot be the sole device of distribution. There must be a division of labor between the parts of the social system in answering to the common sense precepts of justice. Different institutions meet different claims. Competitive markets properly regulated secure free choice of occupation and lead to an efficient use of resources and allocation of commodities to households. They set a weight on the conventional precepts associated with wages and earnings, whereas the transfer branch guarantees a certain level of well-being and honors the claims of need. ... Whether the principles of justice are satisfied, then, turns on whether the total income of the least advantaged (wages plus tranfers) is such as to maximize their long-run expectations (consistent with the constraints of equal liberty and fair equality of opportunity).

Finally, there is a distribution branch, Its task is to preserve an approximate justice in distributive shares by means of taxation and the necessary adjustments in the rights of property. Two aspects of this branch may be distinguished. First of all, it imposes a number of inheritance and gift taxes, and sets restrictions on the rights of bequest. The purpose of these levies and regulations is not to raise revenue (release resources to government) but gradually and continually to correct the distribution of wealth and to prevent concentrations of power detrimental to the fair value of political liberty and fair equality of opportunity. ... The unequal inheritance of wealth is no more inherently unjust than the unequal inheritance of intelligence. It is true that the former is presumably more easily subject to social control; but the essential thing is that as far as possible inequalities founded on either should satisfy the difference principle. Thus inheritance is permissible provided that the resulting inequalities are to the advantage of the least fortunate and compatible with liberty and fair equality of opportunity ...

I now wish to give the final statement of the two principles of justice for institutions ...

*First Principle*
   Each person is to have an equal right to the most extensive total system of equal basic liberties compatible with a similar system of liberty for all.
*Second Principle*
   Social and economic inequalities are to be arranged so that they are both:
      (a) to the greatest benefit of the least advantaged ... and
      (b) attached to offices and positions open to all under conditions of fair equality of opportunity.
*First Priority Rule* (The Priority of Liberty)
   The principles of justice are to be ranked in lexical order and therefore liberty can be restricted only for the sake of liberty. There are two cases:
      (a) a less extensive liberty must strengthen the total system of liberty shared by all;
      (b) a less than equal liberty must be acceptable to those with the lesser liberty.

*Second Priority Rule* (The Priority of Justice over Efficiency and Welfare)

> The second principle of justice is lexically prior to the principle of efficiency and to that of maximizing the sum of advantages; and fair opportunity is prior to the difference principle ...

The sketch of the system of institutions that satisfy the two principles of justice is now complete.

# 8

# Constitutional Contract and Continuing Contract

## JAMES BUCHANAN

### The Limits of Liberty

CONSTITUTIONAL CONTRACT: THE THEORY OF LAW
*(Chapter 4)*

Postconstitutional contract has occupied the primary attention of economists for the whole period of their independent disciplinary existence. Despite the concentration of effort on the exchange processes, major analytical complexities remain unresolved. What then may we anticipate when we try to conceptualize constitutional contract, that human interaction in which individual rights may be initially defined, where the very rules for interpersonal behavior may be established, where 'society', quite literally, replaces 'anarchy'? ... The temptation is strong to assert what is essentially the positivist position that a structure of law, a legal system, a set of property rights, exists and that there is relatively little point in trying to understand or to develop a contractual metaphor for its emergence that would offer assistance in finding criteria for social change ...

In order to discuss or to analyze possible criteria for modifying the structure of rights, however, some understanding of conceptual origins may be helpful. As has been suggested, the problem is one of trying to explain and to understand the relationships among individuals, and between individuals and the government. And for this purpose, various 'as if' models of conceptual origins may be necessary, regardless of the facts described in the historical records. Stress should be placed on 'explanation' and 'understanding' since

*Source:* Extracts reprinted by permission of University of Chicago Press from chapters 4 and 5 of J. M. Buchanan, *The Limits of Liberty* (University of Chicago Press, 1975), pp. 53–86.

the temptation to introduce normative statement becomes extremely strong at this level of discourse. Precisely because the conceptual origins are discussed independently of observable historical data, the distinction between positive analysis and normative presupposition is difficult to detect.

Must we postulate a basic equality among men in some original setting in order to derive the structure of a free society from rational, self-interested behavior? We have often answered this question affirmatively, even if implicitly. In the process, we have made our whole 'theory' of conceptual constitutional foundations highly vulnerable to positivist refutation. In this book, I am attempting to explain how 'law', 'the rights of property', 'rules for behavior', might emerge from the nonidealistic, self-interested behavior of men, without any presumption of equality in some original position — equality either actually or expectationally. In this effort, I make no claim to have escaped all normative influences. But I should argue that the approach taken is less normative than the familiar one which says, in effect, that any logical analysis of law *should* be based on the *as if* presumption of personal equality. We can substantially strengthen the foundations of freedom if we can succeed in demonstrating that, even among men who are unequal, a structure of legal rights can be predicted to emerge, a structure that retains characteristic elements that we associate with the precepts of individualism.

## Personal inequality

Consider, then, some initial setting in which men are not equals. Following economists' practice, we can discuss inequality in two separate attributes: (1) tastes or preferences, and (2) capacities. It is necessary to avoid explicit the tendency to slip exclusively into the familiar classification of persons by personal endowments of 'goods', presumably measured in commodity dimensions. This procedure amounts to neglecting the very problems addressed in this chapter, to presuming that individual rights to commodities, to goods, have already been defined.

In the fundamental sense required for the analysis here, an individual possesses no 'goods' or 'resources'. He can be defined initially by a preference or a utility function on the one hand and by a production function on the other. The preference or utility function describes the rates at which the person is willing subjectively to trade off goods (and bads) one against the other. The individual's production function is less familiar. He will have, inherent in his physiological makeup, a set of capacities (skills, talents, abilities). These capacities, when exercised in a specified environmental setting, define for the individual a potential relationship between inputs (negative goods or bads) and product (positive goods). This relationship is his 'production function'.

As noted, persons may differ from each other either in tastes, in capacities, or in both. Or, persons identical in both tastes and capacities may find themselves in environmentally different situations relative to their capacities ... The position attained by a person is dependent on three basic elements: his preferences, his capacities, and his environmental setting ...

## Anarchistic interaction

Consider two individuals who are wholly isolated from each other; each on his separate island with no social contact. Each man would attain a personal behavior equilibrium, as determined by the interaction among his utility function, his basic or inherent capacities to convert input into output, and the natural environmental setting that he confronts ...

This two-Crusoe world is, of course, purely anarchistic. There is no law, and there is no need for a definition of individuals' rights, either property rights or human rights. There is no society as such. Nonetheless, this two-Crusoe world provides a useful starting point from which to begin consideration of the world where personal conflict may emerge. Suppose that the persons, whom we shall name A and B, no longer exist in complete isolation, but that, instead, they now find themselves in some spatially limited area, on the same island. This change, in itself, need not modify the preferences of either person, although such an effect should not be ruled out. The environmental setting of each person will, however, almost surely be modified. In the absence of law, each person will now consider the other as a part of the environment that he faces. The effects of this upon the rate at which bads may be transformed into goods may take on several patterns.

In a world of scarcity, mutual exploitation of the natural environment insures that, for each person, the terms-of-trade with his own environment are worsened relative to those confronted in the isolated setting where one person, alone, faces this environment. In effect, the natural environment becomes 'common property', and the familiar reciprocal externality relationships emerge. Most economists would perhaps tend to stop the analysis at this point with little or no consideration of the remaining possibilities. But a second, and very different, sort of influence may operate. If production is not simultaneous with actual consumption of goods, individuals may store goods for future use. In this situation, the presence of B may prompt A to devote effort, a bad, to concealing hoards, and to defending and protecting these hoards from predation by B. Since this effort might otherwise have been used to produce goods directly, A's net rate of transformation is adversely affected by this necessity for defense.

An offsetting effect may, however, work in the other direction. Because of the presence of B, A now has available to himself a new opportunity. He may secure goods that were not available to him in the strict Crusoe setting. If B is known to be producing, and storing, goods, A may find that locating and taking these stocks from B is more productive than producing similar goods on his own. This effect, if it should predominate, tends to shift A's production function in a favorable manner. Once the prospects for defense and predation are recognized, it is clear that individuals may differ in their talents for these activities and that such differences need not be directly correspondent to their relative capacities as direct producers. Furthermore, individuals may differ in their tastes for defense-predation efforts relative to direct production efforts . . .

This sort of interaction may be analyzed in externality terms, even if we are working with a model without law and rights of property. It is useful to think of the reciprocal external diseconomy model in which each person's behavior imposes harm on the other. Consider, first, the behavior of A in producing goods in the environment that is shared, but without overt dispute. That is to say, let us postulate initially that A and B allow each other to attain private adjustment independently of disturbance. Each man uses his talents as best he can to maximize utility on the assumption that the other will not take stocks from him and that he, in turn, will not take stocks from the other. This is strictly an arbitrary starting point, and it will not represent a final equilibrium in the interaction sequence . . . Note that, at this position, A and B need not have equal quantities of the good, nor need they be accepting equal quantities of the bad to secure the position indicated . . .

This arbitrary starting point does not qualify for a behavioral equilibrium because, in this position, each person has some incentive to initiate conflict, to engage in predatory activity . . . Equilibrium [is the] point [at which] neither person has an incentive to modify his behavior privately or independently. In this equilibrium, each person may be expending some share of his efforts in defending his stocks from the other, another part in taking stocks of the other, and another part in producing goods directly. The position of independent adjustment equilibrium describes the outcome or result that could be predicted in a genuinely anarchistic order. The distribution has been called the 'natural distribution' by Winston Bush, and the two-person model may, of course, be extended to apply in a many-person setting.

I have emphasized in several places that there is no presumption of equality among persons in this independent adjustment or natural equilibrium. A second important principle is that this position cannot itself be attained contractually. Until this natural equilibrium is itself attained, there is no basis from which persons can negotiate contracts, one with another. The generation of this independent adjustment equilibrium is, therefore, the precontractual stage of social order, if indeed we can use the word 'social' at all here ...

## Disarmament and the emergence of property rights

In natural equilibrium, each person uses resources to defend against and to attack other persons. Each person would be better off if some of these resources could somehow be turned to the direct production of goods. The most basic contractual agreement among persons should, therefore, be the mutual acceptance of some disarmament. The mutual gains should be apparent to all parties ...

Positions that embody mutual gains must involve lower outlay on defense-predation for both parties. Suppose that such an agreement is reached ... Note precisely what this agreement embodies. The contract is one of bilateral behavioral exchange. Individual A agrees to give up some share of his own defense-predation effort in exchange for a related behavioral change on the part of Individual B. There is no incentive for either person to take this behavioral change unilaterally, and there is nothing in the initial agreement, as such, which requires or even induces any acceptance by the other of the legitimacy of either person's command over goods, either in the preagreement or postagreement stage. Mutual acceptance of 'ownership rights' is not a part of this preliminary disarmament agreement. On the other hand, by negotiating such an initial agreement to limit defense and predation, 'law' of a sort has now emerged. The two persons accept limits to their own freedom of action, to their own liberty. The first leap out of the anarchistic jungle has been taken.

## Conquest, slavery, and contract

In the discussion of anarchistic interaction to this point, I have assumed implicitly that all persons will exist as independently acting defenders and predators both prior to and after a natural equilibrium is attained. If personal differences are sufficiently great, however, some persons may have the capacities to eliminate others of the species. In this instance, the natural equilibrium may be reached only when the survivors exercise exclusive environmental domain.

The complete elimination of other persons may not, however, be the most preferred course of action by those who possess superior capacities. Even more desired might be the state in which those who are 'weak' are allowed to exert effort in producing goods, after which the 'strong' seize all, or substantially all, of these for their own use. From this setting, the disarmament contract that may be negotiated may be something similar to the slave contract, in which the 'weak' agree to produce goods for the 'strong' in exchange for being allowed to retain something over and above bare subsistence, which they may be unable to secure in the anarchistic setting. A contract of slavery would, as other contracts, define individual rights, and, to the extent that this assignment is mutually accepted, mutual gains may be secured from the consequent reduction in defense and predation effort. This may seem to represent a somewhat tortuous interpretation of slavery as an institution, but it is explicitly designed to allow the analytical framework developed here to be fully general.

## Trading equilibrium and direct production

The underlying postulates [of the argument] do nothing toward insuring that a final post-trade position where all gains are exhausted will be coincident with ... the allocation or result that would obtain in the absence of all defense and predation effort. This direct-production position, in which each person retains for his own use those goods that he himself produces, given his own capacities, his tastes, and his environmental situation, may or may not be Pareto-superior to the natural equilibrium ...

The relationship between the position of equilibrium attained in the absence of law, and the ... position attained when each man keeps all that he produces, is important because of the dominant role that has been assigned to the latter in the historical discussions of property rights, notably those discussions in the natural-law tradition, and especially as represented in the theory of John Locke. In the conceptual origins of contract that have been developed here, there is no fundamental distinction between the position which allows persons to retain goods privately produced and any other position. The only distinguishable position, prior to contract, is ... the natural equilibrium (E).

If the direct-production position is Pareto-superior to E, by which we mean only that both parties secure higher utility levels in the former position than in the latter, there may well be a strong attraction toward settling the negotiations at this point ... An agreement to eliminate all predatory behavior might be a plausible outcome under this setting, in which case each person's production from the natural environment that he confronts becomes his 'property' in some positive sense. The law might begin to take on positive features in a manner akin to that rationalized by John Locke.

The predominant role that has been assigned to the direct-production position may be based on the implicit assumption of natural equality among men. If we allow interpersonal differences to exist in the natural state, however, there is no assurance that the position attained in the anarchistic equilibrium is Pareto-inferior to the direct-production position ... At least one of the two persons may be better off, in utility terms, in anarchistic equilibrium than he would be if required to depend exclusively on his own production efforts (as in the slavery example noted). This outcome might emerge if the two persons were widely different in the ability to produce goods, either from a difference in natural capacities or from a difference in environmental situations. Also, such an outcome might arise if one person retains moral inhibitions against predation while the other does not, or even if one person values liberty of action so highly that he willingly sacrifices protection of goods produced.

When the direct-production position is not Pareto-superior to E, positive property rights to goods directly produced will not emerge from conceptual contractual agreement. Something other than an agreement on mutual limits to behavior is required to leap from the Hobbesian jungle in this case. Such an agreement on limits must be accompanied by a transfer of goods or endowments

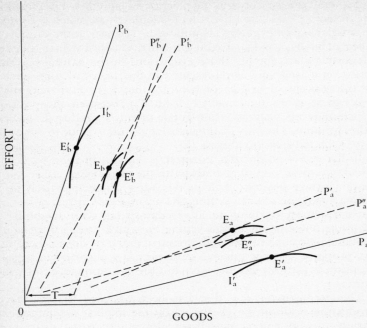

EFFORT

0

GOODS

*Figure* 8.1

before a contractual settlement can be reached, and property rights positively established.

This may be illustrated with a ... geometric construction ... In figure 8.1, effort is measured along the ordinate, and goods along the abscissa. Individual A is either favorably situated or is more capable of producing goods than individual B. The production function for A, if he is not interfered with by B, is shown by the curve $P_a$, which lies along the abscissa for an initial range, indicating that A can secure some goods without an outlay of effort. Individual B, by contrast, faces a much more unfavorable direct-production prospect. In the absence of all interference from A, he faces the production function shown by $P_b$. The direct-production position ... is attained when A attains point $E_a'$ and when B attains point $E_b'$. In the situation where no rights of property are assigned, B may well find that his most productive expenditure of effort lies in predation, in stealing goods that are produced by A. If A undertakes no defense or protection effort, the anarchistic production function faced by B might be like that depicted by $P_b'$, along which B would move to position $E_b$. This activity on the part of B would, of course, modify the situation faced by A. He would, privately, face the production function shown by $P_a'$, if he undertakes no responsive action. In order to illustrate the relevant relationships in a diagram like figure 8.1, we shall assume that A does not find it advantageous to respond to B's predation. A's new equilibrium position would be that shown at $E_a$. Since we have assumed that A undertakes no defense or protection efforts, his actual production function is not modified, but he is producing a portion of his goods for B. The anarchistic equilibrium is that position indicated by the two points $E_b$ and $E_a$ in figure 8.1. It is clear that, for B, this is a more favorable situation than that which he attains when property rights are assigned in goods that are directly produced. Hence, B would never agree to the direct-production position. Contractual arrangements must include something over and beyond limits to behavior. In this setting, A might achieve B's agreement to respect an assignment of rights to goods that are produced privately or independently if he transfers to B some initial quantity of goods or endowments. One such transfer can be depicted on figure 8.1 by the amount T, as indicated. If this is transferred to B, his direct production function shifts to $P_b''$, and his attainable private production equilibrium to $E_b''$, which is on a higher utility level than $E_b$. The production function for A is shifted leftward by the initial transfer, to that shown by $P_a''$, but the attainable equilibrium along this function at $E_a''$ is superior in utility terms to $E_a$, the anarchistic result. Upon this transfer, B will agree to respect the assigned own-product of A and A will agree to similarly respect the assigned own-product of B. Positive rights may be established, once the initial transfer has taken place to bring the parties into a setting where the direct-production assignment is, in fact, Pareto-superior to anarchistic equilibrium.

Despite the extremely simple and abstract nature of the geometrical models presented, the conclusions are significant for an understanding of the conceptual emergence of individual rights. The analysis demonstrates that there is no necessary basis for any initial agreement that will simply acknowledge the rights of persons to retain those stocks of goods that they can wrest from the natural environment by their own labor ... To secure an initial agreement on positive claims to goods or to resource endowments, some transfer of goods or endowments may be required. That is to say, some 'redistribution' of goods or endowments may have to take place before a sufficiently acceptable base for property claims can be established. As the simple two-person model indicates, there may be many such redistributions that will meet the minimal requirements. Once any of these transfers takes place, if one is required, and/or behavioral limits are mutually accepted, positive rights of persons in stocks of goods or in resource endowments capable of producing goods may be settled. From this base, trades and exchanges in the postconstitutional stage ... can be implemented. These trades may, in utility terms, shift all persons to positions that overwhelmingly dominate either the natural equilibrium in anarchy or that distribution of goods and endowments that is settled on the initial establishment of positive individual rights.

## Defection and enforcement

To this point, attention has been concentrated on the conceptual bases for the formation of an initial social contract. The analysis has been aimed at isolating and identifying the mutuality of gain to be secured from a primal disarmament agreement accompanied, if necessary, by some unilateral transfers of goods or endowments. In this initial inclusive contract, all parties gain from the potential elimination of socially wasteful outlays on defense and predation. At the immediate postcontract stage, persons claim positive rights in stocks of goods, in resource endowments, and in specific spheres of activity. To this point, we have implicitly assumed that the set of rights agreed to will be respected by all participants.

This assumption cannot, of course, be justified. Even at this most elementary level of examination, the problem of enforcing contractual agreements must be introduced. Straightforward utility maximization will lead each person to defect on his contractual obligation if he expects to be able to accomplish this unilaterally. This may be illustrated in figure 8.2, which presents a two-by-two matrix for the two-person example. We are interested only in the net payoffs received by each of the two parties, A and B, in each of two possible positions. Each party has two behavioral options; he may keep his agreement, which amounts to respecting the defined rights of the other person. This is the action indicated by the 0 row and column of the matrix. Or, alternatively, each person may abide by no agreement and act strictly in narrow self-

|  |  | B | |
|---|---|---|---|
|  |  | Respects Rights 0 | Respects No Rights V |
| A | Respects Rights 0 | Cell I 19, 7 | Cell II 3, 11 |
|  | Respects No Rights V | Cell III 22, 1 | Cell IV 9, 2 |

*Figure 8.2*

interest. This option is defined by the V row and column. If both persons take the V option, and refuse to abide by contracts made, the result is equivalent to that which was described earlier as the natural anarchistic equilibrium. If both persons respect the terms of contract, both are better off, and the 00 result in figure 8.2 represents the contractually agreed-on set of rights discussed earlier.

The numbers in the cells are utility indicators for the two persons, with the left-hand numbers indicating utility levels attainable for A, the right-hand numbers those attainable by B. As the numbers indicate, each person has an incentive to defect on the agreement provided that he expects to be able to do so unilaterally. If A defects, while B respects A's rights, the result is in Cell III, which is the most preferred of all positions shown for A. Similarly, if B defects, while A respects B's rights, a Cell II result emerges, which is the most favorable of all positions for B. The situation is analogous to the classical prisoner's dilemma in game theory. Any positive structure of rights is, therefore, extremely vulnerable to defection if continued adherence to the contractual basis depends on voluntary and independent 'law-abiding'. In our illustration, A can obtain three units of utility by defaulting unilaterally from the result in Cell I; Individual B can gain four units by defaulting unilaterally and securing a result in Cell II And if both persons defect, the system lapses back into a Cell IV outcome, and ultimately to the anarchistic equilibrium discussed.

In the simplified two-person interaction illustrated, however, it is surely plausible to suggest that rationality precepts will direct each person to adhere to the initial contractual terms. Each person will recognize that unilateral defection cannot succeed and that any attempt to accomplish this would plunge the system back into a position that is less desirable for everyone than that which is attained upon adherence to contract. As the payoffs or utility indicators in figure 8.2 suggest, neither A nor B would allow the other person to defect and get away with it. Once a defection has occurred, the other party can improve his own position by bringing the system back to the Cell IV position.

It is important to recognize explicitly the behavioral motivation that lends stability to the contractual solution in the two-person setting. Each person may respect the agreed-on assignment because he predicts that defection on his part will generate parallel behavior by the other party. Each person realizes that his own behavior influences the subsequent behavior of the other person and does so directly.

It is precisely this aspect of the interaction that is modified, in kind, as we shift from a two-person to a many-person setting. As more parties are added to the initial contractual agreement, in which an assignment of rights is settled, the influence of any one person's behavior on that of others becomes less and less. As an element inhibiting individual defections on an initial contract, this influence tends to disappear completely after some critical group size is reached. In large-number groups, each individual rationally acts as if his own behavior does not influence the behavior of others. He treats others' behavior as a part of his natural environment, and he adjusts his behavior accordingly. In this large-number setting, man ceases to be a 'social animal' at least in this explicit behavioral sense. This setting remains analogous to an n-person prisoners' dilemma, but it is one in which fully voluntary compliance with contract, or law in any form, cannot be predicted. Each person has a rational incentive to default; hence, many persons can be predicted to default and the whole agreement becomes void unless the conditions of individual choice are somehow modified.

This relationship between voluntary adherence to mutually-accepted rules of social interaction, whether these be ethical standards or property-rights assignments, and the size of the interacting group is familiar, but it does have specific relevance to our analysis here. The problem of enforcing any original contract becomes more difficult in large than in small groups. Any set of property rights, any legal structure, becomes more vulnerable to violation, and hence requires more than proportionate outlay on enforcement in large than in small. In respect to the conceptual origins of law and contract, this relationship alone suggests that contractual or quasi-contractual arrangements commence among individuals (families) that are involved in relatively small-number settings, with movement toward more inclusive contractual order taking the form of arrangements among smaller groups. These complexities are important, but they need not occupy our attention here.

If individual parties to an initial contract in which property assignments are established mutually acknowledge the presence of incentives for each participant to default and, hence, recognize the absence of viability in any scheme that requires dependence on voluntary compliance, they will, at the time of contract, enter into some sort of enforcement arrangement. Individuals' claims to stocks of goods and endowments will be accompanied by some enforcement institution that will be aimed to secure such claims. The nature of this enforcement contract or institution must be carefully examined. Each person will receive some benefit from the assurance that his established claims will be honored by others in the community. And there are mutual gains to all parties from engaging in some joint or collectivized enforcement effort. Enforcement of property claims, of individuals' rights to carry out designated activities, qualifies as a 'public good' in the modern sense of this term.

Enforcement is, however, different from the more familiar examples of public goods in several essential respects. In order to be effective, enforcement must include the imposition of physical constraints on those who violate or attempt to violate the rights structure, on those who break the law. It is this characteristic that creates problems. There is no obvious and effective means through which the enforcing institution or agent can itself be constrained in its own behavior. Hence, as Hobbes so perceptively noted more than three centuries ago, individuals who contract for the services of enforcing institutions necessarily surrender their own independence.

Consider, say, a hundred-man community. In the absence of enforcement, let us say that B violates the contract that settles all property claims. He does so by stealing goods from or by interfering with the designated personal liberties of A. The latter will, of course have some incentive to react privately by a counterattack on B. But if this becomes the general pattern of behavior, the system rapidly degenerates toward the precontractual position of anarchistic equilibrium. Individuals C, D, E, . . ., however, have no direct interest in punishing B for stealing from or interfering with A. They have an indirect interest insofar as such punishment makes their own claims more secure, but unless they make such a connection in their own conception of enforcement, they may be reluctant to approve particularized punishment. This problem may be handled by an agreement by all persons on the purchase of the services of some external enforcing agent or institution that will, in all particular cases, take the enforcing-punishment action required. The 'public good' is the generalized security of rights or claims, and not the particular enforcement action which produces this security.

In an idealized sense, the enforcing institution is necessarily external to the parties that reach agreement in the initial contract. The analogy to a simple game may be helpful. Two boys mutually acknowledge some division of marbles between them, and they seek to play a game. Each boy may know, however, that his opponent will have a strong incentive to cheat unless he is closely monitored. They agree and appoint a referee or umpire, inform him about the specific rules under which they choose to play, and ask that he enforce adherence to these designated rules. This is precisely the functional role assigned to the state in its law-enforcement task. The state becomes the institutionalized embodiment of the referee or umpire, and its only role is that of insuring that contractual terms are honored.

This analogy exposes a recurrent fallacy in many discussions of property rights and of the role of the state in enforcing these rights. Enforcement of claims is categorically different from defining these claims in the first place. Claims are conceptually agreed upon by all parties in the constitutional stage of social contract. The state is then called upon to monitor these claims, to serve as an enforcing institution, to insure that contractual commitments are honored. To say that rights are defined by the state is equivalent to saying that the referee and not the players chooses both the initial division of the marbles and the rules of the game itself.

## The protective state and the productive state

The distinction between the constitutional and the postconsti-tutional stages of social contract allows us to interpret the state, the collective agency of the community, in two separate roles. Failure to keep these roles distinct, in theory or in practice, has produced and continues to produce major confusion. At the constitutional stage, the state emerges as the enforcing agency or institution, conceptually external to the contracting parties and charged with the single responsibility of enforcing agreed-on rights

and claims along with contracts which involve voluntarily negotiated exchanges of such claims. In this 'protective' role, the state
is not involved in producing 'good' or 'justice', as such, other than
that which is embodied indirectly through a regime of contract
enforcement ...

This legal or protective state, the institutions of 'law' broadly
interpreted, is not a decision-making body. It has no legislating
function, and it is not properly represented by legislative institutions.
This state does not incorporate the process through which persons
in the community choose collectively rather than privately or
independently. The latter characterizes the functioning of the
conceptually separate productive state, that agency through which
individuals provide themselves with 'public goods' in postconstitutional contract. In this latter context, collective action is best
viewed as a complex exchange process with participation among
all members of the community. This process is appropriately represented by legislative bodies and the decision-making, choosing
process is appropriately called 'legislation'. By sharp contrast, the
protective state which carries out the enforcement task assigned to
it in constitutional contract makes no 'choices' in the strict meaning
of this term. Ideally or conceptually, enforcement might be
mechanically programmed in advance of law violation. The participants agree on a structure of individual rights or claims that is to
be enforced, and violation requires only the findings of fact and
the automatic administration of sanctions. A contract or a right is
or is not violated; this is the determination to be made by 'the
law' ... Properly interpreted, 'the law' which is enforced is that
which is specified to be enforced in the initial contract, whatever
this might be ... As noted, 'the law' steps beyond the bounds of
propriety when it seeks, and explicitly, to redefine individual
rights ...

## Rules as indirect rights

To this point in the discussion of constitutional contract, we have
assumed that agreement is reached on the limits to behavioral
interaction and on the positive set of claims to endowments of
goods, accompanied by some enforcement contract with the protective state. In an all-private goods world, this would be the end
of it. Trades and exchanges among persons in postconstitutional
stages would more or less naturally emerge. However, when we
allow for the presence of jointly shared collective or public goods

and services, the collectivity as the productive state and its rules for operation must be taken into account. The political constitution, which in our context is only one aspect of the broader constitutional contract, becomes important here, and the rules for making collective decisions concerning the provision and the cost-sharing of public goods must, themselves, be settled at the ultimate constitutional stage of negotiation. It would be of relatively little moment to define an individual's nominal claims to goods only to leave these claims fully vulnerable to unconstrained political exploitation.

An earlier work, *The Calculus of Consent*, written jointly with Gordon Tullock, was devoted largely to an analysis of the constitutional choice among rules for making collective decisions ... The present analysis differs from *The Calculus of Consent* in this fundamental respect; here I am trying to analyze the initial contract that assigns rights and claims among persons. This difference allows collective decision rules to be interpreted in a somewhat modified setting, namely, as an integral part of a more inclusive contract rather than a strictly political constitution superimposed on some previously negotiated settlement. In the earlier book, we argued that the criterion of acceptability or efficiency lay in agreement, in unanimity ... When we recognize that the rules for collective decision-making at the postconstitutional stage are also to be settled as a part of the initial contract, we have available ... another dimension for adjustment.

Consider the calculus of an individual whose position in anarchistic equilibrium is not significantly worse than that which he expects to secure under a simple disarmament agreement. When he also recognizes the problems of enforcement, including those which involve constraining the enforcing agent, this individual may be quite reluctant to enter into the basic social contract at all. Suppose, however, that one of the many clauses in a proffered contractual settlement states that 'public goods' are to be financed by progressive income taxes, and that the person in question has either higher-than-average expected demands for public goods or lower-than-average income-wealth expectations. This proposed part of the larger social contract now represents, for this person, a positive supplement to the set of claims that he might otherwise secure from the unamended disarmament agreement. The collective decision rules present him with something akin to additional 'rights' and upon which he may place a positive value. He may be motivated to enter into the constitutional contract under such conditions, even without a unilateral transfer of goods, although this would be an alternative means of making the proposal attractive to him.

## The constitutional mix

The inclusive constitutional contract embodies elements that may appear in alternative combinations or mixes. The terms must include, first of all, some statement of limits on the behavior of any person with respect to the positions of other persons in the community. This element was referred to earlier in this chapter as the disarmament contract. As they enter genuine society from anarchy, persons lay down their arms; they accept rules governing their own behavior in exchange for the like acceptance of such rules on the part of others. Secondly, the basic contract must define the positive rights of possession or domain over stocks of goods, or more generally, over resource endowments capable of producing final goods. These endowments include human capacities (the rights to one's own person which have been widely discussed in the theory of property), as well as nonhuman factors, including domain over territory. These ownership rights or claims may simply reflect the pattern of possession established directly when interpersonal interferences are eliminated, which we have called the direct-production imputation, but, as the analysis disclosed, certain 'exchanges' of resource endowments or goods and behavioral constraints may be necessary before clearly acknowledged ownership imputations are possible. Along with the limits on behavior and the rights of ownership, the inclusive constitutional contract must also make explicit the terms and conditions of enforcement. This set of terms will specify in detail the operation and limits of the protective state that is established as the enforcing agent. Finally, the basic contract must define the rules under which the collectivity must operate in making and in implementing decisions concerning the provision and financing of 'public goods'. This set of terms will specify in detail the operation and the limits of the productive state, the legislative aspect of collective organization. The rules and institutions of this productive state may, in themselves, incorporate several dimensions. The contract should indicate the allowable range over which collective action may take place. That is to say, some restrictions on the type of goods to be provided and financed collectively must be included. At least in some rough sense, the dividing line between the private and the public or governmental sector of the economy should be settled in the basic constitution. Within these defined limits, allowable departures from unanimity in reaching collective decision should be specified. Such departures need not, of course, be uniform over all decisions. Institutions for cost-sharing, that is, tax institutions, may also be imbedded in the inclusive constitutional structure.

It is not my purpose here to develop criteria for efficiency in constitutional contract in any specific setting. The mix among the various elements in this inclusive settlement will be functionally related to several identifiable characteristics of the community of individuals. This will include the size of the membership itself as well as the environmental setting. The features of the anarchistic natural equilibrium, whether or not this is ever actually realized, will influence the relative positions of individuals and groups in the final constitutional settlement. The degree as well as the distribution of the inequalities among persons will be important in this respect. Individuals may differ, and may be thought to differ, in relative capacities to produce goods and to secure gains by predation on their fellows. These differences, along with differences in individuals' tastes for productive and predatory activities, will have predictable effects on the initial settlement. Expectations about demands for publicly provided goods and services along with expectations about relative income and wealth levels will also affect individuals' willingness to accept rules for collective action.

The most significant point that emerges from this very general discussion is the interdependence among the several elements in the constitutional mix. Contrary to orthodox economic methodology, the rights of persons to property, the rights to do things privately and individually with physical resources, cannot be treated in isolation from those rights which are indirectly represented by membership in a collectivity that is constitutionally empowered to make decisions under predetermined rules. Consider, for example, the position of a person who holds nominal ownership rights to an income stream from a scarce and highly-valued resource (human or nonhuman). This private ownership claim may be tempered by the membership rights in the collectivity, the governmental institutions of the community, that are held by others persons, membership rights that may offer other persons some indirect claims on the differentially higher income stream in question ...

This approach allows us to look somewhat differently and in a positive manner at the perplexing issue of income-wealth redistribution. Under certain constitutional structures, those persons who are relatively 'poor' do not properly claim, on the basis of overriding ethical norms, a share in the economic returns or assets of those who are relatively 'rich'. They *may* claim some such share indirectly on the basis of commonly held membership in collectively-organized community under specified constitutional contract. The relatively 'rich', in their turn, may legitimately expect their 'private rights' to be respected and honored, and violations of these rights enforced, only as a component part of the more inclusive contractual arrangement which predictably requires that they pay differentially higher shares in those goods and services provided jointly for the whole community. In this larger and more inclusive contract, all individuals and groups should find it advantageous to adhere to the rules established, to respect the claims as tempered, and to conduct themselves in such fashion as to attain maximum individual liberty within the constraints of acceptable order.

CONTINUING CONTRACT AND THE STATUS QUO<br>*(Chapter 5)*

## The ethics and economics of contractual obligation

One of the continuing criticisms of any contract theory of social order is closely related to the timeless attribute of the model. As noted earlier, many critics have opposed the contractarian explanation on the grounds that, historically and empirically, no formal contracting among individuals was observed to take place. More important, they have suggested that, even if some such original compact might have taken place historically, there is nothing which binds men who did not themselves participate in the contractual settlement, nothing that binds them to honor commitments which they could not personally have made.

This is an important and relevant criticism of a contractarian argument that has essentially ethical foundations, and which seeks to locate the legitimacy of social order in implicit contract. Contractual obligation, expressed by the willingness of individuals to behave in accordance with specified terms, depends critically on explicit or imagined participation. Individuals, having 'given their word' are 'honor bound' to live up to the terms. This remains true even if, subsequent to agreement, these terms come to be viewed as 'unfair' or 'unjust'. Defection or violation runs counter to widely accepted moral codes for personal behavior. When existing rules for social and political order, including the definition of individual rights, are simply inherited from the past, no such moral sanctions may be present.

This is the setting descriptive of the real world, and the question must be asked: Why will persons voluntarily comply with the rules and institutions of order that are in being? ... Under what conditions are individuals most likely to adhere to the inherited rules of order, most likely to respect and to honor the assignment of individual rights in being?

This question can only be answered through an evaluation of

the existing structure, *as if* it were the outcome of a current contract, or one that is continuously negotiated. Individuals must ask themselves how their own positions compare with those that they might have expected to secure in a renegotiated contractual settlement. If they accept that their defined positions fall within the limits, they are more likely to comply with existing rules, even in the acknowledged absence of any historical participation. This approach offers a means of evaluating social rules, legal structure, and property rights. But one point needs to be made in passing. That set of rights which might be widely accepted as being within the limits of what we may call here the 'renegotiation expectations' of individuals will not be uniform over communities and over time. As the [earlier] analysis demonstrated, the contractual terms, including the mix among the several elements in the constitution, will depend directly on the personal differences that exist in fact or that are thought to exist. The degree and distribution of these differences will not be uniform as among separate groups. This suggests that there can be no resort to idealized general standards through which a legal or constitutional structure in a particular community at a particular stage of historical development might be judged. At best, an observer can make some inferences about existing institutions from his assessment of the behavior of individuals living under them ...

In recognition of individual motivation for defection, any legal structure will include rules for enforcement and for punishment of violators. On strictly economic grounds, there is no a priori reason why an individual would defect more quickly from rules and institutions that do not fall within his reasonable renegotiation expectations set than from those that do. Even for the person whose assigned rights in the status quo seem to be more favorable than he could reasonably expect to secure in a genuinely renegotiated settlement, the incentive to violate law is present, provided he expects to be able to accomplish this unilaterally and to escape punishment. Again, in a strictly economic calculus, whether a person will violate the terms of existing contract, whether he will abide by the set of legal rules, institutions, and rights in being, will depend on his assessment of the probability of and the severity of punishment rendered by the enforcing agent. This expected value is directly dependent on the willingness of the community, acting through the protective state, to make commitments to enforcement and punishment. These commitments, in their turn, are functionally related to the levels of voluntary compliance predicted. And, as noted, these levels will depend on the strength of ethical constraints on individual behavior. Through this sort of causal linkage, we can trace the relationship between enforcement and the 'distance' of the status quo from the set of 'renegotiation expectations'.

Consider an example. Suppose that there is, in fact, an initial contractual settlement, and that only nominal violations are predicted to occur in early periods of the agreement. For a given resource outlay on enforcement, a specific degree of adherence to contractual terms is guaranteed. For purposes of illustrations, say that only .001 percent of all behavior is explicitly violative of agreed-on rights. Time passes, and the structure of rights is not modified. But sons inherit fathers' positions in the community, and sons no longer feel themselves ethically committed to the initial contractual terms. More important, the existing rules may not be within the set of renegotiation expectations of at least some members of the second generation. For both of these reasons, more sons than fathers will respond to the strictly economic motivations for default. With the *same* enforcement, therefore, we should expect to find that the percentage of behavior that is violative of 'social contract' rises to, say, .01 percent. That is to say, more persons will 'break the law' unless it remains in their strictly economic interest not to do so.

There are two ways that the community might respond to an increasing 'distance' between the status quo and the set of renegotiation expectations for a large number of its members. It may, first of all, increase resource commitments to enforcement, along with the accompanying moral commitments required, thereby making departures from the set of rights defined in the status quo more costly to potential violators. Second, the community may attempt to renegotiate the basic agreement, the constitutional contract itself, so as to bring this distance back to acceptable limits. The first alternative may be extremely difficult to implement, and, indeed, there may well be pressures for reducing rather than increasing enforcement-punishment commitments. In practice, the only alternative may be that of attempting to renegotiate the basic constitutional contract, at least along some of the margins of possible adjustment. Before such renegotiations can be discussed, however, we need to define the status quo more clearly ...

## Prior violations and the status quo

What justifies the status quo when an original contract may never have been made, when current members of the community sense

no moral or ethical obligation to adhere to the terms that are
defined in the status quo, and, what is important, when such a
contract, if it ever existed, may have been violated many times
over, both by the government and by individuals and groups that
may have succeeded in evading proper punishment? Does the
presence of any one or all of these negations remove legitimacy
from the status quo?

Again it is necessary to repeat the obvious. The status quo
defines that which exists. Hence, regardless of its history, it must
be evaluated as if it were legitimate contractually. Things 'might
have been' different in history, but things are now as they are. The
fact that government may have violated implicit terms excessively
and repeatedly does nothing toward modifying the uniqueness of
the status quo . . .

Evaluation of the status quo as if it were legitimate may yield
results in either direction. The set of rights in existence at any
point in time may or may not deserve the putative legitimacy that
it claims. If it does not, or more correctly, if there are aspects of
this set that do not, there should exist means of adjustment which
could be agreed on by all or substantially all of the members of
the community. Adjustment that must be imposed coercively can
scarcely represent in itself a restoration of 'legitimacy' in any
genuine meaning of the term. This sort of change would, instead,
amount to still further violation of the implied contract.

Consider a situation where, due either to a change in the relative
capacities of persons or to explicit past violations of an agreed-on
set of terms, the status quo has come to define a set of individual
rights that are clearly inconsistent with the renegotiation expectations of a large majority of the community's membership. That
is to say, the relative positions of persons cannot, through any
stretch of the imagination, be reflective of the relative positions
that might be attainable after a detour into anarchy and out again
into a new constitutional contract. In this case, it should be rational
for those who seem differentially favored in the status quo to
accept reductions in the measured value of their assigned rights. If
they do so, constitutional change can emerge through agreement,
as previously discussed.

Those who are or may be differentially favored in the status quo
may not, however, accept this as the rational course of action.
Especially if they can control the activities of the enforcing agent,
the government, they may consider their relatively advantageous
positions invulnerable. They may be unconcerned about the alleged
illegitimacy of the structure of individual rights in existence. It is

this sort of setting that invites breakdown into disordered anarchy or revolution with a potentially new natural equilibrium in the offing followed by some new constitutional order. ... Agreed-on and quasi-contractual readjustment offers the only effective alternative to such progressive deterioration in legal order, to continued violations of the implied contract by government and by individuals alike, to accelerated decline in the legitimacy of the whole constitutional structure, to general reduction in the stability and predictability inherent in the ordinary operation of the legal-political environment.

Insofar as they have discussed changes in status-quo imputations of individual rights, political economists have probably confused the issues. With only a few exceptions, political economists, along with other social scientists and social philosophers, have been unwilling to search for and to analyze the potential opportunities for voluntary or contractual changes in the constitutional order. Instead they have felt themselves obligated to propose changes that are derived from external ethical criteria, changes that are presumably to be imposed on the existing structure. This sort of discussion has tended to distract effort and attention from the less romantic but more productive approach involved in working out possible compromise modifications that would be agreeable to large numbers of persons in the community.

# 9

# The Balance between Rights Individually Held and Rights Collectively Held

JAMES S. COLEMAN

Robert Nozick has written a book[1] which, like that of John Rawls before him, has excited the attention and intense interest of non-philosophers. This is an unusual situation for moral philosophers to find themselves in, and it is useful to ask why the sudden interest and attention. Moral philosophy has addressed two funda-mentally different kinds of questions. One is the question of what actions are moral: what kind of criterion can one use to judge the morality of an action. The Golden Rule is one such moral principle for action; Kant's Categorical Imperative is another. The second question, however, is at a completely different level than the first. It asks what is a moral, or just *society*. Thus, the second question is not concerned with individual actions, but social policy and the nature of the state.

When moral philosophy confines itself to the first question, those ordinary persons not enmeshed in philosophical debate are unlikely to be roused into defense of or attack upon the new principle. However, when moral philosophy addresses the second question, it is not merely offering to the ordinary person a criterion by which he can judge his own action. It is also offering a prescrip-tion which, if it is accepted and put into practice by others, affects the organization of society and of the state within which the ordinary person must live. When the principle advanced concerns the rights that various parties have to portions of individual or social products, the social acceptance of those theories is of direct and central interest to the ordinary person. He is no longer indiffer-

This review article is reproduced by permission of the author and *Arizona Law Review* from James S. Coleman, 'The Balance between Rights Indi-vidually Held and Rights Collectively Held', *Arizona Law Review*, 19 (1977), pp. 180−92. Copyright © 1977 by the Arizona Board of Regents.

ent to the reaction of others to the principle, for their reactions may affect him. Moral philosophy has moved out of the closet, and into the arena of political philosophy and political debate.

Basically, Nozick's book concerns the question of the kind of a state, if any, to which rational self-interested men, endowed with a set of natural rights, will agree. However, the central portion of the book addresses itself to the question of what constitutes justice, and how a just society is derived. Nozick here enters the broad political debate on distributive justice and inequality, or, rather, the balance between equality and liberty, which has recently occupied the attention of philosophers as well as social scientists. It is this portion of Nozick's work that I intend to examine.

Nozick fastens upon John Rawls as a prototype of an 'end-result' theorist of distributive justice, who evaluates the justice of a social system on the basis of the distribution of desired goods among its members. Nozick places 'historical' theories in opposition to the end-result theories. A 'historical' theory bases justice not on any distribution, but on the justice of the process by which such a distribution came about.[2] Nozick thus arrives at his own theory, an entitlement theory, which he outlines only skeletally, in which each person is entitled to what he acquires so long as it is acquired through a just process.

Nozick argues, in opposition to the end-result theorists, that any rational self-interested person will not choose to have a portion of his product expropriated and redistributed to others. Such an argument would have no force against the utilitarians, but does have force against those theorists of distributive justice who, like Rawls, attempt to base their theories on the assent of rational self-interested persons. As Nozick asserts: 'End-state and most patterned principles of distributive justice institute (partial) ownership by others of people and their actions and labor. These principles involve a shift from the classical liberals' notion of self-ownership to a notion of (partial) property rights in *other* people.'[3]

Rawls' response to such an argument would rest on his conception of a social contract made behind a veil of ignorance. Rawls' rational self-interested person standing behind a veil of ignorance concerning what the future may hold for him, and recognizing that he may face periods of destitution as well as of plenty, will choose to tax himself when he is well-off, to insure his well-being when he is badly-off. Since all persons stand behind such a veil of ignorance about the future, all will agree upon redistribution to reduce the degree of inequality. The particular rule concerning inequalities that, according to Rawls, rational persons will choose, is that only those inequalities are just which make the least well-off in society better off, in absolute terms, than if the inequality did not exist. As Nozick notes, this particular rule is especially vulnerable, because it supposes, in game theoretic language, that rational persons will choose according to a minimax principle: that they will attach complete weight to the worst possible condition they might face, and none at all to other conditions. Such a principle may be rational in a zero-sum game with an intelligent opponent, but not in a game against nature, which is the appropriate conception here.

Nozick's objection to this approach is more fundamental, however. He argues that choice in the original position behind a veil of ignorance *must* lead to end-result principles of justice, and cannot result in a principle that bases justice on the processes by which the distribution was reached. He expresses it in this way: 'A procedure that founds principles of distributive justice on what rational persons who know nothing about themselves or their histories would agree to *guarantees that end-state principles of justice will be taken as fundamental*'.[4] Because such a procedure automatically excludes process principles, such as the entitlement principle which Nozick presents, it cannot be, Nozick argues, an appropriate procedure for arriving at distributive justice by rational persons with natural rights. Nozick states: 'For people meeting together behind a veil of ignorance to decide who gets what, knowing nothing about any special entitlements people may have, will treat anything to be distributed as manna from heaven.'[5]

To illustrate his point that only end-state principles will be chosen behind a veil of ignorance, Nozick constructs an example:

> Suppose there were a group of students who have studied during a year, taken examinations, and received grades between 0 and 100 which they have not yet learned of. They are now gathered together, having no idea of the grade any one of them has received, and they are asked to allocate grades among themselves so that the grades total to a given sum (which is determined by the sum of the grades they actually have received from the teacher). First, let us suppose they are to give a particular grade to each identifiable one of them present at the meeting. Here, given sufficient restrictions on their ability to threaten each other, they probably would agree to each person receiving the same grade, to each person's grade being equal to the total divided by the number of people to be graded. Surely they would *not* chance upon the

particular set of grades they already have received. Suppose next that there is posted on a bulletin board at their meeting a paper headed ENTITLEMENTS, which lists each person's name with a grade next to it, the listing being identical to the instructor's gradings. Still this particular distribution will not be agreed to by those having done poorly. Even if they know what 'entitlement' means (which perhaps we must suppose they don't in order to match the absence of moral factors in the calculations of persons in Rawls' original position), why should they agree to the instructor's distribution? What self-interested reason to agree to it would they have?

. . . . . . . . . . . . . . . . . . . . . . . . . . . . . . . . . . . . . . . . . . . . . . . . . . .

The nature of the decision problem facing persons deciding upon principles in an original position behind a veil of ignorance limits them to end-state principles of distribution. The self-interested person evaluates any non-end-state principle on the basis of how it works out for him; his calculations about any principle focus on how he ends up under the principle.[6]

This hypothetical example, except for the fact that the choice should have been made at the beginning of the course, conforms to Rawls' 'original position' ideas exactly. Yet it is with this argument that Nozick's position falters. It is true that the decision problem *as Rawls has conceived it* must lead to an end-result principle, and cannot lead to a process principle. But Nozick has too quickly adopted Rawls' conception of the decision problem. As he puts it in his example, 'they are now gathered together, having no idea of the grade of any one of them has received, and *they are asked to allocate grades among themselves. . . .*'[7] Nozick, by posing the problem in this fashion, has forced a narrow choice upon the students, and has thus forced his conclusion. The students have no opportunity to choose not to have collective authority over the grades of each. He did not ask them, behind this veil of ignorance, the prior question of what rights they choose to continue to hold individually, and what rights they choose to allocate to themselves as a collective body. Yet before they have the right, as a collective body, to make a decision of the sort Nozick poses for them, they must decide whether they want to hold these rights as a collective body. Nozick has, by the question he posed to them, done precisely what he shows that Rawls' difference principle does: he has taken from them individual rights and given those rights to the collectivity. There is nothing inherent in the procedure of choice behind a veil of ignorance which leads to that. In fact, it seems likely that if, at the beginning of the course, students were asked to draft a constitution governing the conduct of the class and the allocation of grades, they would choose to retain to themselves, as individuals, the right to demonstrate performance, and would allocate to the instructor or another outside observer the right to assign grades on the basis of these performances.

The statement can, in fact, be made stronger. If at the outset, persons have natural rights held individually, in accord with Nozick's basic theory, then the only kind of choice they *can* make is a choice about which of those rights to retain individually, and which to give up, either to themselves as a collective body, or to another party outside themselves. Because they hold such rights individually, any decision to give up a portion of them to the collectivity must be a unanimous decision. If instead they made a decision as to how the grades are to be divided up among them, any one of them could correctly object that the collective had no right, as a collective, to make that decision. This is not a problem for Rawls, since he implicitly assumes that the social product *is* collectively held. Thus, in Rawls' scheme, the collective does have the right to decide collectively how the social product is to be divided . . .

What Nozick fails to recognize is that this assumption is not at all inherent in the notion of a social contract made behind a veil of ignorance. Thus, it is not this procedure which is incompatible with a process principle of justice; it is the assumption that all resources are collectively held. Because of his use of Rawls' conception of the problem with which rational persons behind a veil of ignorance are confronted, Nozick rejects Rawls' procedure for the wrong reason: it can lead only to end-state principles of justice, and excludes process or historical principles. The problem which Rawls poses to rational people behind a veil of ignorance should be rejected, from a natural rights perspective, because it gives the collective body a set of rights that they do not hold collectively — the right to decide as a collective body how goods in society are to be allocated.

There is an objection which Nozick might still make. The set of natural rights with which persons are endowed may be arranged in two sets: One set held by all persons equally — for example, the right to free speech, or the right to the fruits of one's labor; and a second set, held by persons differentially — those arising from natural abilities, the accident of being born to an attentive mother, or differing material goods. The second set of natural rights ordinarily constitutes what we conceive of as resources rather than rights, so I will call the first set 'rights' (equally held) and the second, 'resources' (differentially held). If we conceive of the natural rights with which persons are endowed as only the first set, then the notion of a social contract behind a veil of ignorance is compatible with knowledge of one's natural rights. All persons begin with individually held natural rights, yet have no idea of their future position, because they have no differential resources. Thus, the veil of ignorance is opaque. The social contract *could* be made; it *would* concern the question of what rights were to remain in individual hands, and what rights were to be given over to the collectivity. It *would* also achieve the goal at which Rawls aimed: to transform interpersonal comparisons into intrapersonal ones, and thus arrive at a state in which the collective would have rights by which it could bring about some sharing by the rich with the poor. This occurs because, at the time of the contract, each person would balance off the utility of having goods taken from him if he was rich, against the benefit of having goods given to him if he was poor. The principle arrived at would of course not be Rawls' difference principle. Instead, it would more likely be some modification of Nozick's entitlement principle, weakened by giving the state some right to redistribute a portion of that entitlement.

Suppose, in accord with Nozick's position, that the natural rights with which persons begin are not merely those which they all hold alike merely by virtue of being persons, but include also the second set, the resources which each person holds differentially. Then, when they come to make a social contract, they will not be behind a complete veil of ignorance about their future positions. Knowing the extent and nature of their resources, the individuals' self-interested calculations will not lead to consensus on the rights to be held individually and those to be held collectively. Those persons who expect to be well-off in the future will want to retain more individual rights, to secure their liberties, and those who expect to be poorly-off in the future will want to have more rights collectively held, to give the collectivity greater power to aid them. In this way, the achievement of a just allocation of rights through the consensus of self-interested persons dissolves, and we are back in a situation of interpersonal conflict – Hobbes' war of all against all.

But what is an appropriate starting place, if we assume a natural rights position, as Nozick does? If we are concerned with a norma-tive theory of justice, we are not necessarily constrained to begin with the total set of rights and resources that are actually found in society. We are completely at liberty to abstract from real persons and ask the following question: At what allocation of rights to the collective would rational, self-interested persons, equally endowed with a set of natural rights, arrive? That such a scenario is a fiction never to be realized does not deprive the result of its moral force. Such an abstraction is possible, and appropriate, if persons (actual persons in society) can agree that the premises (equal natural rights) are appropriate, or perhaps just.[8] Then they must agree that the resulting allocation of rights that such fictional people would arrive at is itself appropriate, or just.

It is not at all clear, if such a fictional scenario is established, what allocation of collective rights would ensue. It is clear that rational self-interested persons would enter into some sort of social contract in which they give over some rights to be collectively held.[9] It is equally clear that the contract would neither be one in which the total social product and all rights are held collectively, as envisioned explicitly by Rousseau and implicitly by Rawls, nor would it be Nozick's full entitlement scheme, in which the full rights to the total product of a person's labors remained with him. Each person would agree, in Nozick's terms, to institute partial ownership by others of his actions and labor, as an insurance premium for the partial ownership of others' actions and labor. I will return shortly to the question of just what considerations might go into this rational decision behind a veil of ignorance.

First, suppose that persons in society cannot agree that an appropriate starting point for a theory of natural rights is the set of equally held rights, but instead contend that the starting must be the *total* set — the resources differentially held as well as the rights equally held. Then we are constrained to begin with this total set of rights and resources, and must address the more difficult task of distributing rights between individual and collectivity when persons are behind only a partial veil of ignorance. Such persons accordingly will not arrive at a social contract in which all desire exactly the same allocation of rights to the collectivity — the state. Yet they will still, if they are rational, want to engage in some sort of social contract, with the same reasons as before, under the equal rights starting point. That the existence of differential resources partially lifts the veil of ignorance does not mean that the veil is completely removed. Persons remain uncertain about their futures, despite their knowledge of their resources, and even despite their knowledge of others' resources. Each person, no matter how well or poorly endowed, will want to reserve for himself certain natural rights with which he begins, in order to use his resources and enjoy the product of his labors without undue constraint. Each person will also want to give over some of those rights to the collective, so that it may use its inherent power when he is in need. Thus, there will be some degree of consensus. The desired division of rights between those individually held and those collectively held will of course differ, and the difference will be related to the resources different persons hold. It will also be related to their differing degrees of self-confidence, their degrees of risk aversion, their capacities for envy, and their desires for freedom versus equality. Accordingly, inter-personal differences will have been narrowed: The maximal rights to be held collectively (as desired by those who have few resources, little self-confidence, high risk aversion, a high capacity for envy, and a taste for equality) will be something short of complete. The minimum rights to be held collectively (by those who have many resources, high self-confidence, no risk aversion, no envy, and a strong taste for freedom) will be something greater than zero. There will remain some interpersonal conflict of interest; a state, which is everyone's ideal, will not be formed. However, the extent of opposing interests will have been reduced. The uncertainty about the future on the part of these rational self-interested persons will have placed upper and lower bounds on the amount of rights to be collectively held.

Can we go beyond this, to say, within these bounds, what social contract will be made, if one will be made at all? This can be answered by envisioning the following procedure. Consider a pro-posal for a particular allocation of rights to the collective, in which each person must make the following calculation in deciding whether it is beneficial for him to assent to such an allocation. In light of the distribution of future situations which he expects to confront, he must weigh the benefit to be expected from full control over his small set of individual rights against that expected from partial control over the larger set of collective rights that he would share as a member of the collective. If the latter benefit is larger, then he would rationally assent to a collective with such powers. The process could be imagined as follows: Each person, endowed with natural rights and resources, some of which are differentially distributed, is asked to accept or reject allocation of a minimal set of rights to a collectivity. This process is continued, increasing the collectively held set beyond this minimum so long as there is unanimous acceptance of a collective with such an allocation. When the collectively held rights have been increased to the point where unanimity no longer holds, the process stops, and a collective is formed, with the maximum set of rights, or power, that all potential members find to their benefit. This maximum would, of course, be the lower level described earlier. The state will have exactly the set of rights desired by the most libertarian, and a smaller set of rights than those desired by those more egalitarian. Nevertheless, they would agree to this state, because they prefer it to any of the more individualistic states assented to by the most libertarian. Why the asymmetry? Because there is an asymmetry in starting point: We begin with rights *individually held*, and move as far toward collectively held rights as unanimous consent will carry us. If we had begun with rights wholly collectively held, we would have moved in the opposite direction, away from collective rights, until we had reached the upper bound, which is as far as we could go with unanimous consent. The region between upper and lower bounds is not one that could be reached by unanimous consent . . .

The reason for beginning with individual rights, according to Nozick, is the normative priority accorded to individual rights. If Nozick's premise as to the inviolability of individual rights is accepted, then any social contract, whether it begins with equal rights or unequal rights, must begin with the assumption of rights individually held.

## WHAT CONDITIONS AFFECT THE DECISIONS OF RATIONAL PERSONS CONCERNING INDIVIDUAL VERSUS COLLECTIVE RIGHTS?

Whether a social contract is made behind a veil of complete ignorance or a veil of partial ignorance, another question can be asked: Will rational persons' choices be affected by the social conditions surrounding them, and if so, how? Although they are behind a veil of ignorance, partial or complete, about their own position in the future, they are not ignorant of the kind of society in which they would find themselves.

The first and most obvious element that would lead rational persons to allocate greater portions of their rights to the state is the existence of collective threats, whether from the natural environment or from external enemies. Eskimos treat many of their resources collectively during the winter months. Similarly, the Essenes in the desert near the Dead Sea 2,000 years ago maintained a largely communal existence. Modern Zionists, resettling the agricultural lands of Palestine, created collective Kibbutzim and cooperative Moshavim to confront both the natural and human environment. Insofar as there can be a reallocation of rights at different times within a state, we see the same thing: In time of war, citizens voluntarily submit themselves to greater central direction and greater taxation than in times of peace.

Somewhat more subtle is the difference between a largely agrarian economy and an industrial economy. In an agrarian subsistence economy, most of a person's essentials are directly satisfied by his own efforts: He grows most of his own foodstuffs, and builds his own shelter. There are good times and bad, but they vary in continuous gradation, for there is no concept of a 'full-time job'. In an industrial economy, on the other hand, most of his essentials are provided by exchange for money obtained from his labor in a 'full-time job'. In good times, he has a job; in bad times, he does not. He cannot subsist by the direct fruits of his own labor in the absence of the job, but must receive aid from some source, or migrate to a place where he can subsist. In addition, the interdependence of the economy would suggest that bad times would be likely to hit many persons at once, and one would be less likely to fall back on resources held by others especially close to him.

Thus it is reasonable to expect that rational persons behind a veil of ignorance about their own position, but knowing the character of the economy, would agree to reserve a larger portion of their product for insurance, perhaps agreeing to a larger tax (and perhaps even a more progressive one), if their economy were an industrial and highly interdependent one, than if it were an agricultural subsistence economy. Furthermore, this rational allocation of resources for collective use would carry with it the rights to use the resources not merely for common defense, but for redistribution to the needy and destitute.

### THE DANGER OF THE STATE

There is one final point that should not be overlooked. When certain rights are allocated to the state, one of the rights that constitutes Nozick's definition of a minimal state, as well as a central portion of any definition of the state in political science, is a monopoly over the use of coercion or violence. By virtue of this right, the state, and whatever faction, majority or minority, gains control of it, gains the power to garner other rights to itself, without the impediment of unanimous consent. It can employ coercion, imposing policies on unwilling citizens, because of its monopoly over coercion. Thus, if there is to be an allocation of rights in a just society, there must also be, within this allocation, some means of protecting against the progressive expansion of rights by the state — an expansion that would create an unjust society from one that was initially just.

It may be that the most fruitful way of looking at these matters is somewhat different. Suppose we begin with a set of persons with natural rights, setting aside for now the question of whether we include only equally held rights or differentially held resources. When these individuals create a state by giving over certain of their individual rights to be held collectively, they create a new 'person', of a different sort, with a derived set of rights. The state is a legal person, with a certain set of rights before the law.[10] Accordingly, the state *acts* as a person, through a set of agents pursuing purposes or goals of the state, just as natural persons pursue their goals.

Similarly, when any group of persons within the state creates another collectivity by giving over certain of their rights or resources to be collectively held, another 'legal person' is created within the state. This may be a profitmaking corporation, a trade union, or an association of some other kind.

A society at any point in time will consist not only of individuals (natural persons), but also of the state (which may have various coordinate parts, such as the executive and legislative branches of the United States government), and of other legal or corporate persons. Conceiving of the society in this way, we can say that one of the principal tasks of natural persons in the society — from whom all rights originate — is to so allocate those rights to corporate bodies that the various corporate bodies and natural persons are able to prevent any one of their number using its rights to acquire further rights without the assent of the owners of those rights. If such acquisition of rights goes unchecked, then all the rights end in the hands of one natural or legal person, which can do as it will to satisfy its interests alone. Within this system, there is nothing to prevent the continual and gross subversion of justice. One hundred years ago in the United States, this danger existed with the greatest force in regard to the emerging and developing corporations. Today, it exists with greatest force in the expanding and aggrandizing state — an infinitely more dangerous problem.

## NOTES

1  R. Nozick, *Anarchy, State, and Utopia* (Basic Books, 1974).
2  Ibid., pp. 153−5.
3  Ibid., p. 172 n. 1.
4  Ibid., pp. 198−9.
5  Ibid., p. 199.
6  Ibid., pp. 199−201.
7  Ibid., p. 199 (emphasis added).
8  It is important to note that the assumption of equal natural rights does not imply equality among all resources. It implies only that those rights which are regarded as 'natural rights', such as entitlement to the product of one's labour, are, at the starting point, held equally by all.
9  Their calculation would balance the utility gain to be expected from rights held collectively (for example, the utility that results from the security of combined forces, which are more powerful than the sum of their individual components, and smoothing out, through redistribution, the resource fluctuations each might experience) against the utility loss which results from loss of full control over rights otherwise held individually.
10  This concept is analogous to the concept of the corporation as a 'person' under Anglo-American common law. Corporations, although recognized as persons under the law, have specifically designated rights, which are more limited than those rights accorded a natural person.

# 10

# Justice as Social Choice

## DAVID GAUTHIER

### I

What the good is to an individual, the just is to society. The parallel is aptly formulated by John Rawls: 'Just as each person must decide by rational reflection what constitutes his good, that is, the system of ends which it is rational for him to pursue, so a group of persons must decide once and for all what is to count among them as just and unjust'. ...

Given our parallel between individual good and social justice, we should be able to determine the principles in accordance with which the rational society pursues justice. These then would be the subject of the theory of collective decision, or social choice. In this way the theory of justice would be part of the theory of rational choice ...

### II

I will propose, and endeavor to make plausible, an account [based on the Rawlsian] formulation ... that society is a 'cooperative venture for mutual advantage'. Social choice must be rational from the perspective of each individual within society. If an individual is to act on, or in accordance with, the principles of social choice or of justice, then she must find that membership in society enables her to pursue her own system of ends more effectively than were she to act on her own, independently of others, in a

*Source:* Reproduced by permission of the publishers from David Gauthier, 'Justice as Social Choice', in David Copp and David Immerman (eds), *Morality, Reason and Truth* (Totowa, N.J.: Rowman & Allanheld, 1985), pp. 251–69.

'state of nature'. We do not claim that all societies may correctly be characterized as cooperative ventures for mutual advantage. We do claim that societies that command the rational support of their members must be so characterized ...

The idea of society as a cooperative venture for mutual advantage links rational social choice with justice. And this aim of justice is to be achieved not by decision-making that embodies a single, social, maximizing procedure, but rather by decision-making through agreement among the individual participants in the cooperative venture. Put differently, the principles of justice are those principles for making social decisions or choices to which rational individuals, each seeking to cooperate with her fellows in order to maximize her own utility, would agree.

## III

Rawls poses the problem of rational agreement on principles of justice as one of individual choice. He insists that 'the parties have no basis for bargaining in the usual sense'. The idea of agreement is idle in Rawls's theory because the individuals who are to agree on principles of justice are placed behind a veil of ignorance so thick that the differences among them are obliterated. Each person simply asks himself which principles it would be rational to accept in ignorance of all particular facts about his talents and aptitudes, traits of character, and circumstances. Each knows that since all persons are similarly ignorant, the reasoning that will convince one must convince all. Thus each may represent himself as deciding on or choosing the principles of justice from behind the veil of ignorance; the principles that anyone chooses must be those that everyone chooses.

Here we do not follow Rawls. His use of the veil of ignorance is ultimately motivated by his insistence that the parties are to seek a conception of justice appropriate to 'free and equal moral persons'. The real differences and inequalities that characterize them are to be dismissed as morally irrelevant. Thus the principles of justice, in Rawls's view, must be related to a prior moral conception of the person. But if we insist strictly on the parallel between individual good and social justice with which we began (and with which Rawls may, to the unwary reader, have seemed to begin), then we may not appeal to this moral conception. Rather, the human person must be viewed in the same way from the standpoint of justice as from the standpoint of good. If the individual is

represented as a maximizer of expected utility, so that his good is
what he chooses on the basis of overall considered preferences,
then justice among several individuals must be that to which they
would agree on the basis of, and only of, their overall considered
preference. Whether our concern be with individual good or with
social justice, a prior moral conception of the person has no place
except insofar as it may happen to enter into and to inform
considered preference.

In rejecting the view that the principles of justice are to be the
object of choice behind a veil of ignorance, we do not remove all
constraints on the circumstances in which they are to be selected.
We suppose that the principles are to provide a basis not only for
making future social decisions but also for evaluating past decisions and existing institutions and practices. We shall therefore
not want the selection to be influenced by actual social circumstances; we cannot allow those factors that we seek to evaluate in
terms of the principles of justice to be assumed in the process of
agreeing to those principles. If we were to consider an agreement
in which each person assumes his existing social position, then we
should in effect allow the status quo to constrain the choice of
principles of justice, although we should have no reason to suppose
the status quo to be itself mutually advantageous or just.

Furthermore, we shall not want the selection of principles of
justice to be affected by the actual capacities of individual persons
as bargainers, or by the ability each person has to advance his
interests in the context of making agreements with others. The
principles of rational choice are defined for an ideal decision-
maker; if their use must be tailored to the capacities of particular
agents, yet we do not suppose that the principles themselves should
be related to the imperfect rationality of real persons. Similarly,
the principles of justice are defined for an ideal society, even
though their application must be tailored to the capacities and
circumstances of the actual members of an imperfect society. We
must therefore suppose that the process of agreement leading to
the choice of principles must be itself ideal, so that the parties to
the agreement, whatever their actual capacities, are to be thought
of as bargainers able to advance their interests equally with their
fellows, and as fully and effectively as possible. We achieve this
ideal conception not by placing the bargainers behind a veil of
ignorance, but rather by taking each to be adequately informed
not only about his own good but also about that of his fellows.
Communication among the persons must be full and free; no one
is able to deceive another about anyone's interests or bluff suc-
cessfully about what anyone is willing to do. The process of

bargaining must be thought of as effectively cost-free, so that the participants are not under pressure, and especially not under differential pressure, to reach agreement. No one is in a position to benefit by his superior ability to outwait the others. Threats are useless to ideally rational bargainers, for insofar as a threat involves the claim that one will act in a non-utility-maximizing way unless some other person accedes to one's wishes, everyone knows that no one would carry out such a threat, so that the attempt to threaten would be idle. In these several ways, then, we require that the process of bargaining exhibit procedural equality and maximum competence among the persons who are to agree on the principles of justice.

It does not follow, either from the insistence that social contingencies shall not affect the process of bargaining, or from the requirement that as bargainers individuals be ideally competent, informed, and rational, that the natural capacities of the actual members of society are also irrelevant to the agreement. Just as each person in determining his own good takes his particular capacities and interests into account, so each person in agreeing on social justice must be expected to take his capacities and interests into account. But no one is thereby able to tailor principles to his own differential advantage, since each is equally able to demand that his capacities and interests be recognized in the content of agreement. Each bargainer thus serves as an ideal representative of the particular person he will be in the social world to be shaped by the agreed principles of justice; thus fairness is assured at the procedural level . . .

## IV

In bargaining, it is natural and seemingly necessary to think of each person as beginning from a base point — a prebargaining payoff that is not called into question by the bargaining situation and that must be realized for the particular individual to be willing to accept any bargain. In our problem the prebargaining payoff may be associated with what each person could expect to gain from his or her own efforts in the absence of any agreed or cooperative interaction. Or more precisely, the prebargaining payoff may tentatively be so identified; we shall have to ask whether there are other constraints that must be imposed on it. For the present we simply assume that the base point is fixed in some way for each person.

It is then natural to think of each bargainer as advancing a claim, reflecting his or her desire to gain as much as possible from agreement, but constrained by the recognition that others must not be driven away from the bargaining table. Since those others must expect to benefit from any bargain into which they willingly enter, they could not be expected to entertain a claim acceptance of which would leave them with a payoff less than they would expect from no agreement, and so less than that afforded by their base point. The desire to benefit maximally, and the need to reach agreement, thus fix each person's claim as the most that she could receive from any possible outcome that affords every other person at least as much as her base-point payoff. Individual expected-utility maximization and mutual advantage prove to be not only necessary but also sufficient to determine all claims.

However, we must beware lest we understand the fixing of claims in an overly simple way. In a situation involving more than two persons, each person's claim must be restricted to those parts of the overall cooperative venture to which she contributes. Otherwise, even if all others were better off than in absence of any venture, yet some would be worse off than with a modified cooperative venture that would exclude the particular person whose claim is in question. One's claim must not be so great that it would be advantageous for others to exclude one from the bargaining table; one must avoid driving them away and one must also avoid being driven away or excluded oneself. Although this is implicit in the idea of mutual advantage, exclusive attention to two-person agreements might lead us to overlook the full extent of the constraint that mutuality entails.

Claims, even though they are compatible with mutual benefit, will in general be incompatible one with another; each will demand the most that would be compatible with her participation in a mutually advantageous venture. Thus to reach agreement bargainers must offer concessions. Given that no one wishes to concede — given that any concession represents acceptance of a diminished payoff — then rational bargainers will endeavor to minimize their concessions. Now the magnitude of a concession is established not with reference to some absolute scale of utility, but rather with reference to the particular bargaining situation; concession is a measure of the *proportion* between the part of one's claim that one abandons, and the entire claim, or gain over one's base-point payoff, that one originally advances. Since the bargainers are equally and fully rational, the maximum concession — the greatest proportion of his or her original claim that any bargainer gives up — must be minimized. Since all benefit from reaching agreement, some set of concessions is rational for all to accept, but a particular set is rational for all only if any alternative would require a concession at least as great as the maximum in the given set.

In bargaining, therefore, rational persons will act on a principle of *minimax concession* – the greatest or maximum concession must be a minimum. This principle may be formulated equivalently as a principle of *maximin relative benefit*. We may measure the relative benefit of an agreement to an individual as the proportion her actual gain over the base point payoff bears to the potential gain represented by her claim. Relative benefit is thus the proportion of potential benefit that one actually receives. And we may now relate rationality, as expressed by minimax concession, to fairness or justice, which we claim is captured by maximin relative benefit. If an agreement is to be considered fair by those party to it, then no one may receive a relative benefit smaller than necessary – smaller than the minimum relative benefit of that outcome which, in relation to the other possible outcomes, has the greatest or maximum minimum relative benefit. Given that all persons benefit from reaching agreement, some set of relative benefits must be fair, but a set is fair only if any alternative would afford some person a relative benefit no greater than the minimum in the given set. Maximin relative benefit ensures that no one's advantage is sacrificed to benefit someone who, relative to the context of agreement, is better placed.

The principle of minimax concession, or maximin relative benefit, is uniquely acceptable to every party in the bargaining situation. Developing a contrast suggested by T. M. Scanlon, we may ask whether a principle is acceptable because any individual 'judges that it is one he could not reasonably reject whatever position he turns out to occupy,' or whether it is acceptable because 'it would be the rational choice for [any individual] behind the veil of ignorance,' or in ignorance of the position he is to occupy. In our view the latter, which is of course what Rawls supposes, is insufficient to establish the impartiality requisite for justice. Impartiality requires acceptability in every position rather than acceptability in ignorance of one's position. The former does and the latter 'does not take seriously the distinction between persons', to turn against Rawls the criticism that he levels at the utilitarians. There is no reason to suppose that a principle that would be acceptable to any person in a hypothetical state of ignorance of all particulars would be acceptable to every person in every possible position that the principle would license. And so there is no reason to suppose that such a principle is truly impartial. Only acceptability from every standpoint that satisfies the principle can meet the demand — both rational and moral — that we make on justice. The idea of rational agreement by all persons on a principle demanding that the greatest concession anyone makes be minimized, or ensuring that the smallest relative benefit anyone receives be maximized, addresses the demand for acceptability from every standpoint.

At this point some examples may be illuminating. These will illustrate the application of the principle of minimax concession to particular situations; they will not relate to the agreement on the principle itself.

Suppose that, in order to take advantage of linearly increasing returns to scale, Mabel and Abel decide to pool their investment funds. Mabel has $600, on which she could expect to gain $180, and Abel has $400, on which he could expect to gain $80. Together they have $1,000, on which they can expect to gain $500. Clearly, Mabel insists on a gain of $180 as her base-point return, since she could achieve that without cooperating with Abel; she claims $420, the total gain ($500) less what Abel could achieve without her ($80). Abel of course insists on $80 as his base-point return and claims $320 ($500 less the $180 Mabel could achieve without him). If Mabel receives $x$ from their agreement, then her concession is the proportion between the part of her claim that she abandons, or $420 less $x$, and her entire claim over her base-point payoff, or $420 less $180.

If Abel then receives $(500 − x)$ from their agreement, then his concession is the proportion between $320 less $(500 − x,)$ and $320 less $80. It is evident that the maximum concession is minimized when their two concessions are equal or, in other words, when:

$$\frac{\$420 - \$x}{\$420 - \$180} = \frac{\$320 - \$(500 - x)}{\$320 - \$80}$$

Solving for $x$, we find that $\$x = \$300$; Mabel receives a gain of $300, and Abel receives a gain of $200 ...

## V

We may give this part of our argument greater precision by deriving the principle of minimax concession from a set of conditions on rational bargaining. To prepare for the derivation, we first define a set C of concessions as *feasible* relative to a situation S if and only if there is a $1-1$ correspondence between the persons in $S$ and the members of $C$ such that, if each person makes the concession correlated with him or her, a possible outcome of $S$ is realized. Next, we define the *magnitude* of a concession $c$ relative to a feasible set $C$ of which it is a member: Let the outcome realized by $C$ have utility $u$ for the person with whom $c$ is correlated; let that person claim a utility $u\#$ and let his or her base-point utility be $u^*$; then the magnitude of $c$ is $[(u\# - u)/(u\# - u^*)]$. It is evident by inspection that this captures our previous account; the magnitude of a concession is the proportion between that part of one's claim that one abandons and one's total possible gain over one's base-point payoff ...

A *minimax* concession in any situation $S$ is then one that is maximum in its set and no greater in magnitude than a maximum concession in each feasible set in $S$. Thus for any situation $S$, every feasible set of concessions in $S$ must have a member with a magnitude at least as great as that of the minimax concession in $S$.

The conditions on rational bargaining then are:

1    Each person $A$ must claim an outcome that affords him or her maximum expected utility, compatibly with affording no person less expected utility than in the absence of an agreement to which $A$ is party.

2    Given claims satisfying condition 1, each person must suppose that there is a feasible set of concessions such that *every* rational person is willing to entertain it; that is, willing to make the concession required of him or her provided the others make the concessions required of them.

3    Each person must be willing to entertain a concession as part of a feasible set of concessions if its magnitude is no greater than that of the greatest concession that he or she supposes some rational person willing to entertain.

4    No person is willing to entertain a concession if it is not required by 2 and 3.

We justify condition 1 by appealing to each person's concern to be included in an agreement and yet to maximize his utility. We justify condition 2 by appealing to the mutual advantageousness of cooperation, and so of agreement on an outcome that can be realized only if all make the concessions required of them by a feasible set. It is not enough for each person to be prepared to make a concession required by some feasible set, since this would not ensure that all were prepared to accept the *same* feasible set.

We justify condition 3 by an appeal to the *equal* rationality of all parties to the agreement. Since each person wants to minimize the concession he makes, I cannot suppose it rational for you to entertain a concession if I would not entertain a concession of equal magnitude. And condition 4 is justified by noting the unwillingness of rational persons to make concessions except where necessary to gain some benefit.

By condition 2 each person must suppose that there is a feasible set of concessions that every rational person is willing to entertain. But every feasible set of concessions contains a concession with a magnitude at least as great as that of the minimax concession. Therefore, each person must suppose that there is a set of concessions that every rational person is willing to entertain, and that requires some person to entertain a concession at least as great as the minimax concession. So each person must suppose that some rational person is willing to entertain a concession at least as great as the minimax concession. Then by condition 3 each person must be willing to entertain a concession at least as great as the minimax concession.

In every situation there is a feasible set of concessions containing no member greater in magnitude than the minimax concession. Thus condition 2 cannot require any person to suppose that there is a feasible set of concessions that every person is willing to entertain and that contains a concession greater in magnitude than the minimax concession. And so condition 3 does not require that any person be willing to entertain a concession greater in magnitude than the minimax concession. Hence, by condition 4, no person is willing to entertain a concession greater in magnitude than the minimax concession. And so each person must be willing to entertain those and only those feasible sets of concessions in which there are concessions with magnitudes as great as, but no greater than, the minimax concession. But this is the principle of minimax concession. Our derivation is accomplished.

## VI

Several problems remain. First, I have left to one side the question of what constraints, if any, are to be imposed in determining the base point for rational agreement on the principles of justice. Is the base point to be identified simply with the outcome if each seeks to maximize his or her own utility in the absence of agreement? Second, I have not considered the problem of compliance with the decisions reached in accordance with the principle of minimax concession. From the standpoint of a particular individual, those actions required of him as part of a cooperative scheme to realize maximin relative benefit need not be those supported by expected-utility maximization. Why then should he comply with the requirements of the scheme? Individuals may have to forgo what we have accepted as individually rational if they are to do what we have claimed is collectively rational. And third, I have not determined the scope of the principles of justice. I have not considered what types of issues are to be decided by an appeal to minimax concession. Here I can only sketch an approach to these difficult questions.

The first two issues are connected. The rationale for compliance with principles of justice is related to the selection of the base point from which concession, or relative benefit, is calculated. As an initial approximation, the base point may be associated with the payoff each person could expect in the absence of cooperation. Society would then be viewed as a venture beneficial to each person, not in comparison with no interaction, but in comparison with noncooperative interaction, with others. But will such a venture be welcomed by each participant? Suppose that there are some persons who prefer cooperation to noncooperation, but who also prefer no interaction to noncooperation, and perhaps even to cooperation. From their standpoint society is a venture entered into primarily to reduce the costs imposed on them by state-of-nature interaction of a noncooperative kind. But their willingness to participate in such a venture, and in a particular distribution of benefits from it, may then be dependent on the presence of whatever factors forced them to acquiesce in the disadvantageous interactions of the state of nature. They may insist that they have no reason to participate *voluntarily* in social cooperation unless the benefits they receive are related to an agreement they would make either from a base point of *no* interaction or from a base point determined by noncooperative interaction that they would consider advantageous in relation to no interaction. Although we cannot argue this point here, we should maintain that voluntary compliance with the terms of cooperation — and so compliance with the principles of justice or social choice — is rational in general only if the base point is not itself considered disadvantageous in relation to no interaction. And this is in effect to say that the state of nature, as determining the base point for social agreement, is to be conceived in Lockean rather than in Hobbesian terms.

An example may suggest the rationale for this position. Consider the present situation in South Africa. We may suppose that interaction between blacks and whites is largely noncooperative and imposed by the power of the whites. Suppose that a sophisticated defender of the South African system were to point out that everyone, black and white alike, could benefit were the repressive apparatus required to maintain the present system of apartheid to be dismantled and replaced by genuine interracial cooperation. Of course, our defender would insist, the present distribution of goods and services must be taken as the base point; each person is to get what he now has, plus the cooperative payoff resulting from dismantling the repressive apparatus.

Black South Africans would be unlikely to give such a proposal serious consideration. Were the present coercive framework of interaction to be dismantled, they would not find it rational voluntarily to maintain a system resting on the distribution of benefits and costs that apartheid upholds. They would not agree to a cooperative venture taking the present noncooperative state of affairs as the base point.

A second example is suggested by the rise and suppression of the Solidarity trade union in Poland. As the repressive apparatus maintaining the power of the Communist minority was relaxed, it became evident that the members of Solidarity were not prepared to accept the existing distribution of power as the base point from which future social cooperation would proceed. Hence, martial law brought the radical innovation of free workers in a workers' state to an end.

Introduction of the Lockean state of nature moralizes the base point for social cooperation. Thus moral factors enter into the derivation of the principles of justice. But the manner of their entry must be carefully noted. Only those moral considerations are introduced that are necessary to attain rational compliance with the principles. In effect, the principles of justice have moral force; they require each person to refrain from seeking his or her greatest expected utility if and insofar as this would conflict with carrying out decisions based on the principles. For this to be rational, a further moral factor must be introduced — the requirement that no one benefit at the expense of others in any interaction taken for granted in determining the base point. But this moral factor is introduced only to ensure the rationality of compliance with the principles of justice. Thus it, like the principles themselves, are ultimately derived from purely rational considerations. It is not introduced as an independent moral element in the argument in the way in which Rawls introduces the conception of moral persons or in which Nozick introduces natural right. It is not an a priori constraint on what each person may do, unmotivated by the idea of a cooperative venture for mutual advantage.

I have offered no demonstration that, to be rational, compliance requires the Lockean constraint on the base point for agreement. I have not demonstrated that compliance, insofar as it overrides individual expected-utility maximization, is *ever* rational. The arguments needed to establish the position sketched here must be reserved for another occasion.

## VII

What is the *scope* of social choice? In conceiving of society as a cooperative venture for mutual advantage, we immediately limit *social* choice, and so the principles of justice, to those contexts in which each person rationally forgoes *individual* choice based on principles of expected-utility maximization. Each must expect to benefit from cooperation. Thus pure redistribution — redistribution from the base point established in a Lockean state of nature — cannot be a matter of rational social concern, and it cannot be justified by an appeal to rational principles of justice or social choice. Pure redistribution must be the effect of private charity, not public justice.

There are two primary aims that afford persons reason to agree to and comply with principles of social choice: to ensure protection and to increase production.[1] *Protection* is to be understood not primarily in reference to external threats, but internally; society protects each of its members against the force and fraud that characterize the interaction of persons in a Hobbesian state of nature. In effect, the protective role of society is to guarantee a Lockean framework for interaction. But in providing this guarantee there are, strictly speaking, no alternatives among which society may choose, no goods whose distribution raises a problem of social choice. Justice requires that each individual's fair base point be maintained. Insofar as there are ways of accomplishing this that differ significantly for the individuals protected, we must suppose that in affording protection society also provides further goods the distribution of which does give rise to a genuine problem of social choice. But then this further distribution is not itself part of the strict assurance of protection, and it must be assessed rather by the standards appropriate to production. The protective role of society may best be conceived as the guarantee of *rights*.

The goods of *production* fall along a continuum whose end

points are those familiar categories distinguished by the economist — private and public. Given that protection is assured, so that force and fraud are eliminated from the interactions of the members of society, then purely private goods are efficiently produced through invisible hand processes in which each seeks his or her private gain — or, in other words, through interaction in which each seeks to maximize his or her expected utility. But there is then no place for social choice in determining the production and/or distribution of these goods. Given the efficiency of the market in which only individual decisions are required or permitted, it is not possible that each should expect to benefit from superseding individual decision by social decision. The market ensures mutual advantage — that is, a Pareto-optimal outcome — without any need for co-operation, and it does so in a manner that, being dependent only on the voluntary choices of individuals, transmits the moral characteristics of its starting point to its outcome. If each individual's base point satisfies the Lockean constraints, then no question of justice arises with respect to efficient market interaction.

Public goods, however, raise different problems. If each person acts privately to maximize his or her expected utility, then the possibilities of free-riders and parasites lead characteristically to the underproduction of public goods and overproduction of public bads. There will be too few lighthouses and too much air pollution. Here, then, is a further role for social choice, and here the principles of justice come into their own. In deciding how public goods are to be produced and distributed in excess of the quantities that individuals would voluntarily supply if each were to maximize his or her expected utility in the absence of cooperative arrangements, we must appeal to the principle of minimax concession.

In a recent book Andrew Levine attacks the coherence of liberal democracy, basing part of his argument on the claim that liberalism constrains the scope of democratic choice. But of course the core idea of liberal democracy is to combine the requirement that social choice equally reflect each person's concerns and interests with a clear limitation on the sphere appropriate to such choice. This limitation is effected by an appeal to the idea of individual liberty. We make it more precise by replacing the idea of liberty with that of voluntary *ex ante* acceptance of social-choice, rather than individual-choice, procedures. As individual's liberty is guaranteed insofar as the scope of social choice is determined by an appeal to what she would rationally accept as an improvement on the Lockean state of nature. We have argued that an individual — any individual — would rationally accept the social provision of public goods, on the basis of minimax concession or maximin relative benefit, but reject the social provision of purely private goods. In the nineteenth century the workings of liberal democracy were clearly flawed by a failure to accept fully the role of society in the provision and distribution of public goods. This failure continues to infect libertarian theory. In the twentieth century the flaw has increasingly been a failure to accept fully the role of the market in the provision of private goods, which infects socialist and welfare-state theory. But the liberal democratic project is in essence the political embodiment of the conception of society as a cooperative venture for mutual advantage, which is itself the key to understanding the theory of justice as part of the theory of rational choice. What remains is to find a battle cry more inspiring than 'To each so that the minimum proportion of potential benefit is maximized'.

#### NOTES

1 The protective/productive distinction is taken from James M. Buchanan.

# 11

# A Contractarian View of Respect for Persons

## B. J. DIGGS

Our moral heritage includes two ideals that seem often to conflict. On the one hand, there is an ideal of moral freedom or autonomy, which in different forms was extolled by Locke, Rousseau, Kant, J. S. Mill and others. On the other hand, there is an ideal of a social order and social morality, supported by reason because they serve the common good, which we inherited from the Greeks. Although each of these ideals has been weakened, partly by combat with the other, both are alive and the conflict is yet to be resolved.

Some contract theories may be regarded as attempts to salvage what is best from the two traditions; although contractarians regularly emphasize the equal freedom of individuals, some also issue principles, moral or political, that are said to command universal rational assent. This paper delineates the most basic features of a moral contractarianism that results from assuming that the two ideals, in forms in which they would receive wide support, are reconcilable. Part I outlines the ideals in these forms and proposes a way of reconciling them. Parts II to IV explain the formalist contractarian requirement of respect for persons that follows from the proposed reconciliation. Part V indicates the importance of this contractarianism by comparing it with Rawls' use of 'the Original Position'.

## I

The ideal of moral freedom was perhaps most simply expressed by Rousseau when, in distinguishing this kind of freedom from others,

*Source:* Reproduced by permission of *American Philosophical Quarterly* from B. J. Diggs, 'A Contractarian View of Respect for Persons', *American Philosophical Quarterly*, 18: 4 (October 1981), pp. 273–83.

he wrote of a 'freedom to obey a law that we prescribe for ourselves' (*Social Contract*, I, 8). But in the form in which it is supported today, this freedom was described better by Mill when he said 'The only freedom which deserves the name is that of pursuing our own good in our own way . . .' and then added that 'Each is the proper guardian of his own health, whether bodily, or mental and spiritual. Mankind are greater gainers by suffering each other to live as seems good to themselves, than by compelling each to live as seems good to the rest' (*Liberty*, *I*). Although certain differences between these passages may be noted, they agree well enough for our purposes. The idea of a freedom to govern or direct one's own life runs through them all; this 'government' is presumed to comprise such activities as investigating and weighing alternatives, setting goals, deciding on principles and plans (including 'plans of life,' as Mill called them), and acting accordingly. The conception of a 'personal self-government' is undoubtedly hazy and its proper limits are poorly defined. Nevertheless, the proposition that persons should be allowed to develop their own views of 'how they ought to live' and 'run their own lives' would be warmly endorsed by most in our society, and for many reasons.

If persons were not allowed to direct their own acts at all, they would be treated as mere 'things', and, if not to a considerable degree, they could not develop the abilities that are needed in order to assume responsibility as persons (for taking care of themselves), as role-holders (for doing jobs), or as members of society (for understanding and following laws, etc.). Moreover, a high degree of freedom is essential if they are to discharge these 'responsibilities' well and enjoy the rewards of the activities involved — if they are to live 'examined' and interesting lives, do innovative or exceptional jobs, and critically assess and reform the laws and institutions of their society. Rousseau's claim that one's humanity depends on one's freedom, and Mill's, that one's 'worth as a human being' depends on it, seem well-supported (*Social Contract*, I, 4; *Liberty*, 3).

The ideal of a social morality that serves the common good and commands the support of reason is equally strong. Today, few subscribe to Greek perfectionism, many regard society as a battleground of opposed interests, and some regard morality as an instrument of oppresion. Yet, in our society, almost all believe that people should respect one another's basic rights because everyone benefits. Moreover, most people teach this kind of morality to their children and believe that if children do not come to accept it,

they will suffer. .... Most of the above appears to be true even of
those who claim to be highly sceptical of morality. Subgroups of
our society do not always advocate the same morality but they
have great confidence in the reasonableness of their own. Even
those who strongly criticize our social morality usually do so
because they regard it as unjust in certain respects, and they argue
that we should accept their views for the reasons they give.

As described, these two ideals are not necessarily incompatible.
If there are 'moral articles' that there are good reasons to accept,
and if persons, governing themselves, freely accept these articles
for these reasons, then there will be harmony. Moreover, if it is
thought best not to violate people's freedom even though they do
not accept these articles, there is still no theoretical incompatibility.
But when freedom is put first, the matter may look quite different:
if individuals are free to govern themselves in whatever manner
they think best, is it really the case that there is a social morality
that all with good reason can accept? A large doubt arises because
the reasons for accepting the common morality seem necessarily to
derive from the views of individuals about how they should live,
and experience tells us that their views differ enormously and
often clash. One immediately thinks of Nazis and Jews, Puritans
and atheists, slaveholders and slaves, etc. Past philosophies offer
little comfort.

Matters are not as bad as they appear. The freedom of persons
who live together to govern themselves would itself be in grave
danger if it included a freedom for them to do anything they
please, 'for who could be free, when every other man's humour
might domineer over him?' (Locke, *Second Treatise*, VI, § 57).
The ideal requires an equal but does not allow an unlimited
freedom. Parties cannot live under a common morality when one
seeks to subjugate or exterminate the other; and it would be
absurd to claim that there is an area of reasonable agreement on a
morality no matter what the conflict. Both ideals are *moral* ideals;
proponents of both assume, or argue, that there are overwhelmingly
strong reasons for humans to live in society and, further, that a
common morality offers a sensible alternative to war. In order to
reconcile the ideals, we thus do not need to reconcile such irrecon-
cilable views as were mentioned above.

The problem is rather to find or to invent a set of restrictions
that it would be reasonable for each person to include in the
morality by which he governs himself if almost all were willing to
accept these restrictions — or, to put social morality in a more
positive light, the problem is to determine articles of morality

that it would be reasonable for all persons together freely to subscribe to. If this problem could be solved, then the moral freedom of individuals would be protected, as much as people could reasonably wish it to be, and at the same time these moral restrictions or articles could be defended as reasonable to all who live under them. The two ideals would then be reconciled apparently as well as they can be. A social morality that results from this reconciliation is, of course, itself ideal. In order to distinguish an ideal morality of this kind from other ideals that have been proposed, and from the actual moralities of this world, we shall call it a 'moral social morality'.

The proposed way of reconciling the ideals is 'pragmatic' and 'contextual'. Any morality that people 'reasonably accepted' would limit the goals and ideals that they would be allowed to pursue (or could 'reasonably pursue'), but also, the moral restrictions that they could 'reasonably accept' would depend on what goals and ideals they pursued and wanted to allow. Different peoples, with different goals, ideals, and attitudes toward restrictions could be expected to make different judgments of what restrictions are reasonable, even when their judgments were well-founded. One may begin to wonder whether the proposed reconciliation adequately protects freedom; if security were the dominant goal in a society, massive restrictions on freedom would probably be reasonable. On this account, one might argue that reasonable restrictions, to be moral, must allow each to govern himself to the greatest degree that is consistent with every other having a like freedom, and thus must limit the pursuit of other goals and ideals within this bound. However, it is not only doubtful that all peoples in all circumstances would find a 'solution' of this sort reasonable, but also doubtful that morality *does*, or that the ideal of freedom *should* demand such a 'solution'. The contextualism proposed does not abandon the ideal of freedom; it insists that whatever restrictions are allowed as moral must be able to be accepted for good reasons by each person as articles of his own personal morality, which provides for freedom at just the right place. As we shall indicated latter, in order to guarantee respect for this moral freedom, it would be reasonable for most societies to grant many other liberties.

Some will claim that the ideal morality proposed is vacuous because no one could reasonably accept its restrictions. On their view, it is reasonable for an individual to accept a morality only if by doing so, he can sensibly expect to promote the realization of his goals and ideals as much as possible; and although it is conceivable that a group will find the acceptance of a morality 'reasonable' in this sense, this condition will not in fact be satisfied for any restrictions commonly called moral. An actual morality, on this view, is a compromise between opposed interests, and a rational person will not let himself be bound by one. Fortunately, however, this 'egocentric reasonableness' is not the only kind. Each individual can find it reasonable to accept restrictions if others do so because doing so is 'more satisfactory overall' than following egocentric reason, in which case there is a 'reasonableness to all together' that differs from the former. One would naturally expect a morality to be 'reasonable' in the latter sense, not the former. Although morality has a 'positive' as well as a 'negative face', no one would expect it never to block one's path.

Moreover, in view of human beings' extreme dependence on one another, and the social character of so much of human life, it is hardly surprising to be told that the reasonableness of an individual's views about how he should live is partly a function of what is reasonable to others. When people engage in social practices or exercise institutional roles, in ordinary games, in the family, in voluntary associations, in their jobs, and so on — and they are so occupied for much of their lives — they do not as a matter of fact expect 'reasonable solutions' to be determined solely by reference to their own views. Yet they freely substitute this 'common reasonableness' for a 'reasonableness' conceived solely in terms of their own goals and ideals. There are two well-known general explanations of this willingness (apart from necessity, its mother) namely, the disadvantages of war and the advantages of peace. Among the latter are all the goals that morally supported institutions make available, and the quality that is added to these goals by the moral 'endorsement' of the institutions. (Compare cohabitation as a goal, first, with legal marriage, and then, with 'moral marriage', marriage 'in the sight of' the moral community — or any other familiar role one might want to exercise.) 'Egocentric reasonableness' is often not just self-defeating (with respect to goals that one may have without morality) but thoroughly unenlightened (with respect to the 'quality of life' that morality affords).

## II

There are other indications, some of which are given below, that the suggested 'way of reconciliation' is plausible. But at this point we shall not defend it further. In order to examine the character of a 'moral social morality' as we have called it, so that it can 'speak for itself,' we shall simply assume that there are moral articles or moral ways of acting that it would be reasonable for each person to subscribe to, together with others, in freely governing himself.

Since a morality is action-guiding, we regard this assumption as essentially practical. Thus the next question is: how is a person required to act if he accepts the assumption that there is a moral social morality (at least for his society) and if he seeks to act morally toward his fellows? If the reasons for subscribing to moral articles give decisively good reasons for acting on them when others do, and for trying up to a point to get them to do so when they do not, which seems reasonable, then each person is directed to join others whenever possible in acting in the ways the articles specify. (A morality, since it is practical, is conceived more accurately as dispositions to act in moral ways, or as virtues, than as articles to which allegiance is sworn.) One who seeks to act morally must thus try to determine what ways of acting toward his fellows can be freely accepted, for good reasons, by them and himself; and if they act in these ways, or can be got to, then he must do so too ...

However, our assumption in one respect is incomplete. If a moral social morality is to be a reality, not just a possibility, more is needed than a set of articles that persons together *can* freely and reasonably accept; in addition, they must actually subscribe to and act on these articles for the reasons that make it reasonable to do so. Thus, if a people want to achieve such a morality, they cannot *impose* even moral ways of acting on one another; they must not use coercion, propaganda, or the like, but rather treat one another in a manner that encourages them all to subscribe to or endorse these ways of acting freely and for good reasons.

When this latter requirement is added to the former, each person who seeks to act morally is told to: Join others whenever feasible,

1  in acting in ways that each person together with others can reasonably and freely subscribe to as a common morality and

2  in treating each person in ways consistent with the person's developing and freely exercising his capacity as a rational being to govern himself.

(We might call this the Imperative of a moral social morality.) At times it may be impossible to satisfy both requirements but one is told to try. (If either part of this Imperative is interpreted broadly, the other part is unnecessary. However, since the first requirement narrowly interpreted is so frequently at odds with the second narrowly interpreted, we retain the more complex statement of the Imperative.)

We now propose the double requirement in the Imperative as a 'practical analysis' of the common moral idea of respect for persons. Respect for a person is usually thought to include both a kind of consideration of the person's interests and well-being, and an acknowledgment of his freedom to govern himself. We shall try to show that this analysis captures the common notion of respect in what follows.

If one acts on the Imperative, how will one treat fellow members of the moral community? How will one act toward others whom one respects? Although responding to these questions involves several large issues that cannot be discussed here, the main features of the answer are clear. Undertaking the task of finding out what ways of acting are reasonable to others and oneself at once distinguishes the moral agent from the egoist, except perhaps accidentally .... How will the moral agent determine what is reasonable to others as well as to himself? The task as it concerns others is a counterpart of the task as it concerns oneself. For the purposes of this paper we interpret 'what is reasonable' to any person, primarily in terms of the 'life plan' that he, in governing himself, would choose after putting it to the test of certain 'canons of rationality' ... and secondarily, in terms of the kind of social order that would most accord with this person's developing and following his rational life plan. The philosopher understandably will recoil when threatened with such a topic. But in the real world one cannot recoil for long because each of us is regularly confronted with problems that require this complex kind of rational assessment.

One who follows the Imperative will be *as concerned* to determine what is reasonable *from the other's point of view* as from one's own. This involves more than 'putting oneself in another's shoes', as this expression has sometimes been interpreted; one must try to determine what is reasonable to others, not what would be reasonable to oneself if one were in the other's position in certain limited respects. If a Nazi ... is to act morally toward Jews, he needs to ask Jews what they think, not to ask himself what he, a Nazi might think if he were a Jew — this 'universalizability' requirement is too weak. Some seem to believe that one cannot be faithful to one's own principles and at the same time adopt the views of others. But surely there is something wrong with one's convictions if they do not allow others freely to form their own; and if living with others is a problem, one needs to take a look through their eyes in order to find a rational way of solving it. (To some extent we do this every day; since ordinarily we have neither the power nor the desire to shove our ideas down others' throats, we try to act in ways that respect others' views as well as our own.) ...

When one has done one's best to look at a moral issue through other's eyes and through one's own, the moral task is just underway. If the Imperative's first requirement is to be met, it is necessary to determine what is reasonable to oneself *and* others. Up to this point, so to speak, one has had to be an advocate and prepare a case on whatever issue is in question for every party, and now one must assume the position of a 'moral judge', a position that in fact is thrust upon us all. (The position of moral judge is as natural a part of this kind of contractarianism as the 'ideal observer's' position is in some forms of utilitarianism.) A moral judge regards all persons as equal; he gives each an equal voice during the person's 'day in court' and tries to fashion decisions that all can accept. The attitude or virtue that is perhaps most often associated with the judge's position is impartiality or, perhaps better, fairness; as with Rousseau's compact, the moral court substitutes a moral equality for physical inequality. This equality, let it be remembered, derives from the conditions that have to be met if persons are to live morally with one another.

But, one will ask, what principles are there to guide a moral judge to 'reasonable decisions'? The Imperative's 'constitutional' requirements, so to speak, which generate the 'office' of moral judge, will also be his basic procedural principles. But how is he to carry out these procedures and, more specifically, how is he to determine what is reasonable to all parties? Often what is wanted in response to this kind of question is a set of clear principles or a decision procedure. Instead of trying to supply the impossible, we ask our questioner to consider how he and others determine 'reasonable solutions' to problems they have. The considerations that enter such decisions, and lead us to call them reasonable are many, diverse, and usually the result of slow and sometimes painful accumulations. There is no *a priori* standard; one is more like a judge in a courtroom than a 'studier of the law' in Locke's state of nature. One who has an equal concern for opposed parties may try first to find a solution that equally benefits both; if 'other things are equal', that should be reasonable to both. If a solution of this kind is impossible, one may try to divide 'the cake', or, if it cannot be divided, one may recommend 'taking turns'. The principle in these cases seems to be 'equal benefits to all parties'. But introducing new cooperative projects may lead the parties to be less interested in how products of old projects are divided; pooling resources for use in mutually interesting cooperative activities may offer more permanent solutions. If merit enters the problem, one may try to find meritocratic principles that all have good reason to accept. If need enters, one may *first* try to find a minimum that no one would be willing to do without. If competition is desirable, one may try to find rules governing the competition that give each an equal chance. If decisions must be made and disagreement is inevitable, one may decide on majority rule; at the same time, if the basic procedural principles are not to be imperilled, it will be necessary to grant each individual some elementary freedoms (of the persons, of conscience, of speech and assembly, etc.). Such freedoms can also be recommended for reasons that are independent of 'majority rule'; in a society such as ours, they are among the best available means of seeing to it that the two requirements of the Imperative, and thus the basic procedures of the moral court, are followed. If persons' views are unalterably opposed, a moral judge may still find a reasonable solution; if the persons want to live together, he may grant each an equal liberty 'to go his own way', as in the case of religious toleration. (We will return to this case in the final section). And so on; criteria of 'what is reasonable' are gradually accumulated. But in some cases, let us grant, there may not be 'reasonable solutions' by any accepted standards; a moral judge may have to point out that, if people want to live together, they simply have to act as if there were and invent some.

In trying to get his decisions accepted by others, the moral judge must give special attention to the second requirement of the Imperative, and not fall prey to the temptation to substitute coercion, propaganda, and the like, for rational discussion and argument. He would do well to bear in mind that the moral role of judgment and mediation, along with that of moral sympathy, never ends. Each new issue poses a threat. Moral relations between persons are constantly being strengthened or weakened, lost or gained. Often the problem is not so much getting persons to act in the way morality directs as forging a morality that will offer common direction.

After one has rendered a fair judgment in a case and had it accepted by the 'interested parties', the Imperative imposes an additional demand on one. This is the demand to be trustworthy or to 'keep one's part of the bargain'. If persons do achieve a rational acceptance of common moral articles, and then proceed to violate these articles, then as Hobbes said, the agreement would be 'in vain'. One might derive the requirement to be trustworthy as a 'material' moral principle, by showing that persons together would have decisively good reasons to accept it. Certainly, something like Rawls' 'principle of fairness' can be rationally agreed to if anything can, when it is applied to a co-operative moral community. However it seems quite natural to regard the requirement to be trustworthy as an additional requirement of respect ...

On the contractualist view the disposition to respect persons is thus a very fundamental virtue, whose practice depends on a number of ancillary virtues, principally, moral sympathy, fairness, and trustworthiness. One who respects others will be even more concerned to live in moral ways than to attain one's other goals. If we think of a moral community as constituted of persons who develop goals and exercise their individual capacities to govern themselves, then respect is the primary virtue of persons considered as its members.

### III

The Imperative can also be used to clarify the idea of fundamental human rights. If we think of there being rights correlative with the two requirements of the Imperative, each person will have a double right to respect, a right to be treated in ways that are both reasonable to him as well as to others and also in ways that are consistent with the development and exercise of his capacity to govern himself. Since the idea of a moral social morality was developed by asking what conditions must be satisfied in order for persons to live under reasonable moral views of their own, it may appear that we assumed such rights at the beginning, and then generated the requirements as an essential condition of the rights being honored. From this point of view one might regard the requirements as basic moral duties with correlative rights constituting a fundamental human right to moral respect.

As they have been asserted, however, the requirements do not constitute an *unconditioned* duty to respect others, and the correlative right to respect would not be unconditioned either. The Imperative requires one to *join* others in acting in the prescribed ways, and this requires co-operation; it is not something one can do by oneself. (The requirement thus fits the idea of a 'moral community,' which is an ideal of a kind of well-ordered co-operative society.) Earlier we interpreted the Imperative as also requiring persons to act in ways that *promote* a moral community, on the assumption that some of the reasons for persons living under its requirements are decisively good reasons in some circumstances for one's trying to achieve it. But no one can be morally required to promote a moral community regardless of the cost to himself or when the task is hopeless. On this contractualist view, the closest thing to an unconditioned imperative requires one 'to do all one reasonably can do' to promote and to sustain the community, and this, of course, is affected by how others act. Correlatively, on this view, no one can have a moral right to respect regardless of how he acts; one who, for example, greets every reasonable overture by others with force, can make no valid claim on others. Thus, on this view, basic rights belong to persons considered as members or potential members of the moral community, not considered as human beings. This helps explain what happens when a person loses our moral respect: it is not simply that our moral estimation of him falls, but that, since he 'breaks the rules', we are puzzled about 'how we can live with him'.

On the other hand, every person who has not forfeited his right to respect is, it would appear, a potential member of the moral community. And only despair is apt to lead a moral person to conclude that one who has forfeited his right, has done so permanently. How can one be certain that the person before one is in this class? Moreover, from the fact that one has forfeited his right to respect, it does not follow that others ought not to treat him with respect. (In fact, a person who has developed the habit and virtue of respecting others probably cannot suddenly deny their exercise.) The idea of respect, developed in the contractualist manner, derives from the thesis that human beings, with rare exceptions, have the capacity rationally to govern their own lives. To coerce another is to deny him, to the degree that coercion is exercised, the ability to govern himself; as such, it is an affront to his dignity as a human being. The morally sensitive person himself, even when he coerces another justifiably, is likely to find his coercive acts repugnant because they represent a loss to him as well as to the other. Coercion may be the best way out but it robs one of the value of living in a rational way with others; it is a moral defeat. On this view, persons do not have an inviolable right to respect, but whenever possible the moral person will treat others as if they did because of the peril to the dignity of all concerned. The inviolability of persons is part of the moral ideal.

## IV

The analysis of this paper has been almost entirely formal in the following sense: a view (or, if one prefers, a concept) of a moral social morality was developed by taking seriously certain ideal conditions, drawn from our moral traditions, that any social morality must satisfy in order to be moral. This view of morality was then shown to have normative consequences of some considerable force, and an account of respect for persons and correlative rights was given in terms of these consequences. This result simply shows that the idea of respect for persons is embedded in traditional views, especially traditional contract theory. The normative consequences or requirements were not derived by asking what articles of morality it would be reasonable for each person together with others to accept; the derivation of such 'material principles' comes later. Rather they were derived by asking how persons would have to act if a morality, conforming to this view, were to be realized. Not even the possibility of such a morality has been established . . .

It might be helpful to think of Rawls as sharing the views of the earlier part of this paper, but of his apparently having become convinced (along with some of his commentators) that if we take people as they are, no determinate moral principles can be generated. We then can look at his Original Position as a device for determining what persons in a position of equality would choose. If successful, this should greatly enlighten our moral judge. However, we might make a counterproposal, namely, that we rely on the pragmatic good sense and devices of our moral judge. This raises some interesting questions: Will the formal constraints of our Imperative and its setting do the work of the conditions in terms of which Rawls' Original Position is defined? If we assume Rawls' doctrine of primary goods, can we not get whatever principles he can get? In order to throw a little more light on our contractarianism, in conclusion let us briefly comment on these questions.

## V

The glaring difference between the two forms of contractarianism lies in Rawls' use of the Original Position (as an interpretation of an 'initial contract situation') and in the consequent reasoning that leads to his two principles of justice. . . . The form of contractarianism presented here makes no use of an 'initial situation' . . . .

In defining the Original Position, Rawls introduces his well-known 'veil of ignorance', for at least two reasons:

(a) so that all persons will be treated equally as persons, no one having a threat advantage (derivative from natural talents or social position) over any other, and

(b) in order to get a determinate solution to the question 'what are the principles of justice?'

On the argument of this paper, with respect to (a), all persons willing to live under a social morality are entitled to the moral respect of others. Natural talents and social advantages are negated, to the extent that they are, not by no one's knowing who one is, but by each being required, in deciding on moral articles and actions, to show a moral sympathy with others, to honor every other's case *as much as one's own*, and to judge impartially. In brief, no one can favour oneself or make use of a threat advantage because each one is required to seek solutions to moral problems that are reasonable to others as well as to oneself; moral principles must issue from the office of a moral judge. Moreover, any kind of coercion is proscribed by the second part of the Imperative.

However, this way of guaranteeing the moral equality of persons may seem to underscore the soundness of (b), Rawls' second reason for introducing a veil of ignorance. In view of the differences between some persons, emphasized in section I of this paper, how is it possible to get rational agreement on moral principles? To what has already been said, let us add the following:

With respect to this question several points need to be made. First, we know that some actual persons hold practical views that are incompatible with their respecting others and assuming the position of moral judge. Such persons will not agree to moral principles; nor will they be interested in what persons in Rawls' Original Position decide. The issue is whether there are 'reasonable moral solutions' to their differences. Secondly, for the purposes of this paper we have assumed, with our moral tradition, that there are good and decisive reasons for a person to live *morally* with others; although some reasons have been offered, obviously more needs to be said about these reasons. On this assumption, the moral decision problem can be thought of as one that confronts persons who are willing to live with others in a community marked by mutual respect. This fits with the way the two ideals were reconciled in I above.

Even if one grants the assumption and concedes this much, it may appear that no determinate solutions are possible. Our view of reasonableness may be rejected as too pragmatic, too unprincipled.

Nevertheless, it is simply a mistake to think that this view permits any sort of compromise or that it is powerless to generate moral principles. As indicated above, it can be argued with considerable cogency (although we cannot argue the point here) that honouring persons' fundamental rights to moral respect requires, in a society such as ours, an equal distribution of certain ancillary rights and freedoms, which are essential *in fact* if each person is to develop and freely exercise his capacity as a rational being to govern himself. To be sure, even when this argument is properly developed, it will not be an air-tight deductive argument. But to insist on the latter betrays a misunderstanding of the character of arguments for moral principles; such arguments depend on the 'weight of reason' and 'good judgment', for which, fortunately or unfortunately, there is no substitute ... In order to illustrate some of the features of an argument that appeals to what is 'reasonable to all', and to indicate how it goes, let us briefly consider 'toleration'. This should give some perspective on how 'determinate solutions' are possible.

In our argument, any person who seeks a moral solution to the problem of toleration cannot simply regard the problem from his own point of view. Many will be quick to note that seeking a 'moral solution', in this sense, already requires the subordination of one's religion to a so-called 'moral judge' for a supposed 'common weal'. In one sense of 'subordination', indeed it does (a point of which Rawls is well aware). To paraphrase Cicero, a moral community 'is not any collection of human beings brought together in any sort of way, but an assemblage of people ... associated in an agreement with respect to justice and a partnership for the common good' (*Republic*, I. xxv). So long as religious intolerants insist on being intolerant, a moral community is (in this respect) impossible; and if their intolerance is reasonable, a moral community (in this respect) is unreasonable. (Rawls has the same problem to face in a different way. If one in the Original Position seriously considers that he may turn out to be a person who prefers death to toleration, and if his judgment is guided accordingly, no agreement would be possible; Rawls says, and repeats several times, that *if* any principle can be agreed to, it must be that of equal liberty.) However, there surely are powerful considerations in favor of toleration even from the standpoint of an intolerant, including the problem of reconciling his religion and his God with the kind of acts that repression involves ... It is only a very peculiar conscience that will condone such acts. More-over, giving precedence to a common reason need not imply a 'subordination' of one's own conscience in a bad sense (as in a case of 'bad faith' or 'not being true to oneself'). The reasons for being tolerant, as we shall see, are such that one does not have to sacrifice one's integrity of self-respect in order to be tolerant.

When one confronts the problem of toleration from the moral point of view, *after* having assumed the position of 'moral judge', ... what will one decide? The right of *each* member of the community to moral respect, derived from a fundamental condition of persons living morally with one another, establishes (to use Rawls' phrase) a 'benchmark of equality'. Now *each* person's case must be heard; *no* person can be disregarded if we are to live morally with *him*. (One cannot honestly supress a person's views in the name of protecting 'the spiritual health' of a community and at the same time include that person as a self-governing member of the community.) Even if a person were a minority of one, this fact would give no reason for suppressing his views. We can hardly regard the sacrifice of his conscience to 'the greatest happiness' as reasonable to him; and if we are to honour his basic rights, he must be given the liberty to follow his own conscience, or as much liberty to do so as is granted to any other. The social power and position of a 'majority party' does not justify it in denying one rights that are essential to one's being a member of a moral community, and it gives a minority no non-coercive reason for bowing to the majority's views. (On the contrary, power, position, wealth and the like invite the question whether these are held in accordance with principles that all can freely and reasonably accept.) Finally, an appeal to 'public order' would appear to justify, at most, temporary expedients. In short, it is very difficult to see what solution a moral judge could adopt other than a principle of toleration or equal liberty. Each person's right to develop his own view of good and to govern himself must be honoured so far as possible, and a principle of toleration allows each person to follow his conscience and practice his religion to the greatest extent consistent with every other being able to do the same.

This line of argument for toleration (in which the formal constraints of our imperative have taken the place of the 'veil of ignorance', and in which reasoning designed to allow each and every person to govern himself has taken the place of the 'mutual disinterested' reasoning of persons in the Original Position) appears to be as cogent and as convincing as Rawls' own line of argument. ... How is he to succeed unless we are impressed by what persons in a position of equality (under the constraints and conditions of the Original Position) would decide? ... And for us to be so impressed, or to care about what free and equal persons would fairly agree to, it certainly appears that already we must have considerable respect for one another, in the sense of this paper, and be interested in finding reasonable solutions to the differences and problems of actual persons ...

In our argument for toleration, notice that no explicit mention was made of what Rawls calls 'primary goods'. But this omission may be deceptive. Freedom of conscience, as we interpreted it, is so much involved in the exercise of one's 'right to develop a rational life-plan and to govern oneself' that we could make a case for this freedom without positing it as a primary good — which only shows that the goodness of this freedom (and of this right) is built into our view of mutual respect (a point that should be obvious from the way this paper began). It is a virtue of the present view that mutual respect is put at the centre of the moral stage, where it belongs even on Rawls' view. Much of the force of Rawls' theory depends on one's regarding society as basically co-operative, and mutual respect is the foundation of this co-operation.

However, it should be fairly obvious that arguments for rights that are ancillary to the most basic (and an effective interpretation of what freedom of conscience itself requires, as well as arguments for other moral articles) would be greatly facilitated if we had a sound doctrine of 'primary goods'. The 'benchmark of equality' could then be extended beyond respect; and the argument for an equal distribution of these goods would be greatly strengthened. For example, if each person could be presumed to want a freedom of expression, and to give this priority over other things that he wants, how could a moral judge deny an equal freedom of expression to each person? Or put differently, how could there be a reasonable agreement among the members of a moral community that did not grant this freedom equally to each person? It is Rawls' doctrine of primary goods, and the order he gives to them, as much as the Original Position, that allows him to reach 'determinate solutions'.

A doctrine of primary goods, although acknowledged to be an over-simplification, offers one way of generating moral principles. As just suggested, if the doctrine is sound, we, as well as Rawls, can make use of it. However, the main line of argument of this paper suggests a different view of moral principles. Perhaps the following will illuminate the difference.

Rawls was not considering the decision problem of a moral judge, who after listening to all sides, has to make 'the most reasonable decision' he can; he was not speaking of deciding cases in the way an actual judge decides, sometimes reasonably notwithstanding great differences between parties. Rawls was developing a theory and seeking a solution to a theoretical decision problem in an 'initial contract situation'; he was trying to generate principles that judges, among others, could (and should) use as a guide; his method did not lead him to look at moral principles, and canons of reasonableness, as partly issuing from concrete decisions, rather than *vice versa*. Perhaps this is sufficient to indicate that one major issue in deciding whether a case can be made for our contractarianism is the issue of how 'reasonableness' and 'determinate moral solutions' are best conceived.

On this subject, we must rest content with a few closing remarks. Reasonable moral solutions, as we try to realize them in our lives, are not solutions to ideal decision problems, implicit in theoretical constructions. We should use such constructions in any way that we can; we need all the help we can get. At the same time, we should be mindful that in living with others, determining what is reasonable is usually not like finding a conclusion that is implicitly contained in premises. Certainly in difficult cases it is more like *devising* a solution (compare what judges do) that, in view of previously accepted principles and canons of reasonableness, and many other considerations and many goals, seems better than any other solution that one can see for the time being. Often solutions are not regarded as reasonable until we have arrived at them, and sometimes only after we have lived with them. Many long for something more definite and more logical, but it is unlikely that they will find it in the moral decisions of this world. And, as usual, there is the *serious* danger that in demanding too much, we will fail to appreciate what is available to us.

# Index